About the Author

Richard Sterling is known as the Indiana Jones of Gastronomy for his willingness to go anywhere and court any danger for the sake of a good meal. His other books include *Dining with Headhunters; The Fearless Diner;* and the award winning *Travelers' Tales: A Taste of the Road.* He has been honoured by the James Beard Foundation for his food writing, and by the Lowell Thomas awards for his travel literature. His lifestyle column 'The Best Revenge' appears monthly in *Code* magazine. Though he lives in Berkeley, California, he is very often politically incorrect.

About the Photographers

Images were supplied by a range of photographers, including Garrett Culhane, San Fransisco, who accompanied the author during research. The photographers are credited on page 200.

From the Publisher

The first edition of World Food Vietnam was edited by Foong Ling Kong and Martin Hughes of Lonely Planet's Melbourne office. Brendan Dempsey designed. Paul Piaia mapped with finishing touches provided by Natasha Velleley. Lara Morecombe indexed. Tim Uden and Andrew Tudor provided technical know-how. Valerie Tellini, from Lonely Planet Images, co-ordinated the supply of photographs. Qynh-Tram Trinh compiled the language section and Peter D'Onghia oversaw its production.

Olivier Breton, Vicki Webb, Joanne Adams, Patrick Marris, Patrick Witton, Quentin Frayne, Gushi Soda, Paul Clifton, Kerrie Hicken and Guillaume Roux provided essential bits and pieces.

Sally Steward, publisher, developed the series and Martin Hughes, series editor, nurtured each book from the seeds of ideas through to fruition, with inimitable flair.

Acknowledgements

The publisher wishes to thank Allison Jones, London, who made helpful suggestions, Guy Mirabella for design concepts and Richard I'Anson for photographic guidance. Also, thanks to Kirsti and Janei Anderson who provided Vietnamese touches, and to Richard Sterling who entertained, provided and was a pleasure to work with.

The author wishes to give special thanks to Miss Pham Nhut Binh Minh whose practical assistance and knowledge were invaluable in Ho Chi Minh City. To Miss Tran Do for her guidance through the shadows. Professors Bui Thi Ngoc Suong and Nguyen Thi Ngoc Tham, two ladies of infinite wisdom and generosity who shared their secrets of the Mekong Delta, and to Miss Luong who kindly guided us to them. Andre Brulhart and Arjen Blom, who shared their rich knowlege of Hanoi. Dr. Hoang Thuy Le, and Miss Nguyen Thi Dong Hai, who helped us unlock several mysteries. And to the Misses Oung and My and Háng and Tuyèn, of Hien and Bob's Place in HCMC who helped us make sense of so much of it, and who knocked our noodles when we needed it.

Warning & Request

Things change; markets give way to supermarkets, prices go up, good places go bad and not much stays the same. Please tell us if you've discovered changes and help make the next edition even more useful. We value all your feedback, and strive to improve our books accordingly. We have a well-travelled, well-fed team that reads and acknowledges every letter, postcard and email and ensures that every morsel of information finds its way to the appropriate people.

Each correspondent will receive the latest issue of Planet Talk, our quarterly printed newsletter, or Comet, our monthly email newsletter. Subscriptions to both are free. The newsletters might even feature your letter so let us know if you don't want it published.

If you have an interesting anecdote or story to do with your culinary travels, we'd love to hear it. If we publish it in the next edition, we'll send you a free Lonely Planet book of your choice.

Send your correspondence to the nearest Lonely Planet office:
Australia: Locked Bag 1, Footscray 3011
UK: 72-82 Rosebery Avenue, London EC1R 4RW
USA: 150 Linden St, Oakland CA 94607

Or email us at: talk2us@lonelyplanet.com

contents

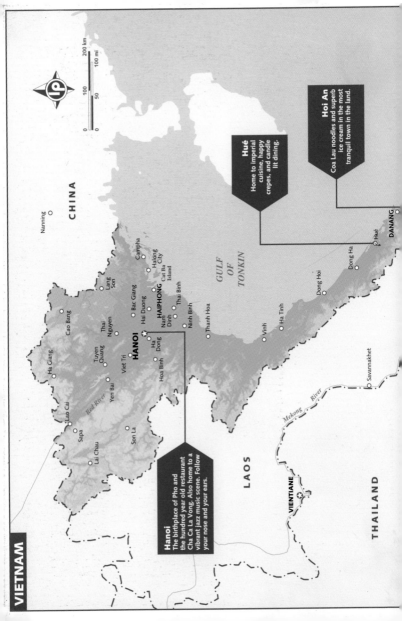

VIETNAM

CHINA

Nanning

GULF OF TONKIN

LAOS

THAILAND

Mekong River

Red River

Lao Cai
Sapa
Lai Chau
Ha Giang
Cao Bang
Tuyen Quang
Yen Bai
Son La
Thai Nguyen
Lang Son
Viet Tri
Bac Giang
HANOI
Ha Dong
Hoa Binh
Hai Duong
HAIPHONG
Nam Dinh
Cat Ba Island
Halong City
Campha
Thai Binh
Ninh Binh
Thanh Hoa
Vinh
Ha Tinh
Dong Hoi
Dong Ha
Huế
DANANG
VIENTIANE
Savannakhet

Hanoi
The birthplace of Pho and the hundred year old restaurant Cha Ca La Vong. Also home to a vibrant jazz music scene. Follow your nose and your ears.

Huế
Home to imperial cuisine, happy crepes, and candle lit dining.

Hoi An
Coa Lau noodles and superb ice cream in the most tranquil town in the land.

0   100   200 km
0   50   100   200 mi

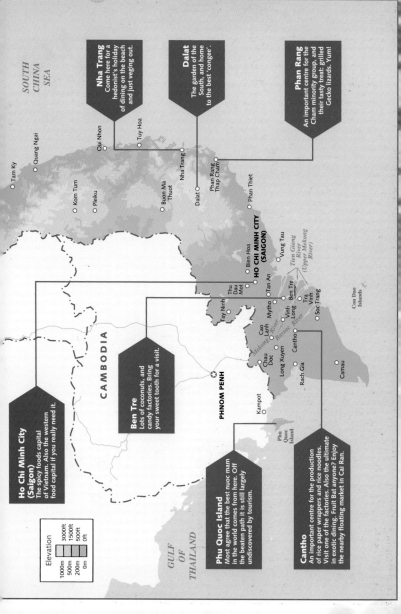

SOUTH CHINA SEA

Nha Trang
Come here for a hedonist's holiday of dining on the beach and just veging out.

Dalat
The garden of the South, and home to the best 'congee'.

Phan Rang
An important centre for the Cham minority group, and their tasty treat; grilled Gecko lizards. Yum!

Tam Ky

Quang Ngai

Qui Nhon

Tuy Hoa

Kom Tum

Pleiku

Buon Ma Thuot

Nha Trang

Dalat

Phan Rang Thap Cham

Phan Thiet

Bien Hoa

Vung Tau

Tien Giang River (Upper Mekong River)

HO CHI MINH CITY (SAIGON)

Thu Dau Mot

Tan An

Ben Tre

Tra Vinh

Tay Ninh

Mytho

Vinh Long

Cao Lanh

Mekong River

Bassac River

Soc Trang

Con Dao Islands

CAMBODIA

Ben Tre
Lots of coconuts, and candy factories. Bring your sweet tooth for a visit.

Chau Doc

Long Xuyen

Cantho

Rach Gia

Camau

✠ **PHNOM PENH**

Kampot

Ho Chi Minh City (Saigon)
The spicy foods capital of Vietnam. Also the western food capital if you really need it.

Phu Quoc Island
Most agree that the best nuoc mam in the world comes from here. Off the beaten path it is still largely undiscovered by tourism.

Phu Quoc Island

Cantho
An important centre for the production of rice paper wrappers and rice noodles. Also visit one of the factories. Fruit Bat anyone? Enjoy the nearby floating market in Cai Ran.

GULF OF THAILAND

Elevation

1000m	3000ft
500m	1500ft
200m	500ft
0m	0ft

People tend to know two things about Vietnam: that it endured a long and painful war, and that it has one of the richest, most varied cuisines in the world.

You'll find no wars within these pages. What you *will* find is all the information you'll need to intelligently eat and drink your way through Vietnam on an unforgettable culinary adventure. Whether on the ground or in your armchair, you're about to embark upon an intimate journey through one of the world's most widely recognised and appreciated cuisines.

If cooking were painting, Vietnam would have one of the world's most colourful palettes. The great diversity of its climate and terrain can produce almost anything which can be eaten. The Vietnamese themselves have no culinary inhibitions and are always willing to try something new. When you combine the two, nothing is ruled out.

The famous dishes such as phở and fresh spring rolls are but the tip of a gastronomic iceberg. In addition to a myriad of foods and preparations, there is a staggering number of sauces and dips limited only by the imagination of each cook. The picture of Vietnamese cuisine is vast and varied, always subject to innovation, and always vibrantly colourful.

You'll encounter the wonderful and the strange, the sacred and the profane. You'll find spices that sing in your mouth, smells that trigger emotions, dishes that amaze by their cleverness and beguile by their sensuousness, drinks that surprise, fruits that will shock and creatures that will make you shriek. Above all, you'll find the people that make up Vietnam's food culture who will charm, frustrate and intrigue you.

You are about to consume a culture. A culture that is still relatively poor in goods but rich in history, art, literature, music and pride. A culture that will reveal itself to you, if you are willing and hungry enough, through the medium of its cuisine. Vietnam lays itself bare in the kitchen and at the table. Its history, its legends and its lore are all reflected in its food and drink. As you navigate these pages, we wish you a good journey and a good appetite.

the
culture
of vietnamese cuisine

Vietnamese cuisine is the sum of many parts. A country that doesn't think twice about eating baguettes with nuoc mam, and grows both artichokes and glutinous rice, is one that revels in its contrasts. It has an enviable natural prosperity, and the cooking techniques showcase the bounty from land and sea to great advantage. Colonialism and foreign influences have led to a blissful marriage of techniques and ingredients. The result? The Vietnamese table.

Historians like to say that geography is fate. Geography is also cuisine, for it determines what foods and what people may shape it. The topography of Vietnam presents virtually every climate and microclimate capable of yielding a crop or animal, whether tropical or temperate, from fish, rice and tea to beef, coffee and cream.

Look at the map of Vietnam. As the Vietnamese are eager to point out, it resembles a **đòn gánh** (a yoke), a bamboo pole with a basket of rice slung from each end. The baskets represent the main rice-growing regions of the Red River Delta in the north, and the Mekong Delta in the south. The other thing to notice on this highly symbolic map of Vietnam is its waters, its 2400km of coastline and its innumerable kilometres of rivers and streams.

Rice cultivation, and the harvesting of the water world provide the cuisine of Vietnam with its two most potent symbols and substances: rice and **nước mắm** (fermented fish sauce). This pair makes up the *sine qua non* of Vietnamese food. With them, Vietnamese cooks can go anywhere and still prepare something at least close to their native fare. Without them, they are bereft.

Rice is both the staff and the substance of life. People call it the 'pearl of the gods', and a meal is not a meal without it in some form. It is more than food; it is history, identity, culture and cult. Any number of myths and legends are associated with it, such as the birth of the Vietnamese people and lines of political succession.

The ubiquitous nước mắm has its legends, too. According to some veterans, American troops fighting in Vietnam could detect Vietcong guerrillas by the lasting aroma of nước mắm. (For their part, the Vietnamese were said to be able to detect the Americans by the smells of tobacco and chewing gum.) Perhaps both sides exaggerate, but the heady aroma of nước mắm is one of the strongest olfactory memories many visitors acquire of Vietnam.

Manual irrigation, central Vietnam

Collecting rice husks for fuel at the rice paper factory outside Cantho City

Nước mắm is a concentrated extract made from salted and fermented small fish. The clear liquid is used as a salty sauce and general flavouring agent in much the same way as soy sauce is used by the Chinese. But it is more. Vietnamese cookery is defined, as much as anything else, by aroma. Even blind people can identify Vietnamese food by the aromas produced by the sparing use of oil, by the smell of fresh and raw ingredients, by the smoky and toasty smells imparted by traditional cooking techniques such as grilling or frying over a wood fire, and by the culinary constant nước mắm.

CELEBRATING MANURE

Manure, both human and animal, is used extensively as fertiliser in the Red River Delta. Some northern people regard manure as sacred, and use it as an object of worship in the ceremonies and prayers for a good crop. The tools used to pick up and transport manure, and the people whose job it is to collect it, have become imbued with guardian spirits. The worship articles for these spirits are a basket and a pair of bamboo tongs with which to pick up the manure. Ceremonial offerings consist of mashed banana on a dish, or caramelised sugar moulded into shapes resembling this kind of fertiliser. After the ceremony, the offerings are shared: old men use special chopsticks to divide the banana or the sugar among those in attendance as shared blessed offerings.

Beach market, Nha Trang

In keeping with its geography, Vietnamese cooking is heavily influenced by China, especially in methods of preparation and kitchen equipment. They share the concept of 'the five flavours', a balance of salty, sweet, sour, bitter and hot (spicy). A dish may be dominated by one or two of the five, but the others will usually play a pleasing harmony in the culinary tune. Stirfry is a common method of preparation but the Vietnamese generally use very little oil, displaying a lighter hand than the Chinese. The frying is more of a gentle simmering in the expressed juices of the food. Lightness and freshness are the goals.

As in China, vegetables play a central role in cuisine, but in Vietnam they are raw as often as cooked. Vietnam's fish and seafood are plentiful, and of great variety. Fish are generally alive at the time of sale to the consumer, and deftly killed and cleaned by the merchant upon selection. Vietnamese cooks rightly point out that fish are more flavourful if they are not deboned before cooking. This can be a problem for the uninitiated, as so many of the fish have numerous small bones. Vietnamese grow up practised in the art of removing them while eating, but foreigners may find the process tiring and frustrating.

Like Chinese food, varying textures such as crunch and chewiness are prized at the Vietnamese table. Indispensable as a seasoning is nước mắm (they seldom use soy); like a judicious splash of Worcestershire sauce, when cooked into a dish it buries itself in the flavours of the food and gives it greater dimension without altering its basic character. Also important are the fire spices, chilli and black pepper. Normally they are not cooked into the food but served as condiments, and are used as commonly as salt. Sweet spices such as star anise and cinnamon, and pungent ginger are common. Vinegar is not widely used – acidity is provided by tamarind and lime.

The Vietnamese have three styles or manners of cooking and eating: comprehensive eating, or eating through the five senses; scientific eating, which observes the dualistic principles of yin & yang; and democratic eating, or the freedom to eat as you like.

In comprehensive eating, the most common form, you eat with your eyes first. Dishes must be attractively presented with a diversity of forms and colours. Then the nose follows: the Vietnamese penchant for aroma is brought to the fore, and each dish must offer pleasant odours of meat, fish or vegetables and a sauce. When chewing, take care to feel the softness of noodles, the texture of the meat, and listen to the crackling sound of rice crackers or the crunchiness of roasted peanuts. And then you taste. The cook must see to it that each dish prepared has its own distinct flavour, and you, the diner, should take note of the differences. A dish might have all the five flavours, but none should predominate.

Scientific eating concentrates on the dualistic philosophy of yin & yang, in this case a balance between hot and cold. For instance, a fish stew would be seasoned with salty fish sauce which is yang, but balanced by the yin of sugar. Green mangoes (yin) should be taken with salt and hot chillies (yang); grilled catfish or duck (yin) must be eaten with ginger (yang). This kind of eating is said to contribute to the good health of both mind and body.

Democratic eating is when you eat for the sake of eating. Everybody does it, but no one wants to make a habit of it.

Baguette seller, Cantho

History

Lengthy borders and coastlines have made Vietnam historically open to the opportunities and dangers of foreign influences and invasions. It seems that every aspect of the culture, from religion to family to government, has been shaped to some degree by foreign powers – not only China and France, but by such bygone kingdoms as Champa. Vietnamese cooking represents no less an amalgam of these influences that, as in other facets of national life, creates a truly unique identity.

A thousand years is a long time, longer than we in the west can generally conceive of, at least in national memory. But that is how long China ruled Vietnam, beginning in 111 BC. At that time the 'Viet' people were a clan-based society practising slash-and-burn agriculture and leading lives not unlike those of the hill tribe minorities of today. Chinese rule was often egregious, but it was also

> ### Vietnamese Riddle
>
> Five boys use two poles. They chase a herd of white water buffalo into a dark cave.
>
> What is this?
>
> A hand using chopsticks to eat rice.

enlightening in arts, literature, government, religion and science, and in the development of the civilised table. From China, Vietnam learned to use chopsticks, to stirfry with oil, and to eat noodles and bean curd. The Chinese taught Buddhism in Vietnam, which led to sophisticated vegetarian cookery. But the most significant and lasting lesson taught by the Chinese was the cultivation of rice. Without this endowment from China, Vietnam would be a quite different culture.

From China came the Mongol herdsmen in the 10th century. They brought beef into the Vietnamese diet, which enabled the development of the national dish, **phở** (rice noodle soup, see the Staples & Specialities chapter). Moving southward, away from China, other nations began to exert their effects on Vietnam. Indianised Cambodia radically broadened the spectrum of Vietnamese cooking by introducing the Indian curries and spices common to their cuisine. The Vietnamese embraced but adjusted the use of the spices to produce recipes that accommodated the Vietnamese desire for aroma more than for a fiery sensation. Thailand and Laos lent a wide range of flavours such as shrimp paste, lemongrass, mint, basil and chillies.

When the French arrived in the 19th century they brought with them their philosophy of food and eating, an interest in and a respect for good quality ingredients and a well-developed sense of how to use them. Ruling the country for nearly a century, the French enriched Vietnamese

Unloading boats at Hoi An

cuisine. They brought in the technique of sautéing, and new crops such as asparagus, avocados, corn, tomatoes and wine. Vietnamese cooking is arguably the only Asian cuisine that can nearly always admit wine successfully to the table. The French also gave the Vietnamese an appreciation for baguettes, beer, café au lait, and ice cream. Vietnamese sandwiches made of French bread, pâté, salad vegetables, and nước mắm or chilli sauce are popular throughout the country.

The French method of long simmering bones and meats has also been adopted for the making of most Vietnamese soups (see Phở in the Staples & Specialities chapter). French culinary terminology is common. For example, the spice lemongrass is sometimes referred to in Vietnam as **citronelle**, and a paste of mashed shrimp with spices is called **pâté**.

SOUP ESPIONAGE

Edward Landsdale, Chief of US Psychological Warfare Operations in Vietnam in the 1950s, had this to say about the soups of Vietnam: "Anyone who wants to see the Vietnamese at their gregarious best and to find out what the public is saying about current events need only to go on a gastronomical excursion among the soup stands. It's a delicious way to take a political survey".

Unique

Vietnamese cuisine has taken on many influences over the centuries, and will continue to do so. And yet it will always retain its distinctive character by the way its cooks use these foreign influences. Vietnamese people like to compare their nation to a house with four walls, each with an open window. The four winds may blow, and enter the house and rearrange the furniture, but the winds that blow in always blow out, and leave behind the same table and chairs. The Vietnamese take delight in combining complementary ingredients to form new flavours with contrasting textures that are uniquely Vietnamese.

Chả giò (spring rolls) are a good example. They are based on the Chinese egg rolls, but the method of preparation and ingredients result in a quite different taste and smell. The rice paper wrappers might be filled with shrimp or other seafood and vegetables, rolled up and lightly fried. They are normally served with a dipping sauce made from nước mắm called **nước chấm** (see the Staples & Specialities chapter).

How Vietnamese Eat

A meal in Vietnam is composed of rice and 'something else'. If all you have is the 'something else' then you haven't had a meal, but a snack. If all you have is rice with a little nước mắm, then you've had a meal. Ideally, a meal includes rice, vegetable, fish or meat, and a soup. Soup is taken for its gustatory value and as the liquid or beverage component of the meal. Nowadays it is becoming common to drink soft drinks or beer at the table.

The Vietnamese like to eat three meals a day. Breakfast is usually simple, and may be a noodle soup such as pho, a rice gruel called **cháo** with bits of seafood or meat in it, or a sticky rice cake wrapped in banana leaf and eaten on the fly. Baguettes are available at any time of day or night, and may be eaten plain with a cup of coffee, or filled with whatever is to hand.

Lunch is served at around 11am. People traditionally go home to eat with their families, but others remain in the office or eat at nearby street cafes. People who are near the major markets at lunchtime often pop in for noodles, grilled meats or seafood with rice vermicelli. They are there to eat, but also to chat, catch up on the latest gossip, and stay connected with friends.

Thi Nghe Market, Ho Chi Minh City

Dinner is a time for family bonding. The meal is approximately a repeat of lunch, if it was a proper lunch, with all four components. Well-to-do families might add a few more items, another vegetable, perhaps two meats. Everything is served simultaneously or as it is ready. The dishes are arranged around the central rice bowl and diners each have a small eating bowl. The procedure is uncomplicated: spoon some rice into your bowl, and lay 'something else' on top of it. Take what you like, leave what you don't care for. At the end of the meal, pour a bit of the remaining soup into your bowl to wash out the remaining rice and eat it. Wasting rice is a no-no.

Vietnamese are generally not fond of desserts after meals, preferring fruit if anything, but they do like sweets as a snack. They are taken often and at any time of day. Vietnamese will eat whenever not eating becomes boring. Rice cookies, fried bananas, sweet potatoes, coconut candy, lotus seeds in syrup are all popular snacks. And people will go a long way for ice cream if they have to.

FOOD FOR THOUGHT

One day I wandered Hanoi alone and I found myself in a little restaurant eating delicious, chewy sausage balls wrapped in tangy lá lốt (betel) leaves and grilled to crispness. The place was bright and airy and beautiful silk paintings decorated three of the walls and the buffet lined the fourth. A Vietnamese man purchased his lunch and, though other tables were empty, he sat down with me. He smiled a greeting but said nothing. We ate in silent company, smiling politely now and then. It was clear to me that the man wanted nothing more than to eat with me, though I could not fathom why.

Finishing his meal, he pointed to one of the silk paintings, a still life of a table set with food and what I took to be a grace written beneath. He smiled again and spoke, apparently trying to explain the painting to me. I nodded and smiled, but he was insistent and got up and pointed to the words under the picture. He gesticulated and gestured and explained. I finally took out my notebook and copied it down, and he seemed satisfied. He even patted the notebook as I put it back in my shirt pocket.

He went his way. I put the inscription in a pouch along with the recipe for Delilah Prawns and other things to be translated when I got home, and forgot about it.

The Vietnamese neighbour who did the translating smiled when he saw the scribbled notes. "An old, old proverb", he said. "In food, as in death, we feel the essential oneness of humanity".

Table Etiquette

Sit at the table with your bowl on a small plate, chopsticks and a soup spoon at the ready. The small plate can be used for discards and scraps. Napkins (serviettes) are not usual at the Vietnamese table. You will see them in restaurants catering to tourists, but you would do well to carry a handkerchief with you for the purpose.

Each place setting will include a small dipping bowl at the top right-hand side of the bowl for the nước mắm, nước chấm or other dipping sauces, depending on the complexity of the meal. There may also be a dish of chilli sauce, as well as sliced fresh chillies or a tiny dish of salt, pepper and lime juice.

CUSTOMS WITH CHOPSTICKS

There is a Vietnamese tale about a woman who marries a handsome man from another province. She knows that he has a younger brother, but she has never seen him. She goes to live with her new husband and his family. At supper in the new home with her new family, her husband and his 'younger' brother take their seats. To her surprise, they are identical twins; one is only minutes older than the other. She cannot tell them apart, but does not wish to let her husband know this. She waits until dinner starts and the chopsticks are distributed. One of the brothers hands a pair to the other, the act of deference from the younger to the elder.

Dining etiquette varies regionally. In the north and centre, the oldest man will sit nearest the door and everyone else is arranged in descending order according to age. The elder starts first by putting food into his bowl. Younger members will request permission from their elders to start. If you are a guest, allow your host and any elders to sit first. You will then be shown where to sit. Opposite the host is the seat of honour. The northern host will often take morsels of food from each dish and place them in your bowl. Southerners will urge you to help yourself.

When serving yourself from the central bowls, use the communal serving spoon so as not to dip your chopsticks into them. When you pause between eating, place the chopsticks across your eating bowl. Do not stick them into your rice and leave them – that is a funerary practice. To begin eating, just pick up your bowl with the left hand, bring it close to your mouth, and use the chopsticks to spoon in the rice and food.

CHRISTOPHER BRASSEUR – Faces of Gastronomy

Where do you find what is possibly the best ice cream in Vietnam, so good that people drive all the way from Danang to Hoi An every Sunday for a taste of it? The Tam Tam Cafe, operated by Frenchman Christopher Brasseur. Think of the movie *Casablanca*, a scene in Rick's Café Américain. But here 'Rick' is a French windsurfer and, though he'll be happy to serve you gin, he makes the best blessed ice cream we have ever encountered in Asia.

He also has a fine wine list and a European restaurant and bar whose decor and ceiling-fan ambience call up nostalgia for Vietnam's colonial history. The better part of it, that is. The part in which both Vietnamese and French were enriched by their time spent together, when the French learned to eat with chopsticks and the Vietnamese came to love ice cream, and to appreciate a bottle of wine.

"I used to keep a windsurfing shop", he tells us from behind the bar. (Hmmm. Trying to picture him as Humphrey Bogart's bohemian son with a French accent.) "But I got tired of it and came to Vietnam just for the change". (Not to escape a lost love, we wonder?) "I rode the country on a motorcycle for two years. I learned the Vietnamese ways of doing things, of living, and doing a business. I decided I had to settle here in Hoi An, so I called for my companions, Natalia and Franck, and together we started Tam Tam".

The kitchen is immaculate, probably the cleanest example we have seen in central Vietnam. And while the menu is Mediterranean, the cook, Pha, is Vietnamese. "Natalia trained him over a couple of years", Christopher explains. "Now he is the best French cook around. But I make the ice cream".

What flavours does he make? Whatever flavours Vietnam can grow – chocolate and vanilla and coffee, all from fresh beans. Any and all kinds of intensely flavoured tropical fruits (well, not durian) and fruits from the temperate zones grown in the mountains around Dalat: strawberry, peach, apricot etc . "I change the flavours often. I don't like to be in an ice-cream rut".

You will seldom see Vietnamese spending much time or money in an establishment frequented by foreigners as prices are generally too expensive for the locals' budget. But Vietnamese often come to Tam Tam, where Christopher speaks their language. They come to steep themselves in a little history (or maybe a little romance), to soak up a bit of the ambience that is an almost lost part of their legacy, and to have a fine dish of ice cream.

Here's looking at you, kid.

Vegetables and colonial buildings, Hanoi

The Vietnamese eat with gusto, and noise. Slurping is not considered impolite, although belching is. Politely spitting out fish bones is okay – just try not to spit them into anyone's lap. Vietnamese like to interact with their food, almost to play with it. There are many dishes that call for rolling and wrapping at the table; for adding this or that; grilling or boiling at the table; for assembling or disassembling. Dishes of crab or shrimp often require the dexterous and extensive use of fingers and little picks and other implements to shell them. It can make for a time-consuming process, but that is what the Vietnamese like, any excuse to linger over food, with friends or family. After a messy meal of much interaction and disassembly, you will often be given a finger bowl. Foreigners often mistake its purpose because it is usually filled with weak tea, a fine cleansing agent. Just remember, tea for drinking comes in little cups.

staples
& specialities

From the land comes rice, and from the sea and waterways fresh fish for nước mắm. Together they form the bedrock of Vietnamese cuisine. In supporting roles are the myriad pungent roots, leafy herbs and aromatic tubers which give Vietnamese salads, snacks, soups and stews their distinctive fragrance and kick. But there are constants – for the Vietnamese cook, freshness and a balanced combination of flavours and textures are paramount.

Rice

Vietnamese have a reverence for rice. It is the 'staff of life', not only at the table but in the economy and culture. The majority of the people of Vietnam gain their livelihood by some direct involvement with its production, transport or sale. Vietnam is the world's third-largest exporter of rice, ranking only behind the US and Thailand. The Vietnamese language has numerous words to describe it at every stage of its growth and progress, from paddy to table.

Women transplanting rice, Ba Be

Mothers tell their children that in their next life they'll always be hungry if they waste rice. But they would never say such a thing about wasting chicken soup. Rice is grown in Vietnam in dozens of varieties, each with its own texture and aroma, unique flavour, colour, and amount of gluten. Many Vietnamese can tell what kind of rice is cooking just by the smell.

Sifting grain, Quang Nam, Hoi An

Shopping for rice is a bigger job than one might imagine. Housewives like to buy their rice from a regular dealer upon whose information and advice they rely. The quality and quantity will be discussed in great detail, and if the talk goes on the customer will expect some tea and candies. Just as different flours are used in a western kitchen, different rice types are used for different purposes. As a rule, the long-grain white rice that remains dry and fluffy after cooking is preferred for sit-down meals. When cooked, the grains will be soft but still offer something to the teeth, and will be long and narrow with nicely pointed ends. You might comment on this to your host to show your rice savvy.

Cơm hương giang (a spicy, fragrant variety of rice) is popular in Huế. Vegetarian cookery uses a lot of glutinous rice, **gạo nếp**, as it combines well with legumes and nuts, giving it added nutrition. It is also called 'sweet rice' or 'sticky rice'. There are two types of glutinous rice: the Chinese and Japanese short-grained type and the longer-grained Thai variety, which the Vietnamese prefer. It has a soft, sticky texture and a slightly sweet flavour when cooked. Stuffed with mung bean paste or other savouries, it is the basis of a variety of rice cakes.

To Cook Rice

Every country with rice as a staple has its own varieties of the grain and unique way of preparing it, just as no two European countries have quite the same bread. The method for Vietnamese rice is very exact and produces a unique texture. Put the desired amount into a pot and spread evenly. Place the tip of your index finger on top of the rice and pour water into the pot until it reaches the first knuckle. If that is flying too much by the seat of your pants, try the following proportion.

2   cups (240g) long-grain white rice
3¼ cups (900ml) water

Put rice and water in a pot together and bring to the boil over high heat. Boil for 3–4 minutes until you begin to see small holes in the water's surface, indicating that the water is being absorbed by the rice. Cover the pan tightly then reduce heat to very low. Cook for 20 minutes. Remove from the heat and, without lifting the lid, let the rice rest for 20 minutes. It will keep hot for an hour with the lid on. Fluff before serving.

If you're cooking in a traditional Vietnamese kitchen, you'll be cooking over charcoal, so the heat will not be distributed evenly and hot spots will develop that can scorch the rice. Remember then the rice cooker's mantra: 'three times shift the pot. Nine times stir the rice'.

LEGEND OF GLUTINOUS RICE

There were two brothers. They had to work hard because they had lost their parents. The older brother married and had children while the younger remained single and lived in a separate part of the family's home. The harvest paddy was brought in from the field and divided equally between the two households. One day, the rice reserves were so low that the younger brother felt obligated to help out his older brother's family. At night, the younger brother took several bushels from his storage bin and carried it over to his older brother's storage bin.

The older brother worried about his younger. He thought, 'my brother is alone with no one to comfort him or help him. What would he do if his rice reserves ran low?' One night around Tet, he took a portion of his own rice from his stores to transfer to his brother's. The two met in the storeroom and tears came to their eyes. The falling tears turned into grains of rice more delicious than any other type. People called it **gạo nếp** and it's used to make the traditional **bánh chưng** sticky rice cakes.

Rice is more than a white grain to fill bowl and belly. It can be made into almost anything: wrappers, wine and noodles. **Bánh tráng** is usually rendered in English as 'rice paper', something of a misnomer. We prefer to call it 'rice wrapper'. Round and brittle, it's made from a paste of rice flour, salt and water, and laid out on leaf mats to dry in the sun. Because it adheres slightly to the mat, the rice wrappers have a distinctive cross-hatched design. People use it to wrap Vietnamese spring rolls. You can see this stuff being made by hand in small factories in virtually every community of size. In Cantho, look for the Cantho Foods Processing Company (ask for Mdm Nguyen Thi Phuong, 109 Vong Cung Street, An Binh Villa).

Roasted rice powder, **thính**, adds a mild bitter taste to meat dishes. Rice vinegar, **dấm gạo**, goes into marinades.

Rượu cần (rice wine) is consumed at lunch by men, used in religious ceremonies or to greet guests. City folk consider it a drink for country bumpkins but it's gaining wider acceptance.

While the Chinese and Europeans make their noodles with wheat, Vietnamese use rice. **Bún** (rice vermicelli, the thin variety) is brittle, white, and dried in 25cm lengths. Bún are used in soups and noodle salads, and served at room temperature as a side dish to curried dishes, grilled meats and fried fish. **Bánh hỏi**, another variety of rice noodle, is as fine as angel hair pasta, the thinnest of all noodles. It is used primarily as an accompaniment to grilled foods. **Bánh phở**, (rice sticks) are stirfried or added to soups.

Overleaf: Paddy field, Napa Town

Pho

They call it comfort food. Soul food, even. They call it Vietnam's answer to fast food; a calumny, in our opinion. They call it beef noodle soup, and such it is, but so much more. It is Vietnam in a bowl.

Pronounced 'fer' (say 'fur' with a soft 'r', which is as close as we can come to the correct pronunciation), it is beef noodle soup raised to the nth degree. You can have phở everywhere in Vietnam, but it is almost a cult in Hanoi. According to Vietnamese writer Vu Bang, "to many persons, phở is no longer a dish. They are simply addicted to it, like tobacco addicts". A bowl of pho begins its Mayfly life the day before you eat it. A long, slow simmering of beef shinbones, oxtails and scraps of meat in a great deep pot brings into being a rich, clear consommé. This process alone takes about 24 hours if it is to be done right. The alchemist cooks add their herbs, their spices, their family secrets. Chief among them, and you will always know the aroma of pho by them, are star anise, ginger and cinnamon.

"Good food from fresh ingredients. If you forget this, you cannot cook Vietnamese"
Trin Diem Vy, Mermaid Restaurant

From a distance, its come-hither smell seduces and urges you to reach its source, "just like the clouds of incense that make us quicken our steps and climb the mountains in order to arrive at the pagoda", to use the words of a Vietnamese poet. And indeed a good phở shop is laid out with a touch of poetry. Often it's just a little stand by the roadside, yet the aesthetics are observed. The shopkeeper might hang a small bundle of onions wrapped in mint leaves from a string in front of the shop to scent the air. A votive offering sits on the counter, a few flowers in a corner. The standing vendor deftly cuts rice sheets into noodles and slices meat into nearly translucent thinness.

"Customer", he asks, "what kind of meat do you want today? I have lean meat, cartilage, half meat and half fat". He immerses a sieve full of pre-cooked rice noodles into hot water for a moment, lifts them out, drains them with a shake, and pours them into your bowl. Skilfully, with the eye of the florist, he arranges on top a bouquet of white onion slices, tiny yellow shavings of ginger, perhaps something green. And then, red raw beef, in slices about the size of the heel of your hand.

He deftly lifts the lid of his stockpot and the heady steam billows out, enveloping you in a thin, gossamer cloud of dew that separates itself into those curly wisps of morning in a Chinese silk painting. You know you're about to eat poetry. Ladles of the simmering broth fill your bowl, its heat quickly penetrating the meat, cooking it to perfect tenderness within just a few seconds.

The Maestro has done his part. Now you take the baton. From the garnish tray, add a squeeze of lime juice. Nibble at the beansprouts to test their crispness. If they pass the test, add a few to the soup. And a dash of chilli sauce and garlic sauce or fish sauce. Lastly, sprinkle it with coriander leaves, or mint leaves, or basil. Or all of them. With your chopsticks in your dominant hand and spoon in the other, thrust deeply to the bottom of the bowl. Lift the noodles above the surface and let the dressings you've added subsume into the body of the work. Lay the noodles back to rest. In the next minute the flavours will marry. You can record the ceremony with your nose, as the aroma becomes more complex, with many subtle undercurrents that rise and fall.

When it is done you have before you a study in opposites, a bowl of yin & yang. It is hearty yet delicate; complex and straightforward; filling but not bloating; spicy and comfortably bland. It is everything in the right proportion, the 'golden mean' of the table. So, enjoy. Pull the noodles up with your chopsticks and slurp them into your mouth. Then slurp a bit of broth from your spoon. Again use your chopsticks and layer a few noodles into your spoon, and top that with a mint leaf and a piece of meat. Dip the spoon into the soup and take it all in one bite. Follow it, if you dare, with a small bite of green chilli from the garnish tray. We often like to take all the delicious soup first, then ask for more to be poured over the solid foods. We've never been refused or charged extra.

This full and balanced meal in a bowl will cost you well under US$1, and we have rarely seen anyone who could eat it all. In the north the people eat it at any time of day or night. In the south it's popular for breakfast, especially among farmers and labourers. It's cheap, filling and delicious. It has plenty of carbohydrates to fuel the body, enough protein to keep the body together, and plenty of the liquid one needs in the tropical heat. It is artistry, practicality, and economy. It is seductively delicious.

Pho (Beef Noodle Soup)

Ingredients
Beef Broth
1.5kg	oxtail, chopped into sections
1.5kg	beef shanks
3.5l	water
3	pieces fresh ginger, each 2.5cm long, unpeeled
1	large yellow onion, unpeeled and cut in half
4	shallots, unpeeled
500g	Chinese radishes, cut into 5cm chunks
3	carrots, unpeeled, cut into chunks
4	whole star anise
6	whole cloves
2	cinnamon sticks
1/4	cup (60ml) Vietnamese fish sauce
	salt

Beef, Rice Noodles and Accompaniments
250g	beef round, in one piece and at least 5cm thick
500g	dried flat rice stick noodles, 6mm wide
1	large yellow onion
2	spring onions (scallions)
2	fresh small red chillies
1	cup (30g) fresh coriander (cilantro) leaves
1/2	cup (15g) fresh mint leaves
1	lime, cut into 6 wedges

To make the broth, combine the oxtail, beef shanks and water in a large pot and bring to a boil. Meanwhile, preheat a broiler (griller). Place the ginger, onion and shallots on a baking sheet and broil (grill), turning frequently, until browned on all sides, 1–2 minutes. Set aside. When the water reaches a boil, using a large spoon or a wire skimmer, skim off the scum from the surface until the liquid is clear of all foam, about 10 minutes. Add the browned flavourings and the radishes, carrots, star anise, cloves and cinnamon to the pot. Reduce the heat to medium low, cover partially and simmer gently for 3½ hours to concentrate the flavour. Remove from the heat and let cool. Strain the broth through a sieve into a bowl, discarding the contents of the sieve. Let stand until the fat rises to the surface. Using a large spoon, skim off the fat and discard. Add the fish sauce and salt to taste. You should have about 8 cups (2l) of liquid.

Meanwhile, soak the dried rice noodles: place them in a large bowl with warm water to cover and stand until soft and pliable, about 20 minutes. Drain and set aside. Cut the beef across the grain into paper-thin slices about 5cm wide by 7.5cm long. Set aside.

To serve, bring the broth to a boil. Reduce the heat to low to keep the broth warm. Thinly slice the onion and spring onions and the chillies; set aside.

Bring a large pot three-quarters full of water to a boil. Add the noodles and boil until tender, about 1 minute. Drain and divide the noodles evenly among 6 soup bowls. Top each evenly with the onions, a few slices of the beef and some chillies. Ladle the hot broth over the top. Garnish with the coriander and mint. Serve with lime wedges.

Serves 6

STAPLES

CHE

The Hanoi speciality of **chè** (a dessert or sweet snack made of green mung beans) is now popular throughout the country. It's best in Hanoi and you'll see it throughout the city in shops and markets. Hanoians love to snack and so there is a kind of chè for every occasion, each with different ingredients and appearance. The most popular type is a thick liquid with the consistency of custard which must be eaten with a spoon.

Che is eaten anywhere at anytime – you'll see it in shops and markets throughout Hanoi – and is popularly served in a tall glass with shaved ice on a hot summer day. It's really a combination of ingredients and each shop has its own special formula. The most well known che among Hanoians is **chè thap cam** (chè of 10 ingredients), made from a base of sweetened cooked green mung beans and coconut milk, to which is added small cherries, slices of dried banana, a deep green jelly-like agar-agar, steamed coconut paste and dried coconut shavings, crushed peanuts, lotus seeds and dried apples. It has a textured taste adventure with every bite and it's a good pick-me-up on a hot and thirsty summer's day.

There are three chè street stalls next to each other at the start of Hang Dieu Street in front of the Hang Da Market which sell a typically delicious chè thap cam.

It is common to make an appointment to meet friends in a chè shop. The one in the alley at 72 Tran Hung Dao is always crowded with people but since it is unseen from the street, it is hardly noticed by the uninitiated. This shop adds some unusual ingredients like lychees, apples and custard apple which add to its visual effect. It also adds marble-sized coloured balls of steamed rice flour paste filled with exotic sweets. Even the ice here is special; ground so fine that it quickly melts in your glass.

On Phan Chu Trinh and Hai Ba Trung streets there is a chè called **chè thái**. It is more orange in colour and thicker in consistency. There are fewer additional ingredients in che thai, which has the consistency of a thin pudding. 'Chinese' **chè bánh trôi tàu** is an excessively sweet, almost black, syrup spiced with ginger and served for its medicinal and warming properties on a cold day. Added to the liquid is an egg-shaped rice flour paste filled with sesame seed, coconut and peanuts. The shops on Cat Linh and Hang Dieu sell this.

Dry chè is yellow and comes in the form of a cake which you can eat by hand. Many small portable stalls sell this, and it makes for a sweet energy-giving snack for a busy day in Hanoi.

– *Barbara Cohen*

Nuoc Mam

This is the one ingredient that is quintessentially Vietnamese. It is different from fish sauces made in other countries, and lends a distinctive character to Vietnamese cooking. The simplest way to describe it is as the liquid drained from salted, fermented fish. It is very often used as a dipping sauce, and takes the place of salt on a western table. It can be mixed with garlic, chilli, sugar, vinegar and fresh lime to make the dipping sauce **nước chấm**. Every cook varies the ingredients a little, depending on what is to hand, or on taste to achieve a good blend.

All along the length of Vietnam's coastline and in the deltas people brew nước mắm. Different combinations of fish and a few secret ingredients can add or change colour and flavour, and the result is many different local blends.

Wherever and whatever, the process is the same. The fish, usually small anchovy types, are alternately layered with salt. (Nước mắm makers often produce their own sea salt by boiling seawater over a rice husk fire, and scooping off the salt as it crystallises on the surface.) The salted fish are left in huge wooden barrels for up to three months, then the liquid is drained through a tap at the base and poured back into the barrels and left for another three months. It is drained off again, strained, and is then ready for sale, or it can be aged further. The flavour improves over the years, making aged nước mắm like fine wine to a connoisseur.

During the American/Vietnamese war, several Vietnamese expats living in France imported large quantities of superior nước mắm and put it into storage for aging. It is now said to be at its peak. Most Vietnamese will never travel to France, but government officials on official trips are said to seek out the aged nước mắm with the fervour of French wine masters.

The islands of Phu Quoc, off the southernmost coast, are thought to produce the best nước mắm, praised for its clarity and flavour. As with olive oil, the best grade is from the first draining. It is usually very dark in colour, very viscous and heady, with the label marked **ngon** or **thượng hạng**, indicating its high quality. Cheaper grades are made after the first grade has been drained off. Fresh water is added to the mash and, after pressing, a clearer, lighter product can be drained off. This nước mắm is used in cooking.

Nước mắm neophytes often find it repellent when raw, but cooked with other ingredients it highlights their flavours while losing most of its own. Hotels and restaurants often assume that foreigners will not like nước mắm, and so serve them soy sauce instead. Unless you are a vegetarian, do not allow this to happen. Insist on the real thing. You will not have been to Vietnam otherwise.

Nuoc Cham (Dipping Sauce)

No Vietnamese table is complete without a dish of nuoc cham for dipping and drizzling. It is as ubiquitous as rice.

Ingredients

1–2 cloves garlic
1   red chilli, stem and seeds removed
2   teaspoons sugar
$^1/_4$ fresh lime
$2^1/_2$ tablespoons water
2   tablespoons nuoc mam

With a mortar and pestle, pound the garlic, chilli and sugar into a paste. Squeeze in the lime juice. With a paring knife, remove the pulp from the lime and pound it into the paste. Add water and nuoc mam and mix well. Makes 1 cup (250ml)

Herbs & Spices

Vietnam first came into western consciousness via spices. Roman traders landed here in 166 AD as they worked the spice route. The Portuguese stayed longer and did more for the business in the 16th and 17th centuries. By the time the French arrived Vietnam was known in the west as a land of spice. While rice and nước mắm define Vietnamese 'food', it is spices that define Vietnamese 'cuisine', the study, practice and development of the kitchen arts. There could be no phở without them, just plain beef noodle soup, and nothing to wax rhapsodic about. But the picture of Vietnamese cuisine is painted in vivid colours. And this is the palette:

Bạc Hà (Mint)
The best is said to come from Lang village near Hanoi. Of the numerous Asian mint varieties, the round-leafed mint, a tropical variety of spearmint, is the one most commonly used by Vietnamese cooks. This fragrant herb is indispensable to Vietnamese cookery.

Bội Hương (Star Anise)
The dried pod of a tree of the *Magnoliaceaes* family, said to come from China. Mainly grown in the Lang-Son region (north Vietnam), this spice has cloves that resemble an eight-pointed star. Not related to aniseed, it yields a strong liquorice flavour and is an essential in phở.

Bột Nghệ (Turmeric)
The ground powder of a ginger rhizome of the ginger family. Deep yellow in colour, this spice is often used as a dye as well as in curries.

Gừng (Ginger)
Not as common in Vietnamese dishes as Chinese, but still an important spice for both its gustatory and medicinal properties. It is added to fish, seafood and organ meats. Its pungent aroma can be used to neutralise any 'too fishy' smells in fish.

Hoa Huệ (Chives)
Thin, stiff flowering stems from Chinese chives, with a flower bud at the tip of each stem. Sold fresh by the bunch, the stalks are tender and taste mildly of garlic.

STAPLES

Hột Điều Đỏ (Annatto Seeds)

The seed of the 'lipstick plant' is commonly used as food colouring. The seeds are fried in oil to extract the orange colour, then discarded.

Mía (Cane Sugar)

Raw, brown and refined, sugar is an essential element of Vietnamese cookery, especially in the south. Sugar cane is widely cultivated in Vietnam as a food crop and as a source of sugar. In Vietnam, the pressed juice from the canes is served as a drink in summer, and people enjoy simply chewing on the peeled stems and spitting out the fibres.

Ớt (Chillies)

Vietnamese cooks generally use two varieties. The large, elongated red or green chilli, resembling the Italian pickling variety, is mildly hot, and used sliced or whole, or cut into a 'chilli flower' for garnishing finished dishes. The other is a tiny, fiery hot chilli called 'bird's eye chilli', used for seasoning.

Ngò (Coriander/Cilantro)

Vietnamese cookery as we know it would not exist without coriander, also known as cilantro or Chinese parsley. The leafy green herb is highly fragrant, with a clean, refreshing taste.

Rau Quế (Basil)

Also known as Thai basil, a herb with an exceptional mild aniseed flavour. It is necessary for garnishing phở. In the tropics holy basil, which has purple stems and flowers, is commonly used.

Riềng (Galangal)

This bears a slight resemblance to a small 'thumb' of ginger but tends to have white and purple colouring. It is not a substitute for ginger. Dried galangal is used only in soups and stews. In the spirit world, galangal represents silver; ginger represents gold.

Xả (Lemongrass)

Also called citronella, lemongrass is an aromatic tropical grass that informs both Vietnamese and Thai cuisine. It imparts a lemon-like taste and smell without the acidity. Use the whole stalk, usually cut into sections and slightly crushed with the dull side of a knife blade.

Flavouring Agents & Sauces
Bánh Phồng Tôm (Prawn Crackers)
Often called 'shrimp chips', these dried, reddish-pink chips are made from minced prawns, tapioca starch and egg whites. They are often eaten as a snack or as an accompaniment to salads.

Hương-Liệu (Five-spice Powder)
Used to flavour barbecued meats and stews, this fragrant, reddish-brown powder is a blend of ground star anise, fennel or anise seed, clove, cinnamon and Sichuan peppercorns.

Đậu Xanh (Mung Beans)
When green mung beans are watered, they develop into beansprouts. Dried green mung beans with the green skins removed are known as yellow beans. They have a subtle flavour and a slight crunch. In Vietnam, yellow beans can be used to make dipping sauces (yellow bean sauce), and they find their way into glutinous rice preparations such as banh chung. The starch from the beans is processed into cellophane noodles.

Củ Kiệu Chua (Pickled Shallots)
These are the very young, tender bulbs of spring onions, packed in vinegar, sugar and salt. They are used as a condiment to accompany grilled foods and noodle dishes or added as a seasoning to sweet-and-sour dishes.

Dầu Hào (Oyster Sauce)
A Chinese condiment made from ground oysters, water, salt, cornflour and caramel colouring, used primarily for stirfrying vegetables, giving them a greater depth of flavour.

Đậu Nành (Dried Soybeans)
Soybeans are the edible dried seeds of the soy plant. Used in the production of bean curd (tofu), and the main ingredient in soybean milk and jellied bean curd.

Đậu Phộng (Peanuts)

An important ingredient in Vietnamese cooking. Raw peanuts are preferred. The cook will normally toss them in a hot, dry pan to toast them, giving them a deeper flavour and more aroma. Peeled raw peanuts are a common item in the markets. Crushed peanuts are used for texture and flavour in dipping sauces and as a garnish for cooked food.

Dầu Mè (Sesame Oil)

The oriental type of sesame oil is a rich-flavoured, amber-coloured oil obtained from pressed, roasted sesame seeds. It is very intense, so only a few drops are needed in marinades or at the last moment of cooking to flavour certain dishes.

Đường Phèn (Rock Sugar)

Also called 'rock candy' or 'yellow rock sugar' for its close resemblance to a rocky piece of quartz crystal. It is made from white sugar, brown sugar and honey and is much sweeter than regular sugar. It is often crushed with a mortar and pestle and used to season Vietnamese sausages and meatballs.

Đường Thẻ (Palm Sugar)

A type of sugar made by boiling down the sap of various palm trees. It is used as a sweetener and also to help balance saltiness in savoury dishes.

Hạt Sen (Lotus Seeds)

These seeds of the lotus plant resemble large, round peanuts. In the lakes and marshes of Vietnam lotus seeds are abundant, and are eaten raw as a snack, used to add eye appeal to stews, soups (especially in vegetarian cooking) and sweet confections. On festive occasions they are used in the aromatic lotus rice, **cơm hạt sen**.

Hoisin (Hoisin Sauce)

A sweet, piquant brown paste made from soybeans, red beans, sugar, garlic, vinegar, chilli, sesame oil and flour. Though more common in China, Vietnamese cooks often mix it with broth, fresh chillies and ground peanuts to make a dip. It is also used as the chief ingredient in barbecue sauce.

Mắm Nêm (Anchovy Sauce)

A blend of fermented anchovies and salt, bottled and sold as both condiment and cooking ingredient. It is very strong in taste and smell, and is normally diluted when used to make the sauce of the same name.

Lá Chuối (Banana Leaves)

In Vietnam, banana leaves are used to wrap foods for steaming or to enfold food for portability. The food is served in the leaf, but the leaf is not eaten. They preserve moisture, and impart a light green colour to rice but no flavour or fragrance.

Lá Lốt (Betel Leaves)

The peppery leaf of a vine related to *Piper nigrum*, which yields black pepper. The large, round and crinkled leaf is often stirred into soups for its herbal fragrance, used as an outer wrapping for spring rolls, and as part of the standard garnish. Wrapped around beef meatballs and grilled, it yields **bò lá lốt**.

STAPLES

Tương Ốt (Chilli Sauce)

Also known as **lak kiu chuong** this hot sauce is made from ground fresh chillies, garlic, salt, sugar and vinegar. It's used as a table condiment and seasoning in soups, green papaya salad and anything else you might fancy.

Mắm Ruốc (Shrimp Sauce)

This very pungent sauce is made from pounded, salted fermented prawns. It's commonly used to add flavour to soups, salads, dipping sauces, and stirfries of meats or vegetables.

Mè (Sesame Seeds)

Sesame seeds are used both hulled and unhulled. A common ingredient in Vietnamese cookery, they are toasted in a hot, dry pan, then crushed to release their flavour. Used in dipping sauces and marinades, and sprinkled on sweet confections.

Men (Yeast Ball)

Also known as 'wine ball', men is normally sold in pharmacies. It is a dry yeast used in making rice wine. Small, round, greyish balls are usually sold in pairs.

Nuoc Dua (Coconut Milk)
The main ingredient in Vietnamese curries and sweets, this is the milky liquid squeezed from grated and heated coconut meat. The clear juice inside the shell is called coconut water; it is mainly used as a beverage or as a meat tenderiser. Coconut milk can be the vehicle for almost any sauce, savoury or sweet. Simply add what flavourings you like, such as curry powder, or sugar and vanilla extract, and simmer for 30 minutes.

Ingredients
2   medium-sized coconuts, shelled, meat grated
5   cups (1.25 l) boiling milk or water for a less rich product

In a food processor fitted with the steel blade, blend the grated coconut and half of the boiling milk until the coconut meat is finely ground. Let steep for 30 minutes.
   Pour the liquid through a fine sieve or cheesecloth into a large bowl. Squeeze out as much of the liquid as possible. Repeat the process with the same coconut meat and the remaining boiling milk to make a second pressing. Discard the coconut meat. Combine the two extractions.

Nước Hoa (Flower Water/Essences)
In Vietnam, flower waters and essences are popular for flavouring sweet drinks and desserts. Most popular are jasmine, grapefruit and orange-blossom water. They are produced by pressing then heating and distilling the fresh petals of these flowers.

Tan Xai (Preserved Vegetables)
A mix of pickled Chinese cabbage and seasonings, a bit like Korean 'kimchee'. It is sold in small crocks in the markets. Very pungent, and used only in small amounts to add flavour to soups and noodle dishes.

Thạch Cao (Gypsum)
Chemical agent used as a coagulant for bean curd.

Kim Châm (Lily)
The buds of a special type of the *Hemerocallis* lily. Also called 'golden needles'. The gold-coloured dried buds are added in combination with tree ear mushrooms and cellophane noodles to stirfries, soups and vegetarian dishes.

Thạch Đen (Grass Jelly)
Also known as agar jelly in Chinese. Made from seaweed and cornstarch, this black jelly is sold sweetened and has cooling properties. It is sold in cans like soda. Try it on ice.

Thạch Hoa (Agar-agar)
A gelatine derived from processed seaweed. It looks like crinkled strips of cellophane. It is widely used in the tropics for jellied sweets, as it sets without refrigeration in temperatures up to 37.7°C.

Tôm Khô (Dried Shrimp)
Shelled, dried and salted shrimp with a pungent flavour. They are usually used in small quantities to season certain dishes such as soups and stirfries, but they can be found sprinkled on cupcakes as well.

STAPLES

FLOWERS FOR THE TABLE

Flowers for the heart? Flowers for your love? How about flowers for your table? Your plate, to be exact. Yes, flowers to eat. Both for your gustatory delight, and for your health. Traditional Vietnamese medicine regards certain flowers as part of its pharmacology. Traditional Vietnamese cooks regard them as tasty.

Flowers of the pomelo tree, whose sweet smell perfumes the nights of late spring, can be distilled into an essence that gives an extra dimension to many desserts.

The frangipani that grows on temple grounds is used for its anti-hypertension properties and taken as a kind of tea.

Lotus stamens are thought to have medicinal properties for the treatment of uterine bleeding and 'loss of libido'. Lotus seeds – flowers to be – may be candied, cooked in syrup or used as stuffing for chicken. They are thought to have a sedative effect.

Jasmine, the traditional symbol of loose morals, has long been popular in tea and candy. White roses steamed with sugar make cough syrup that children are not reluctant to take. Banana flowers are sliced into thin strips and made into a tasty salad. Flowers of **mướp** (luffa) and **bí rợ** (pumpkin) are often eaten fried in peasant homes.

A soup cooked with flowers of the strong-smelling **thiên lý** (cynanchum) is popular among rice farmers and is thought to be a good treatment for gout.

Cha Gio (Spring Rolls)

Yes, they do sometimes seem to be the national dish of Vietnam. When we think of Vietnamese food they tend to be the first thing that come to mind. And they do serve to set the Vietnamese apart from the Chinese, by their use of rice wrappers instead of wheat, and their different fillings. Yes, they're a tasty tidbit. When you wrap them in a lettuce leaf with a sprig of coriander/cilantro and dip them in nước chấm, they are even more so.

And we can't seem to get away from them. They're like hamburgers, or locusts even, in their number. And while we are loath to think of them as McSpringRoll, or as a plague of chả giò, they begin to tire. They all seem to taste the same. Many travellers to Vietnam, or even diners in Vietnamese restaurants in Melbourne, San Francisco or London, feel somehow obligated to down as many as possible, as though the more spring rolls they consume, the more of Vietnam they will taste.

Let us humbly disabuse you of this, if disabusing you need. You could eat your way through the entire nation without ever tasting one of these ubiquitous little morsels and still have had all you needed to thoroughly understand Vietnamese gastronomy. We have nothing ill to say about the little nubbin. We would never counsel you to avoid the chả giò. But we would urge you not to let it define for you, in even a limited way, the cuisine of Vietnam. And just to prove that we have no hard feelings against them, we happily provide you with the recipe so you can have them at home.

Filling

60g	cellophane noodles, soaked in warm water for 20 minutes, then drained and cut into 2.5cm lengths
500g	minced pork
1	onion, finely chopped
2	tablespoons tree ear mushrooms, soaked in warm water for 30 minutes, then drained and finely chopped
3	cloves garlic, finely chopped
3	shallots or white part of 3 spring onions, finely chopped
1/2	can (200g) crabmeat
	teaspoon freshly ground black pepper

Assembly

20	sheets dried rice papers (banh trang)
4	eggs, well beaten
2	cups (500ml) peanut oil

Accompaniments

> basic vegetable platter (lettuce, mint leaves, coriander, and cucumber slices)
> grated carrots

2   quantities Nuoc Cham (see recipe earlier in this chapter)

Combine the filling ingredients in a bowl and set aside.

Cut a round rice paper sheet into quarters and lay them on a flat surface. Using a pastry brush, paint the beaten egg over the surface of each piece of rice paper. Give the egg mixture a few minutes to soften the wrappers.

Place about 1 teaspoon filling near the curved side of a rice-paper quarter. Fold the sides over to enclose the filling and continue to roll.

Pour the oil in a large frying pan or wok. Add the spring rolls to the cold oil then bring the heat to moderate, and fry for 10-12 minutes until golden brown.

To serve, arrange the vegetable platter attractively. Have grated carrot and a bowl of **nước chấm** at hand. Take a lettuce leaf and place some of the other vegetables on it. Then take a spring roll and roll it into a cylinder in the leaf. Hold the cylinder with the fingers, dip it into your bowl of **nước chấm**, and enjoy.

Makes 80

STAPLES

Tương Cà-ri (Curry Paste)
More pungent and spicy than curry powder, they are often combined.

Tương Ớt Tươi (Chilli Paste)
A spicy hot mash of fresh red chillies, garlic, salt and soybean oil, this has no relationship to Chinese hot bean paste. Used as a table condiment and seasoning for sauces and stirfries, it is a necessity of Vietnamese cookery.

Nước Tương (Soy Sauce)
A traditional light brown sauce prepared from soybeans, in which the ground beans are mixed with water, roasted rice powder and salt.

Sundries
Bột Báng (Tapioca Pearls)
Teardrop-sized nodes made from the starch of the cassava root. Used as an ingredient in certain soups and sweet puddings to thicken and add texture.

Bột Năng (Tapioca Starch/Flour)
The starch of the cassava root, when added to rice flour, gives a translucent sheen and chewiness to fresh rice wrappers.

Bot Gao (Rice Flour)
The flour made from long-grain rice, it is different from glutinous rice flour, which is made from sweet rice; the two are not interchangeable. Rice flour is the basis for many rice noodle dishes and sweets.

Bột Khoai (Potato Starch)
Used as a binder for pâtés and meatballs.

Bột Nếp (Glutinous Rice Flour)
Glutinous or sweet rice flour is used to make sweet confections.

Fruit & Vegetables

After rice, fruit and vegetables make up the bulk of the Vietnamese diet. If given the choice of abandoning vegetables or abandoning meat, virtually all Vietnamese would eschew flesh and keep the veggies. And they would not be the inveterate snackers and grazers that they are were it not for the gift of fruit. Hardly anyone would go on a trip without a bag of fruit – just go down to a train or bus station and see.

Vietnamese Proverb

Take medicine when you are sick, eat vegetables with every meal.

Fruit

Bưởi (Pomelo)

Like a large grapefruit, pomelos (sometimes called pamplemousse) have thick skins and pith, and yield a sweeter, less acidic fruit than ordinary grapefruit. The coast of central Vietnam produces the most prized varieties between August and November. They are often sold on the street and in train stations as a popular snack. They are often eaten with salt, or tossed with herbs to make a refreshing salad.

Chôm Chôm (Rambutan)

Fiery red hairy skins give rambutans the look of tiny suns. They have a tender white flesh with a cool sweet flavour. Look for them from May to October, the rainy season.

Đu Đủ (Papaya)

One of many New World crops in Vietnam, there are 45 species of papaya (also known as pawpaw). High in vitamins A and C, when ripe, the large, gourd-like fruit has a refreshing and sweet orange to red flesh, often taken with a squeeze of lime juice to bring out its subtleties. When green it is high in iron and used to make a tangy salad.

Dứa (Pineapple)

Grown chiefly in the Mekong Delta region. Some are very good, others rather dry. You can improve on them by doing as the Vietnamese: use the little packet of salt and red chilli powder that is usually sold with cut pineapple. The juice is sometimes made into a perfumed liquor, or mixed with egg yolk to produce a high-calorie beverage.

Khế (Starfruit)
A five-pointed and shiny-skinned fruit that comes in a yellow, orange or green colour. Cut into cross sections to reveal its star shape. It is intensely juicy.

Măng Cầu (Custard Apple)
A fruit with a bumpy green skin that blackens as it ripens. Its smooth white flesh is studded with black pips – just pull them out and enjoy the sweet custard taste and texture.

Măng Cụt (Mangosteen)
A fruit the size of a tennis ball with a dull purple shell and green sepals. Twist or cut open for the transparent white flesh with a delicious sour-sweet flavour. In the balance of yin & yang, it is the complement of durian.

Me (Tamarind)
Originally thought to be from India, these brown seed pods resembling vanilla beans contain a tart mushy flesh. Its high acidic content makes it useful as a flavouring agent in savoury dishes and desserts.

Mít (Jackfruit)
A giant blimp-shaped fruit containing chewy yellow segments. The intensely perfumed flesh is a good source of vitamins A, B, and C. The wood of the tree is often used for sacramental carvings.

Nhãn (Longan)
Tasty tiny fruits that grow in the Mekong Delta and in the North. Peel open the smooth, light brown skin to reveal a translucent white pulp covering a large black seed. The thicker the pulp, the juicier and more fragrant the fruit.

Ổi (Guava)

High in vitamins A and C, and in the minerals iron and calcium, the pink flesh of the guava is sheathed in an edible green skin. Eat it raw or use it for juice.

Sầu Riêng (Durian)

The king, or jester, of tropical fruits, praised and damned in equal measure. You either love it or hate it. Its Vietnamese name means 'one's sorrows'. You may regret hacking into the armour-like skin of a durian as its aroma will linger long in your memory. But if you hold your breath you can enjoy the creamy dense flesh and its complex flavour, reminiscent, to speak kindly, of avocado, peanut butter, ripe cheese and honey. This gigantic and very expensive fruit is in season from May to August. (For a less complimentary description, see the The Bold Palate chapter.)

(For a less complimentary description, see the The Bold Palate chapter.)

Xoài (Mango)

The fibrous coral-coloured flesh of the mango comes in several varieties. The sweetest are the large rounder ones with bright yellow skin (**xoài cát**) that can weigh as much as 500g. The most prized come from Cao Lanh in the Mekong Delta, and are in season from March to June.

Trái Vải (Lychee)

One of the common sights of Vietnam, you will see clusters of dark red, lumpy lychees throughout the country, especially in the North. Connoisseurs say the best of them come from Hung Yen province, where they are the juiciest and sweetest. Peel open to reveal white flesh covering a black pip.

STAPLES

Vegetables
Bắp Chuối (Banana Blossom)
Looking like a big purple spearhead, sliced finely and soaked in cold water, it is used as garnish for noodle soup, and eaten raw in salads. It has a delicate taste and a touch of alum to dry the mouth.

Cà Tím (Aubergine/Eggplant)
Also known as Chinese eggplant, this long, thin purple variety has a sweet flavour with little bitterness.

Cải Tàu (Mustard Greens)
This has a sharp flavour that adds a nice clean taste when combined with other ingredients. It looks a bit like head lettuce in size and shape, but you'll recognise it because the leaves wrapping the heart have thick stalks. Parboiled, the stalks become tender and succulent and the assertive flavour mellows.

Cải Xanh (Flowering Cabbage)
With yellow flowers, firm, slender stalks and crisp leaves, flowering cabbage is regarded as the best of Chinese cabbages and is much prized by Vietnamese cooks. The taste is mild and the texture tender but crisp.

Củ Cải Trắng (Daikon)
Also known as Oriental white radish, this root vegetable looks like a large white carrot. The flesh is crisp, juicy and mildly pungent, and lends itself well to soups and stews. Also enjoyed raw in salads or pickled.

Củ Đậu (Jicama)
A brown-skinned root vegetable tasting somewhat like a turnip. It must be peeled before use, and may be eaten raw in salads, munched for a snack, or cooked.

Đậu Đũa (Long Beans)
The immature pods of dry black-eyed peas. Just like the name says, long beans (snake beans) can measure up to 60cm (2 feet) in length. Vietnamese call them 'chopstick beans'.

Đậu Hu (Bean Curd/Tofu)
Made from soybeans, and sometimes called the 'poor man's meat'. Pressed bean curd has all the essential amino acids, is low in calories and devoid of cholesterol. It is bland but goes well with other ingredients, giving them no competition for your attention. You can do absolutely anything with it:

Dong Xuan Market, Hanoi

deep-fry, sauté, steam, bake, simmer, grill (broil) or put it in a sandwich. It comes in three textures: soft, for adding to soups or steamed dishes where cooking time is brief; semi-soft, for use in stirfries; and firm, for stuffing and deep-frying.

Khổ Qua (Bitter Melon)

A hard gourd, thought to have healthful benefits. It looks like a fat, knobby cucumber. Green and firm, it has a very crisp texture and a strong, bitter taste. It is often pickled. Before cooking, the seeds and inner membrane are removed and the outer shell is sliced into small, crescent-shaped pieces and fried or added to soups. It is also hollowed out, stuffed with minced pork and braised.

Giá (Beansprouts)

Mung bean sprouts, the most widely available variety, are found everywhere in Vietnam. They are prized for their crunchy texture. They are eaten raw, added to soups or stirfried.

NEW WORLD CROPS

Vietnam without pineapple? Unthinkable. Could you make nước chấm without chillies? Could you even set a proper Vietnamese table without them in some form? Hardly.

And what about tomatoes? If they disappeared, Vietnamese cooks would wail. And yet Vietnam has not always had them. These fruits are all New World crops, that is, indigenous to the Americas.

We don't know when they arrived in Vietnam, or who brought them. But it is reasonable to assume that it was the Spanish or Portuguese who brought them into Hoi An sometime around 1600. Perhaps they were part of soldiers' rations or from the larders of epicurean missionaries (the Jesuits have always been known for their sophistication). Or maybe they were just ordinary trade goods.

Whatever the circumstances of their arrival, Vietnam has embraced them and made them her own. Their importance is reflected in the fact that they are all included in what many Vietnamese, especially in the south, consider a national dish – canh chua cá, hot and sour fish soup (see recipe later in this chapter).

Khoai Môn (Taro)
An oval-shaped tuber with brown, hairy skin. The flesh may be white to creamy, sometimes speckled purple. It tastes a bit like a potato, and is used in the same way by Vietnamese cooks.

Măng (Bamboo Shoots)
Fresh, pickled or dried bamboo shoots are popular throughout Vietnam. Fresh shoots, which have a savoury sweetness and crunch, are peeled and boiled for about 30 minutes before using. Dried shoots are soaked and boiled.

Nấm Hương (Chinese Black Mushrooms)
Expensive but popular for their distinctive flavour and texture. They have thick-fleshed caps 2.5–5cm in diameter, and are light brown in colour with white markings on the surface. Generally, they are very fragrant. Also available dried.

Nấm Hương (Straw Mushrooms)
Pretty yellowish-brown, umbrella-shaped caps – also called 'paddy straw' mushrooms because they grow on straw and rice husks.

Nấm Mẹo (Tree Ears Mushrooms)
Also called cloud ears or wood ears, and named for their shape, which is reminiscent of a human ear. Their texture is somewhat jelly-like and translucent, yet crisp. They are mainly used to add texture to stir-fries, stuffings and vegetarian dishes. Often sold dried, they must be soaked before using.

Rau Muống (Water Spinach)
Unrelated to the true spinach but used in much the same way. An aquatic plant, considered Vietnam's national vegetable. It grows equally well on wet or dry land. It has hollow stems and light green arrowhead-shaped leaves. Vietnamese cooks use it for the contrast in texture between crunchy stems and tender leaves, as well as its spinach-like taste. It is sold by the bunch at Chinese and Vietnamese greengrocers, and finds its way into stirfries and soups, and can be added raw to salads.

Fish, Meat & Fowl

Because of Vietnam's long coastline, seafood has always been a staple and a major source of protein. Freshwater and saltwater species are common and the emphasis is always on freshness, as no refrigeration is available in most places. Crabs, prawns (shrimps), cuttlefish, clams (vongole), eel, shellfish and many species of fin fish can be bought anywhere. Of all the items to be found in a restaurant, the most perishable is fish. And fish gone bad is one bad bellyache. But as a general rule in Vietnam, fish is impeccably fresh. More often than not, it is alive only minutes before it joins you for dinner. If you have a chance to see your fish before preparation, or if you are buying it yourself, check to see that its eyes aren't sunken or opaque, that the gills are ruddy, and the scales intact and adhering to the skin, not flaking off.

Trussed crabs, Hoi An market

Meats in Vietnam vary in quality. Beef tends to be expensive as there is not much suitable land for cattle to graze. It can be tough but usually has a good flavour. In deciding how you want your meat prepared in Vietnam, remember that dry cooking techniques (roasting, broiling, sautéing) work best with the more tender cuts. They are those portions that are least stressed in ordinary movement, and come mainly from the back of the carcass from the point between the shoulders to the tail. Tougher cuts should be cooked with moist or wet heat (stewing, braising, pot roasting). In restaurants throughout much of Vietnam, especially barbecue restaurants, the carcass, or portions of it, is hanging up somewhere in the kitchen. It's okay to go and check it out and select the cut you desire.

Ducks on the way to market, Mytho

Canh Chua Ca (Hot & Sour Fish Soup)

Nearly every country in South East Asia has its own version of sour fish soup. Loaded with fish, vegetables and fruit, this southern Vietnamese version is herbaceous, spicy, fruity, tangy, sweet and savoury. Serve with steamed rice.

Ingredients

1	whole catfish, striped bass, sea bass or red snapper, 1kg
1	tablespoon Vietnamese fish sauce
1/4	teaspoon freshly ground pepper
1	spring onion (scallion), thinly sliced

Soup

1	tablespoon vegetable oil
2	shallots, thinly sliced
3	lemongrass stalks, cut into 5 cm lengths and crushed
6	cups (1.5 l) water or chicken stock
60g	tamarind pulp, chopped
1	cup (250ml) boiling water
1	cup (185g) diced pineapple
1/2	cup (75g) drained, canned sliced bamboo shoots
2	fresh small red chillies, seeded and thinly sliced
1	tablespoon sugar
2	tablespoons Vietnamese fish sauce, or to taste
2	small, firm tomatoes, cut into wedges
1	cup (60g) beansprouts
1	lime, cut into wedges
	salt and freshly ground pepper
	fresh coriander/cilantro sprigs or slivered fresh mint leaves

Fillet the fish, reserving the head, bones and scraps. Cut the fillets into 2.5cm cubes and place in a bowl with the fish sauce, pepper and spring onions. Toss gently to mix, then marinate at room temperature while you make the soup.

To make the soup, heat the oil in a large saucepan over medium heat. When the oil is hot, add the shallots, lemongrass, and the fish head, bones and scraps. Sauté gently without browning until fragrant, 3–5 minutes. Add the water or chicken stock and bring to a boil. Reduce the heat to low and simmer the stock, uncovered, for 20 minutes.

Meanwhile, in a small bowl, soak the tamarind pulp in the boiling water for 15 minutes. Mash with the back of a fork to help dissolve the pulp. Pour through a fine-mesh sieve into another small bowl, pressing against the pulp to extract as much flavourful liquid as possible. Discard the pulp and set the liquid aside. Pour the stock through a fine-mesh sieve into a large saucepan. Discard the contents of the sieve. Bring the stock to a boil. Stir in the tamarind liquid, pineapple, bamboo shoots, chillies, sugar and fish sauce. Reduce the heat to medium and simmer for 1 minute. Add the tomatoes and fish cubes and continue to simmer until the fish turns opaque and feels firm to the touch, 3–5 minutes. Add the beansprouts and season to taste with salt and pepper. Ladle the soup into warmed soup bowls and garnish with coriander/cilantro or mint. Serve with lime wedges.

Serves 4-6

Pork is one of the favourite meats. Everywhere the quality is good and the price cheap, but the pork from Hué is said to be the best. Apparently, it is a smaller beast fed on rice and the trunk of the banana tree, both of which contribute to its superior flavour.

Frogs' legs are good but lamb and mutton are rarely seen. Chinese-style sausages are common in the markets. Then there are those, shall we say, 'unusual' meats...

Why is it that anything unfamiliar tastes like chicken? Perhaps it's because industrially produced chickens from modern farms are so bland that we can compare them to almost anything without too much contradiction. In Vietnam chickens, as well as other fowl, are produced in barnyards where they grow up fat, happy and tasty. As do the ducks. We find them a Vietnamese culinary constant. In the south, chicken often replaces beef in phở.

drinks

While tea is the preferred drink of the Vietnamese, the heat and humidity will have you reaching for anything that can slake your thirst. Whatever you do, make sure you step off the tourist trail. Drinking moonshine through a straw, beer with ice, or tea with lotus flowers may not fire your enthusiasm but it is only when you immerse yourself in the communal drinking culture that you can sample the essential taste of Vietnam.

Alcoholic Drinks
Bia (Beer)

One of the great benefits to humankind brought about by the policy of **đổi mới** (the free market) is a plenitude of beer. It's as common as water and more worthy. You will never be more than a few minutes from beer. And, ironically, you will often be the only one drinking. The average Vietnamese rarely imbibes – partly because it's still expensive for the average elbow bender, and partly because he considers public intoxication bad behaviour. He generally does what drinking he does in private. He might have a beer with his dinner in a restaurant, but you will rarely see him shouting for rounds in a pub. (And we say 'he' because we mean 'he'. Vietnamese women virtually never drink. Or smoke. Or have impure thoughts, at least none that they will admit to.) But travellers are free to quaff as much beer as they like, and the merchants will encourage them.

There is no 'national brand' such as we find in the Philippines with San Miguel, or Thailand with Singha. The beers are quite regional (see the boxed text), and few are distributed countrywide. Some are high volume, some small, some of them could almost be called micro-brews. Most are light and refreshing – like the popular Saigon beer – in keeping with the climate. Some are full flavoured, like the famous 333.

REGIONAL BEERS

The beer map of Vietnam is a patchwork quilt where each city seems to have its own distinctive brew. All the Vietnamese beers are of the pale Pilsner and lager types. Very often they are named simply for their place of origin: Saigon beer, Hue beer, Hanoi beer, Danang beer etc. Although, from Danang, we also find Biere Larue and Lado beer.

In recent years, with the demand for beer on the rise among tourists and the newly affluent of Vietnam, a few Vietnamese/foreign joint ventures have sprung up. San Miguel of the Philippines has invested capital and expertise in the Red Horse brewery of Nha Trang, and Fosters of Australia is now associated with Biere Larue. The best known joint venture is Huda beer which proudly proclaims on the label that it is made with Danish technology – HUe + DAnish = HUDA!

As for taste, the most distinctive Vietnamese beer, in our opinion, is Song Han of the small coastal town of Hoi An. It has a very bold flavour of both hops and malt, and lingers long on your tongue. You either love it or you hate it. Hue beer, similarly, provides no middle ground. Our favourite? Well, although we ought not, we do like to play favourites. We prefer Halida of Hanoi. We just love alliteration.

There is one caution for the beer-loving wayfarer in Vietnam. While the country is awash in good suds, there always has been, and continues to be, a shortage of refrigeration. Even if your beer is served shiveringly cold at a non-air-conditioned location, it won't stay that way long. If it's served just moderately chilled, it's small comfort. If, as will happen, it comes to you at ambient temperature, you might just as well have beer soup. In the air-conditioned pubs and restaurants catering to tourists in the major cities, everything is cool. But if all you go to are the air-conditioned pubs and restaurants catering to tourists in the major cities, that would be uncool, as you would not really have been to Vietnam, in our humble opinion.

So what to do? Go native. Learn how to say **bia đá**, beer with ice. That's right, drink your beer on the rocks. Shocking, yes, we know. Even blasphemous to the western purist. But these beers can stand up to it. Take it from us. When it's 32°C, with humidity to match, the only thing worse than warm beer is no beer at all. Ask for a bucket of **nước đá** (ice).

'But shouldn't we avoid ice?' you ask. 'It's made of the local water, after all'. Well, we can't say that using Vietnamese ice to cool your beer won't make you sick, but we can tell you this: nobody of our acquaintance has ever been sick from it. And we have never been sick from it. And we have resorted to this measure very, very extensively. **Yo!** 'Cheers!' (For more drinking phrases see the Eat Your Words chapter.)

Afternoon shade, Ba Be

BIA HOI

'Tram Phan Tram!'

All over Vietnam, glasses of **bia hơi** are raised and emptied as these words, literally '100%' or 'bottoms up', echo around the table. I've lost count of the number of glasses I've downed in the past hour. The dozen or so empty plastic bottles piling up on the next table and spilling onto the concrete floor provide a clue. Five more litre bottles are delivered to our table and glasses are refilled with ice.

Bia hơi, or 'fresh beer', is Vietnam's version of a draft beer or micro brew. This refreshing, light-bodied Pilsener was first introduced in Vietnam by the Czechs. Decades later bia hơi is still brewed and delivered daily to drinking establishments throughout Ho Chi Minh City and Hanoi and points between. Brewed without preservatives, it is meant to be enjoyed immediately. And enjoyed it is! But don't expect to find bia hơi in the more fashionable haunts, such as Apocalypse Now or Saigon Saigon. Most tourists and expats have never heard of it (too bad!). Ho Chi Minh City yuppies are loathe to admit imbibing (although many do). Bia hơi is the drink of the masses, the working man's refreshment. (A woman drinking bia hơi, especially unaccompanied, verges on scandalous.)

Bia hơi is as much a social experience as a beer, so don't be surprised if you're invited to join your fellow patrons in celebration. Today I raise my glass with four taxi drivers. My Vietnamese is limited, and only one driver, Nhan, speaks a few words of English, but we share the common language of bar patrons the world over – beer. Of course, these gentlemen seem particularly fluent in the local dialect! The volume of their voices rises as the level in the plastic jugs draws down.

Having dedicated countless hours to research, I consider myself a connoisseur of bia hơi and the decidedly downscale establishments where it is served. Bia hơi varies in price, ranging from cheap to dirt cheap. In Hanoi, prices are often advertised by the glass, with 2000 dong (about 15 cents) common. In Ho Chi Minh City, bia hơi is usually served by the litre for around 5000 dong (about 35 cents). Here proper etiquette stipulates bia hơi be poured into a mug over ice. In cooler Hanoi it's frequently served by the glass without ice.

Many neighbourhood establishments consist of little more than a couple of stools and a folding table in the proprietor's living room. Others are sprawling, outdoor beer gardens, reminiscent of those found in Bavaria. Many establishments offer cheap eats to whet your appetite, such as **đậu phộng** (peanuts), **chả giò** (fried spring rolls) and **cánh gà chiên** (fried chicken wings). The more adventurous may wish to sample local favourites **mực khô** (dried squid) or **thịt chó** (dog meat). Whatever your taste, enjoy the laid-back atmosphere and friendly camaraderie.

To locate these purveyors of liquid refreshment look for the ubiquitous hand-painted words 'Bia Hơi' scrawled across a wooden sign. (The temporary nature of the signs allows them to easily be posted or removed depending on availability.) My favourite is a raucous, open-air garage at 6 Hai Ba Trung in Ho Chi Minh City. The Ha Xuyen is the staging ground for a lively afternoon crowd. Myriad street vendors hawk their wares – cigarettes, gum, nuts, dried fish, trinkets and trash, while a cacophony of street sounds serves as background music.

Enthusiasm for quaffing endless rounds of beer seems to be waning at my table; glasses are half-full, the bottles nearly. The proprietor wanders over to our table, leans on the back of my chair with one hand and counts the empty bottles with the other. He mentally makes an adjustment for the food we have consumed and apprises us of the damages: 110 000 dong (about US$7.50). I reach for my wallet, but my new-found friends will have none of it, insisting it's their treat. I thank them and stumble out into the night.

If you think you're ready to try bia hơi, be prepared – drinking with the pros is not for the meek! A western face is a bit unusual at any bia hơi establishment and inevitably attracts curious attention from fellow patrons. Raising your glass in toast more often than not results in an invitation to join a group. Following are my top 10 tips for enjoying bia hơi ... and living to stumble home afterward.

1   Insist on bia hơi – don't allow the attractive girl in the San Miguel T-shirt to sway you to her brand. (Don't worry, she'll still fill your glass with ice!)

2   Buy cigarettes from the girls in the Craven or Marlboro T-shirts. If you smoke, get a carton. If you don't smoke, a pack or two should suffice.

3   Never drink bia hơi on an empty stomach.

4   Beware the dog meat.

5   Learn to say **không**, the Vietnamese word for 'no'. You'll need it for the dozens of vendors who will accost you.

6   Bring plenty of small denomination notes for all the stuff you'll buy from the vendors to whom you told khong.

7   Never fill your own glass with bia hơi.

8   Always fill your companions' glasses with bia hơi.

9   It is considered poor form to lay your head on the table; ditto lying face-down on the floor.

10 Trăm Phần Trăm! *(trahm fuhn trahm)*

– *Martin Wilson, Boulder, Colorado.*

DRINKS

Can

"We call this liquor **rượu cần**", the farmer tells us, "because we drink it through a **cần**". A cần is a straw made from a long, slender bamboo. "We call the bamboo **quân tử**", he continues. "**Quân tử** means a noble man. You understand? The bamboo is straight and elegant, strong and useful, like a noble man should be."

We taste, sucking hard through a long cần straw. It's bittersweet; not too strong, but still warming in the gut. Moonshine never made us feel so noble. We wonder if there is any meaning to the fact that the several can straws stuck into the five-gallon claypot of hooch have been bent by steam and fire into sinuous curves. Perhaps a noble man must be flexible. We sip and ponder. Ponder and sip. Ah! Enlightenment. Without the curve in the straw, our noble drinker would have to stand up and bend over just to wet his whistle. But we sit on little stools in the farmer's house and comfortably booze it up.

Cần alcohol was long regarded as a country bumpkin's tipple. But lately, smart restaurants in Hanoi have been providing it for those who ask ahead. If you walk into a restaurant or home and see on the table a **ché** – what looks like a large flowerpot holding only the wilted stems of giant flowers – it's a good bet there's a cần party in the offing. If you look interested, or interesting, you may be handed a straw and invited to join the little suck-fest. And it is a very convivial way to drink, rather like two straws in a milkshake for a pair of lovers.

Most ethnic minorities in the central highlands make cần, and use it for all kinds of celebrations, religious rituals, weddings, or simply for receiving guests. Its taste and alcohol content will vary, like moonshine anywhere, according to the maker and the season. But the process is the same throughout the highlands: soak sticky rice in water overnight. Add some cleaned rice husks and steam the mixture to a porridgy mass. Add water and yeast made from the leaves of bastard cardamom, pour it all into a che, cover, and wait two weeks. Spend the intervening fortnight gathering noble men in the forest, and teaching them the virtues of flexibility.

Wine

Since the French arrived in the 19th century, Vietnam has not been without wine. Vietnamese cuisine, almost uniquely among Asian cooking schools, lends itself well to wine. In the dark days between 1975 and the early 1990s what wine you could find was apt to be Bulgarian cabernet sauvignon. We were never quite sure whether 'Bulgarian' meant that it came from Bulgaria, or that 'Bulgarian' was just their word for incredibly bad wine. But the dark days are over, and corks can be heard popping throughout the land. Most of the wines available are French. You can see the occasional Italian. And if you search hard you can find a Californian, when you just gotta have Napa Valley. And they are well priced, generally between US$5 to US$10.

Now as to Vietnamese-made wine. Excellent table grapes are grown in the environs of Nha Trang. But they are just that, excellent *table* grapes. Wine grapes have now been introduced to the highlands of Vietnam where the cooler temperatures and plentiful light could produce very good wines. But it will take years for local growers to learn the vintner's arts. Production is currently very small, and the wine virtually unavailable, which in itself is a virtue.

Then there is what is known as 'joint venture' wine. French wines (often poor) are shipped in casks to Vietnam and bottled there. The labels are in French and there is rarely any indication of a wine's joint venture status. But you can always tell. Joint venture wines are always the cheapest.

In purchasing wine, be aware that most Vietnamese merchants don't know how to store wine. Bottles are usually stored standing upright, in brightly lit, unair-conditioned spaces. It is often displayed, like all kinds of merchandise, right out on the street. Corks dry out, air and heat go in, bad wine comes out. After extensive research we have found that shops facing a northerly direction, which have less exposure to the sun, are less likely to have bottle-sick wine. If you buy younger vintages they will have had less exposure altogether to the perils of shipment and storage.

Having purchased a bottle of wine in the tropical heat of Vietnam, the first thing you should do is take it home and give it a cool, dark rest for at least a few hours. Before drinking, red or white, ice it down. Room temperature in Vietnam is not wine friendly. At 30°C, even the boldest red wine will taste like warm water with vinegar.

Don't know where to find wine? Ask any cyclo driver to take you to a wine seller. If he doesn't know one, he knows somebody who does. And lastly: few Vietnamese restaurateurs know about the western custom of charging corkage to patrons who bring their own wine. Shhhhh.

Non–Alcoholic Drinks
The Culture of Tea

The preparation, serving and drinking of tea has a social importance seldom appreciated by western visitors. Serving tea in the home or office is more than a gesture of hospitality. Sharing tea is a ritual. It precedes the conduct of business, scholarly pursuits or meditation, meeting new people and getting acquainted. It's even a prelude to romance. Politicians and tycoons trying to ease tensions at the negotiating table will call for tea to be served, and all will halt until the rituals are performed, and calm restored. Enter a Vietnamese home and, sometimes even before making introductions, you will be offered tea and a moment to collect yourself. Don't refuse, not even politely. At least touch the cup to your lips. At weddings tea precedes and follows the ceremony. Funerals and other farewells are occasions for the drinking of tea. Couples, after a nasty spat, will take tea together rather than 'kiss and make up'. At a party where both tea and liquor are offered, the liquor is borne by servants, but only the host or hostess prepares and serves the tea.

Side-walk tea shop, Ho Chi Minh City

In Thai Binh Province tea is almost a cult. On moonlit nights its devotees set out in boats on the lakes and ponds when the lotus flowers are in bloom, the air heavy with their pungent aroma. They open the about-to-bloom lotus flowers and place a pinch of tea inside each blossom, then close them with ribbon or string. Then they gather the moonlit dew from the lotus leaves. By dawn, the living scent of lotus permeates the tea, and the gatherers have enough dew to add to their teapots. After a few hours of sleep, a blissful afternoon of tea.

All classes of people drink tea. Soldiers drink it in the field; fishermen on their boats; wealthy people in parlours; monks in their monasteries; ladies dressed in **áo dài** and fashionable youths in Levis. A peasant might drink his tea in a banana leaf rolled up into a cone. The rich drink their tea scented with rare flowers; poets and scholars opt for jasmine; lotus for the pure and the chaste, and those who would have you think they are.

In the bad old days, when the government meddled in every aspect of the economy, tea production and distribution were in a sorry state. Tea could be in short supply, and what there was might smell like swamp water. People often turned to artichoke tea as a substitute. By paring out the hearts of artichokes, drying and cutting them finely like tea, they could produce a refreshing infusion, one that many still enjoy from time to time. But it ain't tea. Worst of all, people didn't have time for tea. They had to work from the time they rose to the time they went to bed. They held two jobs if they could. And this is a land of few appliances or electric conveniences. Merely keeping house is a 16-hour-a-day job.

Tea requires time. Time to prepare it, time to contemplate it, time to talk about it, time to savour it. And then time to think back upon it. It must have a good part of an afternoon, or an evening. It is to the average Vietnamese what the finest wines are to the western connoisseur. If you cannot give it its due respect, you must leave it lie.

Now we're in the new days of đổi mới, economic restructuring. The fine teas, grown in the highlands, are again available, abundant, and even cheap. Excellent tea services are everywhere for sale in the markets, and customers are there to buy them. And with the rising prosperity, there is once again time.

Drink seller, Cai Rang floating market, Mekong Delta

Kettle on stove on street corner, Hanoi

The Tea Course

It was during the Nguyen dynasty, with its new capital at Hué, that tea-drinking was elevated to the status of art. In the Hué tradition, a 'tea course' is usually held for three because a traditional tea table is smallish and set against the wall and so has only three sides available. The room would normally be intimate and tastefully decorated, although the tea course may also be held in a garden.

A 'skilful tea drinker' planning a tea course will select the tea service according to the season, so that its patterns and design reflect or complement the weather. Members of the Nguyen dynasty used pots and cups with weighted, rounded bottoms that, if disturbed, would rock a bit, then right themselves. This symbolised the nation's ability to survive despite its historical ups and downs.

A tea course requires a charcoal brazier, a boiling pot, an earthenware pot of cold water (usually rainwater, and, on special occasions, some dew gathered from lotus leaves), a teapot, large and small teacups, tea box, and a few pieces of Aquilaria, an aromatic wood, to add to the fire. Your host will boil the water for a few minutes, then take it off the fire and let it cool to about 90°C. It is poured gently into the teapot, and covered tightly for about five minutes. While the tea is steeping, skilful tea drinkers will comment on the design of the teapot or the fine aroma of the tea, always keeping the tea as the focus of the conversation, as you would do at a wine tasting. From the teapot, the tea is poured into a large cup called the commander cup. From there it is distributed into smaller vessels called soldier cups. This procedure ensures even distribution of the tea's flavour and colour. If it were poured directly from the pot into each cup, the first cup would be more diluted than the last.

As you sip the tea, discuss its taste and any other qualities. Talk of the mood it brings to you. Let the conversation drift to other fine things. Poetry is always a good subject at the tea course. Painting and music. The landscape. But nothing of the past, and nothing of the future. This bit of precious time belongs only to the present.

Coffee

You take a seat. Perhaps a plush chair in the Metropole bar in Hanoi, or a folding chair in a 747 Ca Phe (see the Street Food chapter) in Ho Chi Minh City, or just a little stool the size of your hat on the sidewalk anywhere. You order coffee, expecting a cup of Java to be delivered in a moment, the steamy liquid to be rolling over your tongue and the caffeine rush to follow soon after. But you wait, as much as a few minutes, for in this establishment the water is often boiled one cup at a time when trade is slow. One cup, boiled just for you.

So now you are served. What's this? Not a hefty mug of steaming coffee ready to drink, but a six-ounce glass tumbler with a curious little aluminium pot on top. At the bottom of your glass, half an inch of the palest yellow, sweetened condensed milk, three or four little brunette stains spreading across its surface. Another appears, fallen from the little top pot. Inside the pot the water is ever so lazily seeping into and through the dark-roasted coffee, ground so fine the people call it coffee powder. Minutes pass, and in this long, hot relationship between coffee and water the coffee gives up its entire soul to the water's embrace. You watch. Watch as the liquid falls from the little crucible drop by placid drop, infusing the milk with the fullest measure of the spirits of Arabica and Robusta.

This is strong coffee, and your glass is only half full. Foreigners are often given a small thermos of hot water with which to dilute the brew and give it volume, to make it something closer to what they are used to. But you should try it the Vietnamese way. After all, will you go to Vietnam for things that you are used to? Take slow, tiny sips. Savour each one. Let the flavour resonate on your tongue until it subsides. Let the aroma rise from the back of your throat. Give it time. As much time as was consumed in the marriage of coffee and water in the little chapel on your glass. Give it time, and it will refresh you, and restore you, and give you calm.

Coffee maker, Ho Chi Minh City

Smoothies

There was one bright candle in the dark night of the gastronomic Bad Old Days between 1975 and the early 1990s. A little beacon of cool relief that you could count on finding at any given street corner or roadside rest at any time of day or night. It was the most beguiling combination of Vietnamese artifice and natural goodness: the fruit smoothie. We're not talking the smoothies you get at home in some coffee cum juice bar or amusement park snack shack. We're talking subtlety and sensuality; sensitivity to the nuances of taste, texture and temperature. We're talking about something that, in our humble opinion, can only be produced by the smoothie meisters of Vietnam.

The process begins with a 20cm block of crystal clear ice that has been cooled to only a few degrees below freezing, unlike industrial strength ice that is brought to well below freezing and so is harder and lasts longer. This block of 'warm' ice is set into the maw of a Rube Goldberg-looking machine whose appearance calls to mind a damaged wrought iron sewing machine. A hand-driven crank rotates the virgin ice against evil-looking steel blades that reduce it to the perfect imitation of new fallen snow. Now, into an electric blender, the fruit: the nearly blood red flesh of papaya, or golden chunks of fresh pineapple dripping with its juice, or impossibly sweet bananas, or perfumed mango, or all of them together with maybe a mint leaf. Then a measure of sweet condensed milk from a little can punctured with a knife, and a squeeze of lime juice. Whirl it all together with the freshly made snow until it makes a happy gurgling sound, then stop and no more.

Not in the mood for a sweetie? Then what about avocado? Or tomato? Or both together with a dash of salt and a bite of green chilli, garnished with coriander. Or be bold and have durian!

Smoothie stands were everywhere during the rebirth of entrepreneurship in Vietnam. It was an easy and cheap way to get a start. The venerable Kim Cafe, magnet to backpackers, began as a smoothie stand at the corner of De Tham and Pham Ngu Lao, diagonally across the street from its present location. Like any of its innumerable cousins, it was just a machine, a blender, and a few low chairs in the shade of the eaves of what was the operator's home. Neighbourhood kids played hopscotch on the sidewalk as you sipped a cherimoya–pineapple–watermelon–strawberry–custard apple smoothie in cool defiance of the midday sun.

If they didn't have the fruit you wanted you could bring your own next time and they will make your cusomised smoothie for half-price. Got a bottle of tequila in your bag? Add a nip, and give them a taste, too. Bliss in the Bad Old Days.

Ho Chi Minh City

DRINKS

HOBBY & HABIT

Whether it's an ordinary meeting or an important event, the Vietnamese people have the custom of entertaining guests by offering them a piece of betel, or a cup of tea or coffee. The elderly used to get traditional beverages from nature's roots, leaves, flowers, seeds or herbs. After gathering it they would boil, dry, steam it and do various things to make it good. Sometimes they needed to use their own secret technique in order to get a unique taste. That's a real art. Soft drinks are preferred by the youth today. It's the hobby and habit that decides the beverage for every Vietnamese. Nowadays, the youth also tend to drink coffee at 'coffee gardens'. That means they enjoy the fresh and serene atmosphere while drinking a coffee in the yard with soft music and ornamental trees. That is the moment of meditation which brings the youth away from the bustling life into the inner mind.

– Miss Pham Nhut Binh Minh, Ho Chi Minh City

Whither the ubiquitous smoothie? For the most part, run out of town by Coke, Pepsi, Heineken, Lipton and Johnny Walker. These might be the Good Old Days, but the new prosperity (relatively speaking) has left everyone aching for imports. For *nouveau riche* Vietnam (or should we say *nouveau* not so desperately poor), these are status symbols. To drink Pepsi, foreign beer and scotch says 'I'm making it' – even if they're all mixed together in the same glass.

It goes beyond things to drink. The smart set is even eating frozen TV dinners. Colonel Sanders has hit the beaches and, unlike the US Marine Corps, he is here to stay. Currently, the only place we know of to reliably find a good smoothie is, ironically, the famous French eatery, Camargue, in Ho Chi Minh City. It is offered as an homage to its host country.

But don't despair. The smoothie will come home again some day. Brillat Savarin said, 'Tell me what you eat, and I will tell you what you are'. It is we of the west that are Coke, Lipton and Mr Walker. The Vietnamese are just playing dress-ups with their new money. But they will put their own clothes on again. They will not shun nor forget the better foreign influences. They've kept French bread and wine. They've kept Japanese noodles. They'll keep this and that over time. But the Vietnamese sense of identity will always reassert itself. The people will never forget who they are. They will never forget the taste of Vietnam.

So be of good cheer. The smoothie is not dead. It's just sleeping.

home cooking
& traditions

Enter the Vietnamese kitchen and you'll see that good food comes from simplicity. Essentials consist of a strong flame, clean water, basic cutting utensils, a mortar and pestle, and a well-blackened pot or two. More important is the advice that only a mother or senior member of the family can offer – the tips on how to cook tender squid, cut vegetables finely or roll out a dough for spring rolls.

The Kitchen

Put simply, the bedrock of Vietnamese society is the family. To most Vietnamese it's the greater part of the universe. And the core of the universe is the hearth, around which revolves all that really matters. The kitchen is so sacred that it is inhabited by its own deities (see the boxed text LacThien in Regional Variations chapter). Some people say that there are three kitchen gods who began their existence as humans and who all died for love. Others say that there is only one kitchen god, Ong Tao, who is often depicted as a droll fat fellow who has lost his trousers. (It seems he stood too near the stove and they caught fire.) But whether there is just one kitchen god or three, the spiritual guardian of the hearth must have its due. The most important object in the kitchen is its altar.

> **Vietnamese Proverb**
> Heaven punishes, heaven reprimands. But heaven does none of this when people are eating.

Of more earthly kitchen objects, there are relatively few compared to a French or Chinese kitchen. The typical Vietnamese kitchen is small and decidedly unfussy. You will find little food stored in it on any given day, as there are no means to do so. There is no refrigerator or freezer. There are no shelves stacked with preserves. People make daily, and even twice-daily, visits to the market for the very freshest of everything, from fruits and vegetables and seafood, to freshly killed-to-order chickens, to spices that are ground on the spot. And certainly in such a kitchen there is no dishwasher, save the one with two hands.

Town & Country

There isn't much difference between a Vietnamese peasant kitchen and one in downtown Ho Chi Minh City or Hanoi. Most city kitchens have a pair of electric or gas burners, in addition to a charcoal brazier. In apartment buildings the brazier is a fire hazard, and so is less common. For street cooking, and at market stalls, braziers are the norm. Cooking over charcoal or wood also imbues many dishes with an extra flavour.

Traditional Vietnamese cooks generally squat on the floor while preparing much of their food. They work around the stove on a wet, tiled area, where all utensils, pots, pans and foods can be easily cleaned before and after each use. To the western eye it can look like an untidy, mad scene. But if this be madness, there is method in it.

Country kitchens will often have a large pot as the standard vessel for cooking soups and stocks. Apartment kitchens are often too small for such things. With rice the staple of the Vietnamese diet, a simple rice cooker is always kept on a low fire.

Kitchen, Ho Chi Minh City

One of the most important things in the kitchen, especially a country one, is time. Vietnamese cooking is labour-intensive and time-consuming. Washing baskets full of vegetables and herbs, scrubbing dishes, pounding things in the mortar, and endless chopping and slicing – all without modern appliances – takes time.

One family member has to be on duty just to fan the flames to control the heat because most of the cooking is done over an open fire. The kitchen may not even have running water, so much of the preparation work is done outside, or at a table in a room otherwise used for sleeping or sewing.

THE ANSWER LADY – Faces of Gastronomy

Radio station FM 99.9 in Ho Chi Minh City broadcasts all day. If you are pottering in your kitchen and have a question about cookery between 7am and 7pm, just pick up the phone and dial 1080. The station will patch you through to Mrs Thanh Huyen, the Answer Lady.

Mrs Thanh is not located at the station, but in her cosy home cum cooking school in district 3. She is entertaining us with tea, both hot and iced, and she is, well, answering questions. Two of her students are in the kitchen decorating a cake. Another keeps the tea flowing.

"I've been a cooking teacher for 20 years", she says as she adjusts the folds of her silk dress – she is the very picture of elegance and seems to have chosen her furniture to match her clothes. "I teach Vietnamese cuisine, but I've always had a love of French pastry. I'm not uncommon in that. So I also teach baking".

"My busiest times (answering kitchen queries) are about 8pm and 4am. In the evening people are at home trying to cook dinner for their family after a long day of work. They don't have time to look through books or run to their neighbours, so they call me. Most Vietnamese people are early risers. Many go to work at five or six o'clock but they want to have a good breakfast first. If they are cooking for a wedding feast, they might be at it for 24 hours, almost non-stop. They call at midnight, they call at 2am, they call at dawn. A wedding feast is very important".

"Vietnamese people take their cooking very seriously, don't they?"

"It's one of the things that holds the family together. All the children help, even the boys. So a good Vietnamese man is also at least a fair cook. The kitchen and table are central to the Vietnamese family. So people think nothing of calling me at all hours. I sleep with the telephone", she laughs, "really!"

"Can anybody call you, from anywhere?"

"You can call me from Melbourne or California if you like. But you'll have to speak Vietnamese".

Utensils

The Vietnamese cook uses lots of water, for everything must be kept clean, and boiling and steaming are common cooking methods. So the cook must have mesh, whether in the form of colanders or plastic mesh bowls, or simply bowls with holes to hold the washed herbs and vegetables. When turned upside-down, they are also used to protect fresh food from flies or accidents. You'll find wire-mesh ladles and little wire mesh baskets, for blanching noodles and beansprouts, from most Asian cookware shops.

General Store, Hanoi

TRIN DIEM VY – Faces of Gastronomy

Trin Diem Vy, or Miss Vy as she is known, is the third-generation owner and chef de cuisine at what is now called the Mermaid restaurant (2 Tran Phu Street, Hoi An). It began as a market stall operated by her grandparents when they were young and Miss Vy still uses many of the recipes her grandmother used, from central Vietnam.

Besides operating the restaurant, Vy teaches cookery but here is a traditional home kitchen. "When you come into my kitchen, you come into my home", she says. Vy offers three programmes for the English-speaking traveller – one hour, four hours or eight hours – and it is amazing how much knowledge and skill she can impart in a short time.

And so Vy admits us into her home, into her hearth, into the focus of her days and nights. We are reminded that the Latin word for hearth is 'focus'. At the centre of her kitchen is the ancient source of all Vietnamese cuisine: the earthenware charcoal brazier. Vy has three braziers, and the walls next to them are blackened with years of cooking. The few simple implements hang or lie within easy reach: a ladle, tongs, a curved spatula. Some pots, a couple of sauté pans, and wire racks for grilling complete the setting.

"No woks?" we ask.

"They aren't necessary. We don't fry in quite the same way as the Chinese, and not at the same temperature".

She picks up a handful of greenery and says, "this is your first lesson: good food from fresh ingredients. If you forget this, you cannot cook Vietnamese".

Garlic Infused Oil

Many Vietnamese dishes call for infused oil that is brushed over noodles, barbecued meats, vegetables or breads.

Ingredients

1¼ cups (312.5ml) peanut oil
6   cloves garlic, crushed

Heat the oil in a small saucepan until hot but not smoking, about 150°C. Remove the pan from the heat and add the garlic. Let the mixture steep at room temperature until completely cooled. This oil will keep stored in a tightly covered jar at room temperature for 1 week.

Makes 1¼ cups

Grilled Tuna with Fresh Turmeric

Marinade

1	tablespoon finely minced fresh turmeric
2	cloves garlic, crushed
1	shallot, minced
1	teaspoon nuoc mam
1	small chilli
1	spring onion, thinly sliced
	a pinch each of salt, pepper and sugar
2	teaspoons peanut oil

Ingredients

200g	tuna, cut into bite-sized cubes
1	wood ear mushroom, thinly sliced
1	tablespoon rice vermicelli, soaked 10 minutes
6	banana leaves, about 30cm long or cut to size

Combine the marinade ingredients and marinate the tuna for 10 minutes. Add the wood ear and vermicelli. Brush one of the leaves with a very thin coating of oil, then place the tuna onto the leaf. Arrange it in an even, compact single layer. Fold the sides of the leaf over like an envelope. Lay it folded side down on another leaf and repeat the procedure. Repeat until all six leaves are used. Secure the outer leaf with a thin wire or safety pin. Lay the leaf package on a wire grill over hot coals and cook for 6 minutes on each side. The outer leaves will scorch.

Serves 4

It is surprising how satisfying it is to cook without the modern appliances and conveniences we're used to. When we have the time to cook 'hands on', there is great pleasure in clutching a bundle of fresh herbs. Aubergines are beautiful to look at, and to touch. There is a soothing mantra in the steady slicing of delicate spring onions, and the prayer-like working of mortar and pestle. We feel we have come home.

And so we begin. We learn how to fold rice paper in triangles around a stuffing of carrot, rice vermicelli, and mushrooms, with a tasty pink shrimp on top. We let the tail stick out of the little package. It serves as a handle, and provides the name for this little treasure, **tom phi tien** (flying shrimp spring roll). We have to wrap it tightly and neatly so that it will not fall apart while frying.

We learn the fine points of cabbage leaves stuffed with carrot, manually mixing sugar with grated carrot, macerating it until the sugar has been fully incorporated. We add crushed garlic, dip the cabbage leaves in boiling water to soften them and remove any bitterness, roll the leaves into tight little bundles and cut them into colourful slices.

"We don't use as much sugar as they do in the south", Vy says. "And less coconut. We use more spice than the north, and we are more concerned than either with the dish's appearance. We like to say that you must 'eat with your eyes' as well as your mouth".

Vy shows us what *seems* a simple dish; stuffed squid, one of the most eye-catching in her culinary canon. With the tentacles removed and set aside for garnish, the squid tubes are stuffed with a mixture of rice vermicelli, a few spices, and pork that has been 'ground' with a mortar and pestle so that its texture is silky smooth. "Always use fresh spices when you can", Vy tells us. "Dry spices can produce a floury texture". The squid tubes and tentacles are braised in their own juices with a little nuoc mam and cut into thin circular slices, and served with other garnishes.

"In cooking this dish, and in grilling with leaves, you will see the essence of the Vietnamese cooking technique: you have to be there every minute and be in control of the whole process. You can't put something on the fire and leave it. Everything tuna must be cut to the proper size for the cooking method you'll be using. You have to know the temperature of the dish at all times so that it cooks just right. You have to know exactly when to cover the pot so that the squid will not get tough. In cooking with leaves, if the fire is too hot it will burn through to the food, so you have to raise it up from the fire. If it's not hot enough you have to fan it to make it burn hotter. You have to be in control".

Vy has taken us to the heart of the matter. We exercise control of each process for another hour. We slice vegetables with precision, blanch them with a watchful eye. We bring dying fires back to life with lumps of charcoal and brisk fanning. We fry vegetables in peanut oil infused with garlic (see recipe) because we will fry so hot that fresh garlic would burn. Vy's family fetch more supplies from the market. We are intensely aware of what we are doing, and how, and why. And we are intensely satisfied.

We sit down, triumphantly, to dine in traditional Vietnamese family style with Vy and members of her clan. The convivial table reminds us that eating in Vietnam is no lonely task, but a ritual of sharing. It reaffirms our bonds of kinship, friendship, and of ourselves to the natural world. Before us is a large pot of steaming rice, a tureen of corn and crab soup, and a plate of aromatic leaves that we wrap around a spring roll and dip into nuoc cham. We have tuna with fresh turmeric presented in the leaves in which we cooked it. We have the stuffed squid, looking like a Japanese flower arrangement. And we have heaps of delicious fresh vegetables, without which no meal can be called Vietnamese. This meal is a special experience for us. We have worked closely together to produce it. Now we will consume it, closely together.

For cutting, the cook has an array of small, sharp vegetable knives and dangerous-looking choppers heavy enough to lop off the top of a coconut. You'll also see special knives for chopping lemongrass, and a little wooden device impossible to describe used to julienne green papaya. Even the ordinary razor blade is pressed into service, to shred spring onions into green and white ribbons. Besides the usual knives found in any kitchen, another useful implement used by the traditional cook is a narrow, two-bladed knife, used for carving vegetables into decorative shapes, and to slice thin fruits and vegetables for the various rolls and wraps. Any kitchen will have its supply of metal soup spoons, and teaspoons with long handles, bamboo or metal skewers, and wooden chopsticks.

No Vietnamese kitchen is without a mortar and pestle, which is used to grind together flavouring ingredients such as shallots, garlic, lemongrass and chilli, as well as for making 'ground' meat and meat pâtés.

Add rice bowls, small saucers for dipping sauces, soup bowls, table chopsticks and porcelain spoons, and the kitchen is fairly complete.

Knives & Scissors, Cholon Market, Ho Chi Minh City

Cooking Vessels

The Vietnamese use a wok-like vessel somewhat smaller in diameter and not as deep as a typical Chinese wok for sautéing, deep-frying, and some stir-frying. But they prefer to use metal pans with two small handles and a lid that can be removed with chopsticks or a potholder for the same purposes. These pans might range from 15cm in diameter and 7.5cm deep to one large enough to make stock. Not all families have steamers, but a plate on a trivet (little stand) or metal mesh tray set inside a cooking vessel makes an adequate substitute. Quick steaming can be done with little or no water by placing the food in a covered pan over low heat, where it expresses enough of its own juices to produce steam.

Most kitchens will have some rough claypots. While they appear to be very humble vessels, they are used to prepare some of Vietnam's most popular dishes of meat, fish, rice and vegetables.

Cooking Methods

Grilling over charcoal and simmering in caramel are usual Vietnamese kitchen craft in addition to boiling, deep-frying, stirfrying and steaming,

In common with Chinese practice, Vietnamese food is cut into bite-sized pieces before cooking. Meats are usually marinated in spices and nuoc mam for half an hour or more. Pre-seasoning in this way enhances the flavour of the food and helps to preserve the vitamins and protein in the meat while keeping it tender and juicy.

Before the Vietnamese cook puts anything other than rice on the fire, all ingredients must be ready for the pan and laid out within easy reach and in the order it will be needed. Dehydrated foods, such as dried mushrooms or cellophane noodles, have to be reconstituted well in advance of cooking. Generally speaking, the cook will spend more time at the cutting board than over the stove. Actual cooking time will be very short for most dishes.

The making of spring rolls and such require a practised skill in deftly rolling and wrapping with leaves and rice paper. While there are many different forms in which to cut or fold the leaves or rice papers, the trick to proper wrapping is to keep it from being too tight or loose, so that it will not fall apart or swell to bursting during cooking.

celebrating
with food

When the Vietnamese people celebrate, food cannot be very far away. Most of the holidays and feasts are based on the family unit and the food that they share. While they will rationalise that the festival is to give thanks to the heavens or to bribe the gods so that the new year will be prosperous, no doubt it's also a welcome opportunity for more eating, drinking and merriment.

Vietnam's calendar is full of holidays and feasts which are accompanied by specific foods, as well as weddings and other family celebrations. These occasions are often celebrated with foods that would not be eaten at other times of the year. For example, **chả giò**, the fried spring rolls that are known as **nem sài gòn** or **nem rán** in the north, require so much preparation that they are generally made in the home only for special occasions, or are eaten at restaurants.

> **Tet Blessing**
> Happiness as vast as the southern sea; longevity as lasting as the southern mountains.

It is in these many feasts that the culture, often one of personal reserve and measured emotion, lets slip the fullness of its exuberance. If the daily fare can be said to speak in soft and dulcet tones, then the party food screams, 'Par-tay!' A festive table groans under the weight of conspicuous abundance, its vivid colours holler at your eyes, and even the staid and steady rice, stoic pillar of the national cuisine, is dressed for the fair, tarted up with saffron or turmeric, bejewelled with lotus seeds, wrapped in a package of green leaves and steamed to a perfumy decadence.

For a festival the family coffers are broken open and no matter what the amount of their contents they are deemed insufficient. But they will be well used for racks of roasted squab and game birds. They will go towards the Vietnamese version of Peking duck, sliced into juicy slabs, drizzled with a piquant sauce and wrapped in lettuce leaves to be eaten as little packages of delight. The more highly prized species of fish will be steamed or braised whole, and the cooks will give themselves over to the Chinese penchant for elaborate decoration. Many portents of good fortune will be watched for, and duly noticed, just as surely as Santa Claus will be seen elsewhere in the world. At the feast, remember that the diner who receives the head of the fish will have good fortune, just as one in the west who breaks off the larger half of a wishbone.

In the highly structured Vietnamese society the structure of the standard meal is knocked askew for the feast, symbolising the fact that during the feast the world is a different, better, place. Beer or wine might flow while tea takes a back seat. People, north and south, recall the emperors at Hué and nibble tidbits, perhaps with sips of whisky, before the main repast. And dishes may be brought forth and consumed individually so that they can be savoured and duly commented upon and praised. Attendance at a festive meal in Vietnam will convince you, should you need it, that the Vietnamese do not eat to live, but live to eat.

Tet

Mr Le Van Tran and his family have many visits to make in a short time, for they have many ancestors buried near their Hanoi home. They bustle from one cemetery to another to place fresh earth on the graves and pull the weeds from around them, replacing them with flowers. They light incense to invoke the souls of their dead from the other world, so that they might return to visit the family home.

As early as the beginning of the twelfth moon, the last month of the outgoing year, they have been making their many preparations. Grandmother has been fattening a few chickens on glutinous rice. Some weeks ago, Mother, joined with some neighbours to purchase a 6kg piglet. Grandfather must still purchase some paper on which he will paint the first ideograms at the start of the new year. He must also remember to buy some festive red paper on which to write poems and benedictions and good wishes. The children are anticipating their new clothes.

All of these things must be done in time, and in the hope that the ancestors will come, for on the 23rd day of the twelfth lunar month, the Kitchen Gods will depart the Earth for their annual mission to Heaven. For the next week these deities, who are privy to the family's most intimate secrets and business affairs, will be making their reports to the Jade Emperor (The Creator). By this report Heaven will know if the family hearth is a place of strife or a place of love.

To help secure a favourable report to the Jade Emperor the family will give the gods a farewell dinner, and make offerings of money tucked into bright red envelopes and laid upon the kitchen altar. Part of these gifts will be will be saved for future use, and part spent for Tết amusements. It's the thought that counts with the Kitchen Gods. (Some people say that there is only one Kitchen God. Perhaps that way they can save on the offerings.)

Tết, the Vietnamese Lunar New Year, is not unlike some of the ancient European rites of spring or the Christian Easter. It even recalls some of the elements of the Jewish seder. It is a time of renewal and reaffirmation of life, love, family and community. Tet is considered the first day of spring and carries with it all connotations of rebirth and renewal, both physical and spiritual. The environment and the soul should be purified, so there are many cleansing rituals: the ceremonial washing of hair or bathing, polishing bronze or furniture, or just giving the house a good spring-cleaning.

The word Tết comes from the Vietnamese word **tiết**, literally, the knotty projection between two sections of a stalk of bamboo, an internode, a pause, a conjoining. It is a place, or time, or a means of transition between seasons or between epochs or worlds. And it is the connection that holds all together. Others may say that tiết simply means 'seasons'.

The full name of Tết is **Nguyên Đán**, meaning the 'new dawn'. Officially a three-day holiday in Vietnam, it often spills over through a week. The most important moment is the night of the first new moon of the year. This falls between 21 January and 20 February of the western sun-based calendar, halfway between the winter and spring equinox.

Tết should be a time of harmony, for it sets the tone of the coming year. So for at least three days, one takes extra care to hide anger, and to be polite. Nagging problems are deferred, nagging spouses tolerated. People take the attitude that the coming year might be more positive than the past one if they act as if that has already been realised. Behaviour at Tết is thought to foretell the chain of events of the next 12 months.

On the first day of Tết, the family loads food on a prominently displayed table, the first meal for the ancestors since they have returned to the world of the living. The head of the family offers a grace, then lights three sticks of incense, kneels, folds his hands in front of his chest, bows his head and prays. He whispers the names of the deceased of the family up to the fifth generation, and invites them to partake of the feast the family has prepared.

Tet Proverb

'Trees have roots; water has a source, and when drinking from the spring, one must remember the source'.

Meaning, thanks are offered to those ancestors who laboured long ago to provide for the present generation.

This act of obeisance is known as 'ancestor calling', and is the prelude to the most important and unifying moments for the family – the sharing of a meal together, as a form of communion with their ancestors and with each other. The same ceremony will be repeated for the morning and evening meals of the three days of Tết, reaffirming the connection between family members. So important is this eating together that the Vietnamese do not say that they celebrate Tết. They say that they 'eat Tết'. You may be asked if you will 'eat Tết with your family'. Overseas Vietnamese might say that they are going to Vietnam to 'eat Tết in the homeland this year'. And it does not refer only to the physical act of eating, but also to spiritual nourishment.

On the second day of Tết a wider circle of connection is observed. This is the day for going out beyond the immediate family to visit the wife's family and close friends. A few shops may have opened. Some lottery stands might be selling lucky chances to people who feel their stars are well aligned. People come out on the streets and display their new clothes and have their pictures taken.

On the third day of Tết, the circle of connections embraces the community. Families with school children call on their teachers, patients on their doctors, soldiers on their commanders. People visit astrologers to get a good start on the year's fortunes. And on the evening of the third day the ancestors will depart, the smoke from burning votive objects assisting them in their flight.

Bundling Incense, Central Vietnam

Foods of Tet

All over the cities, towns and villages shops are selling sweets in bulk or in assortments packaged in elegantly arranged boxes to satisfy the sweet tooth of Tết. Dried watermelon seeds dyed red, or sweet green bean sweets are served to visitors with their tea. To the foreign visitor some of the most unusual treats are the sugared, dried fruits and vegetables called **mứt**. Ginger, persimmons, bananas, lemons, tangerines, lotus seeds and sugared winter melons are common, as are salted dried fruits.

The names of many foods served at this time of year are homophones for auspicious qualities. Watch for the 'tray of togetherness', a round dish

BANH CHUNG & BANH DAY

A very long time ago, King Hung Vuong VI of the Hung Bang Dynasty decided to retire from his throne after defeating the Chinese invaders. He thought that he was too old to lead the country. It was time to choose his successor so he could enjoy the remaining days of his life in peace and leisure.

One day he summoned all his sons and said to them: "I am now too old to lead the country and am very tired. I want some peace of mind and to enjoy the remaining days of my life in quiet. I intend to hand over the throne to one of you, but I don't know which one of you would have the ability and wisdom to lead the country. So, I will test your hearts and wisdom. Whoever among you can prepare the best dishes to offer to our ancestors and also satisfy my taste shall succeed me".

Upon hearing this, each prince set out on his journey to every corner of the kingdom to find the most exotic, unusual, and far-fetched foods to present to the King. Among the princes, Prince Lang Lieu was the youngest and poorest, but the most devoted and considerate. Unlike his brothers, he chose to stay home with his father. However, he was so poor that he could not afford to buy any exquisite dishes to offer to the ancestors and his father. He was very sad and worried because he didn't know what to do. It wasn't because he wanted to succeed his father's throne; he just wanted to make his father happy.

One night, after thinking about ways to make his father happy, Lang Lieu was exhausted and fell asleep. In his dream, an old man with white hair approached him and said, "your devotion and caring have touched my heart very deeply. You truly deserve the royal throne of your father. You don't have to go anywhere to find foods – it is just a waste of time and money".

"Of all the foods, rice is the most precious and valuable of all, yet very abundant. You find it anywhere in your father's kingdom. Go and use full of sweets. Candied melon symbolises growth and good health and the red melon seeds represent joy, happiness, truth and sincerity. The lotus seeds are said to increase the size of one's family since the word, hat sen, sounds like 'many children'. The lotus root has many openings wherein lie the seeds, an indication that people should be thoughtful in their actions.

Originally a pagoda ritual only, the laying out of the 'five sacred fruits' – orange, tangerine, green bananas, Buddha's hand (a citron), and pomelo – has become common in shops and homes. These fruits are offered on attractively arranged platters on altars and later shared among friends and visitors.

glutinous rice. Cook it very thoroughly then mould it into a round rice cake, and call it bánh dày. This will symbolise the sky you live under. Do the same with a square rice cake. Stuff cooked bean paste and minced meat in the middle of the square rice cake and call it bánh chưng. This will symbolise the earth. Present these cakes to your father as offerings to your ancestors". Having said that, the apparition disappeared.

When he woke up, Prince Lang Lieu was very happy and set out to do exactly as he was told. The time came and King Hung Vuong summoned his sons to find out what kinds of foods they brought to him. Each of the princes who returned from afar was each sure that his dish was the best, and each had prepared his discovery himself. There were dainty dishes and dishes made with rare ingredients offered to the King for his judgement. Although exotic and delicious, the King was somewhat disappointed with each dish.

Prince Lang Lieu offered his two cakes: one white and round, the other square and green. The King smacked his lips as he ate with gusto and declared them the most delicious. When his son told him how he had discovered it, the King concluded that one so connected with divine support should handle the affairs of the Kingdom. The young Prince was appointed his heir. As King, he shared his secret with his people.

Today, the two cakes are inseparable companions. Every year during the New Year celebrations, the Vietnamese people cook bánh chưng and bánh dày and use them as offerings to their ancestors as well as special gifts to relatives and friends.

Traditionally, the ashes of the hearth should not be touched during the three days of Tết, lest the peace of the household be disturbed. So food to be consumed during the three days of New Year must be prepared beforehand and preserved for several days. These dishes keep and travel well, and allow freedom from cooking during the holiday. Because of these qualities, they were often used by soldiers on the march during wartime.

Other Tets

There are many holidays on the Vietnamese calendar called Tết. The one falling on New Year is the best known and most important example. But others throughout the year are also are celebrated with food. All Tets occur on dates that 'twin' with the month in which they occur, that is, the first day of the first month, the second day of the second month and so on. The even numbers have yin (female) characteristics and odd ones are yang or heavenly (male). One to five are numbers depicting the nascent process where creatures have yet to assume form, that is in spring, six to nine are numbers pertaining to the manifest or the 'solidified'.

On the third day of the third lunar month, some Vietnamese observe Tiết Hàn Thực, or Cold Food Holiday. The legend behind it tells of Gioi Tu Thoi, who followed his prince as a loyal servant for 19 years. Once, when the prince was starving, Gioi Tu Thoi cut a piece of muscle from his own thigh, grilled it (we assume with a bit of nước mắm) and served it to the prince. But when the prince became King he forgot Gioi Tu Thoi's

Banh Uot (Rice Noodle Sheets)
Bánh ướt are usually cut up into 6mm strands for soups and stirfries.

Ingredients
1	cup (120g)	rice flour
1/2	cup (60g)	cornflour (cornstarch)
1/2	cup (60g)	potato starch
1/2	teaspoon	salt
1/4	cup (60ml)	vegetable oil

Combine the ingredients with 3 cups (750ml) of cold water in a large mixing bowl. Blend with a wire whisk. Let the batter rest for 30 minutes.

Brush a baking sheet with oil and set aside with a small bowl of peanut oil.

Brush a 20cm omelette or sauté pan with oil and set over low heat for 3 minutes. Stir the batter. Pour 1/2 cup (125ml) of the batter into the pan. Tilt and swirl the pan to spread the batter evenly across the surface. Cover the pan and steam for 5 minutes or until the rice sheet sets.

Remove the lid and loosen the edges of the rice sheet with a pair of tongs or a fork, and slide the rice sheet onto the oiled baking sheet. Let it cool slightly then coat both sides with oil. Place on an oiled plate. Oil the baking sheet before placing another rice sheet on it.

Use a fairly low heat for this recipe and make sure that the pan is brushed with oil and reheated before adding each batch of batter.

sacrifice and shunned him. Disconsolate, Gioi Tu Thoi went into a self-imposed exile in the forest. Eventually, the King remembered his servant's selfless act, and when he heard of Thoi's plight, urged him to come out to receive his reward. But Thoi refused, and instead, moved further into the jungle. The King set the forest on fire to force Thoi to come out. He was burned to death. For three days (the length of time for a Vietnamese wake), in honour of the good and faithful servant, the people eat only cold foods and raw vegetables. One of these special foods is called **bánh tro** (floating cake), made of glutinous rice flour encasing a pellet of brown sugar. The egg-like shape of the dumpling on the outside represents the heavens and the square pellet of sugar on the inside represents the earth. Egg and square: the yin & yang of life.

POEM

My body is white, my fate is round.
Seven cakes that float and three which sink
It sticks together or is broken apart,
Depending on the hand of the person who
Kneads the dough.
Sink or swim, I still keep my loyal
Soul and true red heart.

– Ho Xuan Huong,
Vietnam's greatest female poet,
comparing herself to bánh chay

Legend says that the Vietnamese people are descended from a union of a mountain spirit, Au Co, and a water dragon, Lac Long Quan. Their mating produced a sac containing 100 eggs. When the eggs hatched there were 100 sons. Fifty went with the mother to the mountains and 50 went with the father to the sea. Thus the Vietnamese nation has water and mountainous elements, and the shape of the cakes represents the eggs, which became the ancestor. When Vietnamese eat bánh tro, they consume their own genesis.

The other dish served on this holiday is **bánh chay**, which is round with a depressed centre. Three of them usually fill up a small rice bowl. They float in a thick, clear yellowish soup which has sesame seeds sprinkled on top. This combination represents the trinity of the sun, the moon and the earth (the three cakes), the earth's water (the surrounding fluid) and the stars (the sesame seeds).

Tet Doan Ngo

In ancient times the king rejected the advice of Khuat Nguyen, a fine and righteous mandarin. Khuat Nguyen warned the King not to travel abroad, but the silly ruler ignored the advice, and died along the way. The next King was no better, and even exiled Khuat Nguyen who, disappointed, drowned himself in a river. Years later, the King, having become wiser, regretted his actions and made a banquet as an offering to the loyal mandarin's spirit by throwing food into the river. But the fish and prawns immediately gobbled it up, a terrible sacrilege. People took to wrapping the food in leaves and tying it with thread of five colours so that the water creatures wouldn't steal the offerings. To this day, people celebrate with riverbank parties and wrap up pretty food packages to throw in the river.

The Giong festival commemorates Saint Giong who volunteered to fight the enemy when he was just a small boy. To give him strength for the battle, villagers fed him seven baskets of local eggplant and rice, and he grew into a giant. The victory is celebrated at an annual festival, with a mock battle and lots of salted eggplant and rice.

In An Ninh village in Hai Hung province, an annual festival honours General Nguyen Huy Tinh who, according to legend, was appointed by Tran Hung Dao to fight the Mongols. On the eve of the attack, the villagers quickly prepared baskets of rice and 15 pigs to feed the soldiers. The Mongols were defeated but the general was killed. He became the village guardian spirit and is honoured every year with a ceremonial pig run. Specially raised pigs are provided by eight different neighbourhoods, and ritually slaughtered. After the sacrifice, teams of village boys race the trussed pigs to fires where they are cooked. The team which presents the most attractive and tasty pig in the quickest time wins. The pigs' heads are brought to the communal house as sacred offerings. On the following day, there is a procession to mark the victory and a party where the rice and pork are enjoyed by all.

Rice Cooking Festival – Thi Cam Village

Rice-cooking competitions are part of many Vietnamese festivals, and sustain the tradition of quickly and skilfully preparing rice for soldiers going into battle.

Thi Cam village, in Tu Liem district, a suburban area of Hanoi honours Phan Tay Nhac, legendary military commander of the 18th Hung King. When his troops were stationed in the Thi Cam area, he organised a rice-cooking contest in the unit. After his death, Phan Tay Nhac was made the spirit protector of the village. In his honour, the village organises a rice-cooking festival every lunar year on 8 January.

Young girl selling food, Hanoi

Early in the morning, the village leaders gather at the communal house with offerings, and a council – comprising notables and experienced cooks – is appointed to organise and supervise the contest. Various teams in the village take part in the contest. Each team is dressed in traditional tunics – white pants with dark long dresses – but with belts in different colours. The contest is divided into three parts.

Fetching Water

One person from each team takes part in this contest. A symbolic military post is set up for the purpose, and the contestants start running from there to the bank of the Nhue River, covering about 1km. Four big bottles of water are waiting for the runners at a designated place on the bank of the river, and if a person can bring a bottle back ahead of the others he and his group are considered the winner of the first stage.

Making Fire

Two people from each team compete in this event, using several thin pieces of bamboo and some straw as tinder. The two people must, by means of rubbing, make fire by friction between two pieces of dry bamboo. This was the traditional method of fire-making in rural areas of Vietnam. The team that kindles a fire first is the winner of the second stage.

Cooking Rice

Six people from each team compete in this part of the contest. Two people have to husk raw rice with a pestle in order to separate rice, bran and rice husk, and to whiten the rice further. Then a small quantity of rice is taken for cooking, just enough for a 'cult' bowl of rice (which is equal to two bowls of rice put together). Rice must be cooked with a straw fire, the burning straw enveloping the whole pot in order to ensure that the rice is well cooked.

In the end, each team's rice is tasted by the worthy judges and the winning team announced. The prize? Just the glory.

From Hanoi, you can find this village by following highway No 11a, crossing Dien bridge (8km from Hanoi), then turning left and going another 3km along the Nhue River.

regional
variations

In a country extending over 300,000 sq km – with varied histories and climates – it's natural that people should produce and perceive food differently. Northern food displays a Chinese heritage, but in the south, where the weather is more tropical, the dishes have a more aromatic, spicy nose. In the middle lies Hué, the capital of Vietnamese imperial cooking, which features a range of sophisticated, refined dishes designed to tempt jaded royal appetites of yore.

Everybody in Vietnam eats barbecued fish, seafood and fresh uncooked vegetables but regional variations are easy to observe. Some of these are due to differences in the climate and soil, altitude and geography. Vietnam has several climatic zones, from the steamy tropical to downright cold; from high mountains to seashores; from river deltas to places where cacti grow. So there is a great variety both in ingredients and their availability. While some dishes are good for the heat, and some are good for the cold, others are a constant throughout the land. Southerners eat spicy curries, people in the centre nibble on delicacies of the Imperial table, Hanoi is synonymous with **phở bò**, and the whole country eats French bread and pork pâté.

The North

In the north, the influence of Chinese food has been both less and more than in the south and centre. The basic tenets of the north's cookery are more closely aligned with China than that of other local regions. Nevertheless, the centre has also taken inspiration from China for its imperial cuisine during the Nguyen dynasty. And the south has been seeing a resurgence, albeit nascent, of Chinese influence since the reopening of the country in the late 1980s. The northerners, stalwarts that they are, maintain tradition.

There is less agricultural variety in the north, so the cookery is less complex. Fewer spices are available than in the south, but the people couldn't do without black pepper. They use a superior grade that is mild, yet intensely aromatic, and with a sweetness that is unique to this land. It helps to characterise the cuisine almost as much as **nước mắm**.

Equally important are the sweet and pungent herbs – basil, mint, coriander, spring onions, and several other tasty leaves that cannot be found outside northern Vietnam. You can grow them elsewhere but they do not taste or smell the same. In the north, then, more than any other part of the country, the taste of the cuisine is the taste of the soil. It doesn't travel well.

Laden with pots near Ho Chi Minh City

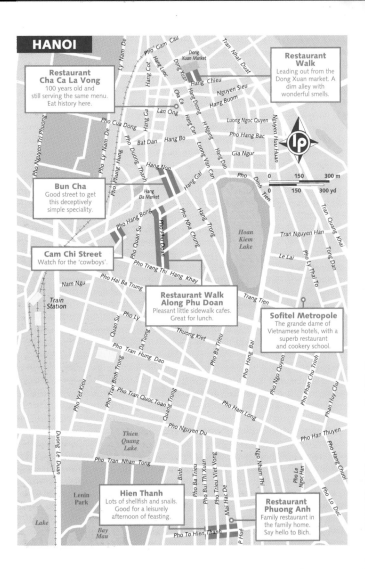

HANOI

Restaurant Walk
Leading out from the Dong Xuan market. A dim alley with wonderful smells.

Restaurant Cha Ca La Vong
100 years old and still serving the same menu. Eat history here.

Bun Cha
Good street to get this deceptively simple speciality.

Cam Chi Street
Watch for the 'cowboys'.

Restaurant Walk Along Phu Doan
Pleasant little sidewalk cafes. Great for lunch.

Sofitel Metropole
The grande dame of Vietnamese hotels, with a superb restaurant and cookery school.

Hien Thanh
Lots of shellfish and snails. Good for a leisurely afternoon of feasting.

Restaurant Phuong Anh
Family restaurant in the family home. Say hello to Bich.

Ly Nam De · Pho Gam Cau · Hang Cot · Hang Luoc · Dong Xuan · Dong Xuan Market · Hang Chieu · Tran Nhat Duat · Nguyen Sieu · Hang Buom · Cho Ca · Hang Duong · Lan Ong · Hang Can · H Ngang · Luong Van Can · Hang Dao · Luong Ngoc Quyen · Pho Hang Bac · Gia Ngur · Nguyen Huu Huan · Pho Nguyen Tri Phuong · Pho Cua Dong · Pho Ly Nam De · Hang Ga · Pho Duong Thanh · Bat Dan · Hang Bo · Hang Non · Phung Hung · Hang Cai · Hang Da Market · Pho Hang Bong · Pho Quan Su · Tho Nhuom · Hang Trong · Hang Khay · Pho Trang Thi · Hang Khay · Nam Ngu · Pho Hai Ba Trung · Trang Tien · Pho · Dinh Tien · Hoan Kiem Lake · Tran Nguyen Han · Le Lai · Tran Quang Khai · Tong Dan · Pho Ly Thai To · Pho Ba Trieu · Pho Hang Bai · Pho Ngo Quyen · Pho Phan Chu Trinh · Phan Huy Chu · Pho Han Thuyen · Pho Hang Chuoi · Pho Lo Duc · Train Station · Pho Ly · Quan Su · Da Tuong · Thuong Kiet · Pho Tran Hung Dao · Pho Yet Kieu · Pho Tran Binh Trong · Pho Tran Quoc Toan · Quang Trung · Pho Nguyen Du · Pho Ham Long · Duong Le Duan · Thien Quang Lake · Pho Tran Nhan Tong · Binh · Pho Ba Trieu · Pho Bui Thi Xuan · Pho Trieu Viet Vong · Mai Hac De · Ngo Nham Thi · Pho Le Ngoc Han · Lenin Park · Hien Thanh · Pho To Hien Thanh · P Hue · Lake · Bay Mau

0 150 300 m
0 150 300 yd

Special Dishes
Bánh Cuon (Rice Rolls)

Bánh cuốn are produced throughout Vietnam, but the Hanoi variety has its own special characteristics. The wrappings are as thin as a sheet of paper, appearing as edible alabaster, soft yet offering something to the teeth. If you see a woman with a basket of these on her head, stop her and get some. In her basket she'll have a jar of fish sauce, a jar of vinegar, a bowl of chilli, some bowls, plates and chopsticks and, below them, layers of rice wrappings. She'll take out a few wrappers, roll them up with mushrooms, shallots, and minced pork or shrimp. Breakfast is served.

The food stalls on the street side and in the markets go further when serving this dish, offering grilled pork, fried bean curd, maybe some vegetables with the rolls. They would be pre-assembled and kept warm in a steamer. If you're really lucky, they'll add a drop of coleopterous essence (a highly aromatic secretion from the gland of a type of beetle), although this will cost you as much as US$2 extra for a dish that otherwise would cost only 50 cents. The coleopterans have been losing habitat for 50 years now, and are as hard to find as truffles. Synthetic essence is now being manufactured – it ain't the same but think of the homeless beetles.

Bun Cha

Bún cha is simply grilled pork served on a bed of cold rice noodles and dressed with a few herbs. Deceptively simple. Like so much of Vietnamese cookery, you will know bún cha by its aroma, and you will always be able to find it by just following your nose. Vietnamese writer, Thach Lam, says, "when you are hungry and stand or sit at a place where the wind brings to you the fragrant smoke, you may feel like becoming a poet. The blue smoke looks like the fog or dew in the slope of mountains, and the drop of fat sputters on the burning coal like a whisper, while the hand fan gives the impression of a moving branch. All attractive to the mind and to the belly".

The meat is always cut from a piece of well-marbled pork, and must be grilled with a pair of fresh bamboo tongs. It is marinated in a mixture of sweet, hot, sour and salty, and the resulting product tastes like none of its constituent flavours, yet more than the sum of its parts. But, like so much of the north, what gives the Hanoi bún cha its characteristic taste and smell are the minty herbs, most often from nearby Lang village.

As important is the method of grilling. It really can't be done in the home because of the smoke produced. And without the smoke ... well, it just won't do. So vendors do it all, and become consummate masters at it. Their stove is usually very small. Often it's just an old biscuit tin or a discarded ammunition box with a few pieces of burning charcoal inside. The vendor may or may not have a permanent place of business.

He might just show up on a street corner, fire up his humble stove and commence operations. With his new pair of bamboo tongs, made fresh every day, he puts the marinated meat over the fire and fans it just enough to make the coals burn red but not too red, just barely hot enough to do the job. The trick is to blacken the outside without drying out the inside. The cook aids this process by letting enough fat drip onto the coals to make the smoke, which then rises and permeates the meat.

Bún cha sellers are quite common. Watch for the blue-white smoke of the grill curling up in the still morning air. Follow your nose. Fifty cents to a dollar will feed you well. Well-known bún cha shops are on Hang Manh and Nguyen Khuyen streets.

DON'T MISS

- Pho
- A cooking lesson at Metropole
- A visit to the December 19 market
- The Cam Chi cowboys
- At least a walk through, if not dinner at, the Nhat Tan dyke
- Cha ca at Cha Ca La Vong
- A cup of tea or a beer on the shore of Hoan Kiem lake in Hanoi

Snail Dishes

In Hanoi there is a type of snail living in ponds and lakes that grows to the size of a golf ball, has a streaked colour, and, while chewy, is very tasty. They are called **ốc**. **Bún ốc** are boiled snails dipped in **nước chấm**, placed in a bowl of rice vermicelli with snail consommé poured on top. You can find the itinerant sellers on street corners and markets. Diners, lounging around the vendor, take their bowls of noodles with the steaming hot snails just scooped from the cooking pot.

You can get bún ốc in many seafood restaurants. **Ốc ngoi** are minced snails mixed with onion, garlic and mushroom; rolled in ginger leaves and stuffed in the shell; then stewed. Pull the ginger leaf out and the rest comes along. **Ốc hấp bia** are snails stewed in beer. The beer helps to tenderise the meat, and imparts an extra flavour. Try also **ốc xào cả vỏ** (shelled stir-fried snails), **ốc cuốn chả** (rolled snail), **bún ốc khô** (dried noodle and snails).

Lau (Hot Pot)

The **lẩu** comes from China. It is a turban-shaped pan containing stock, in the middle of which is a charcoal stove (now alcohol fuel is used). The stock is kept simmering throughout the meal. The lẩu is placed in the middle of the table, around which is a variety of foods, including rice vermicelli, pig's heart, liver and kidneys, goat meat, eel, onion and vegetables. The less adventurous might opt for shellfish, river fish or chicken. Put as much food as you'd like to eat into the pot, give it a stir, and in about five minutes you're ready for dinner. Keep replenishing the pot as you go. It's rather like fondue, and just as convivial and fun. Depending on the ingredients used, it might be called **lẩu dê** (goat meat), **lẩu lươn** (eel meat) or **lẩu thập cẩm** (with many different kinds of meat). This dish always figures on the menu of deluxe restaurants and is referred to as hot pot or steamboat.

(see Hanoi map)

THE CAM CHI COWBOYS

Hanoi is not only known for its special dishes, but also for the tactics of some of its restaurateurs. You can observe this along **Cam Chi** (food) Street (see Hanoi map). The bánh sellers and phở makers are so eager for your custom that they will leap upon you and literally try to drag you into their establishments. If you pull away, another will grab you by your free arm and 'urge' you into his establishment. Think you can escape this treatment by arriving on a motorbike? Ha! Eager young men will stand directly in your path and grab the handlebars like cowboys wrestling a steer and try to kidnap you into their masters' dining room. We have even, in our angry mood, tried running them over (gently), to no avail. And if you escape from one, you'll be nabbed by another. On Cam Chi Street you are doomed to dine. Around the corner on Ha Trung Street this does not happen. The restaurants are sedate, normal and polite. It's just a Cam Chi phenomenon.

Curiously, this form of direct marketing by physical assault is not considered a crime. It isn't even bad behaviour, and rushing off to find a cop will get you nothing but a smile of bemusement.

Don't feel that you've been singled out. Everybody, even the Vietnamese, are subject to ambush by the Cam Chi cowboys. It's just their way of advertising, so don't let it dissuade you. It's actually a good show. When you reach the street, make a mad dash for no 3. It has a good vantage point, decent food and the staff are relatively calm. During the slow times, or when they get bored, they might join the pack to see if they can rope in another. So sit back with a bowl of hot noodle soup or a cold beer. Relax. Take bets on which cowboy will rope the most dogies.

The Centre
Hué

The mid-19th century emperor, Tu Duc, was a picky eater. He demanded that his food be markedly different from what anyone else might eat. Since Hué lacked the agricultural diversity of the south, the imperial kitchens had to show an enormous amount of ingenuity by refining and redefining ordinary dishes until they became something special to set before the king. Tu Duc wanted his eating to be viewed as art, ritual, and sensory pleasure all at the same time. He also elevated tea-drinking to art and ceremony, laden with intellectual meaning and aesthetic significance, as in China and Japan.

Tu Duc caused the food of Hué to be characterised by well-decorated, sophisticated, multiple-dish meals. His chefs are said to have been able to cook over 2000 dishes, as every meal for the king had to consist of 50 dishes, and the emperor was not to be served the same meal twice in a year.

The imperial city dominated central Vietnam in the early 19th century to the 20th, and the food reflects this status. In the north or south, food is placed on the table with one large bowl containing each dish. In Hué, despite the socialist government, they remember the emperor. Food is presented in many small vessels so that the table looks like a king's. Service is

Trays of meat, Danang

more formal, and seating arrangements are given more attention. Pork sausages known as **nem**, savoury soups and sweet or salty rice cakes are typical fare. Vegetables such as potatoes, tomatoes, asparagus, artichokes and cauliflower are grown locally and widely used.

A deeply aromatic shrimp sauce known as **mắm tôm** or **mắm ruốc** is made here and informs a lot of the dishes. Its preparation is similar to that of **nước mắm**, but shrimp is used instead of fish. The sauce is used as a dip, and its pungency is such that even some Vietnamese find it too strong. But you should try it, at least once. Just hold your breath.

Fixing the nets in Hoi An

METROPOLE – Faces of Gastronomy

We find it astonishing, even dismaying. Thunderation! We find it criminal the lack of Vietnamese restaurants in the international-class hotels in Vietnam. You can find French and Italian restaurants aplenty; Korean or Japanese if that is your fancy; you can get American or continental breakfast; you can find sushi, barbecue or borscht; Belgian waffles, Chinese noodles and Mexican tacos. But where is the grand hotel in Vietnam that harbours a restaurant dedicated to serving you the national fare?

As we write there is only one candle to light this culinary darkness, one soft voice in the gastronomic wilderness. Fittingly, it is in the grande dame of all Vietnam's hotels, the Sofitel Metropole in Hanoi, 15 Ngo Quyen Street.

The restaurant is called the Spices Garden, and it's operated by the unlikeliest pair of gastronomes in town: Madam Thi Kim Hai of Hanoi and Chef Didier Corlou of France. Perhaps, they *are* the likeliest pair to run this establishment. We like to think of it as pure Vietnamese with a *soupçon* of French. French not so much in the kitchen, but in the great traditions of grand hotel service and excellence.

Mrs Hai has been a cook since graduating from the Vietnam Tourist School and joining the Metropole Hotel in 1978. She worked her way through the ranks to become Head Vietnamese Chef in 1996. "The hotel has always had a French restaurant too", she says, "but I grew up with my mother's cooking and I want to stay with it". Besides what she learned from her mother and at school, she continued to make it her business to taste far and wide, from traditional phở at street stalls to the expensive fare of indoor restaurants.

Didier Corlou trained in Cannes, put in a few years in some top French restaurants and headed off to explore the world, and in the process became enchanted with Asia. He is married to a local Vietnamese woman and seems as well married to Vietnam. He continues to develop an already detailed understanding of Vietnamese cuisine and rarely lets a day go by without taking a bowl of phở on the street. "Soup is the essence of Hanoi cuisine. And that essence is found in the herbs that grow here. Nowhere else does the dill or the basil, for example, taste the same."

So intimate are they with street fare that they have 'brought the street indoors' at the Metropole. Periodically they hold a 'street fair' poolside in the hotel. Wonderful things that they have culled from market stalls and kerbside cafes are available to hotel guests who might not otherwise see or taste them.

But they think it's not enough to fill you full of Hanoi goodness just once or twice. They want you to be able to take it home with you. So they have started the Metropole Cooking School. Classes begin with a walk to the local market. Accompanied by the chefs, the students (that's you) get a chance to learn all about local ingredients and how to deal with the merchants. Cooking demonstrations follow in the hotel kitchens and participants have the chance to get some hands-on experience. You don't even have to be a guest of the hotel, just call ahead to make a booking.

Hit Lon Nuong Ong Tre
(Marinated Pork Cooked in Bamboo)

Ingredients
1kg lean pork shoulder
3   tablespoons sugar
4   tablespoons fish sauce
30g shallots, chopped
50g spring onions, sliced
2cm piece ginger, peeled and chopped
1   chilli, chopped
2   bamboo tubes, each measuring 25cm long x 7cm in diameter
2   large pieces banana leaf
     kitchen string

Thinly slice the pork shoulder. Heat 3 tablespoons of sugar in a heavy pan over low heat. Stir constantly until the sugar has melted and begins to turn golden. Remove from the heat and stir in the fish sauce. Return to the heat and stir until the two are completely blended.

Marinate the sliced pork with the caramelised fish sauce, shallots, spring onion, ginger and chilli for 30 minutes.

Cut the bamboo into 2 pieces lengthwise. Clean them very well. Clean the banana leaf. Line the inside of the bamboo with leaf. Stuff the pork into 2 bamboo halves and cover with the other halves. Wrap the banana leaf tightly around the bamboo. Tie the bamboo with kitchen string, and grill on a charcoal fire for about 20 minutes.

Serve hot with some rice noodles or plain rice, coriander leaves and a very light fish sauce.

Serves 6 as a main course

Cua Hap Voi Bia Va Gia Vi
(Steamed Crab in Beer & Herbs)

Ingredients
1   whole crab, about 1.5kg
    salt and pepper
30g ginger, julienned
1l beer
1   bunch dill
2   tablespoons light nuoc mam
    lemon juice
2   chillies, chopped

Clean the crab well, and rub the inside and outside with salt, pepper and a little julienned ginger. Cover the crab and marinate for 15 minutes. Pour the beer into a steamer, bring to a simmer, and steam the crab. Sprinkle some crumbled dill branches and ginger julienne on top. Serve hot with nuoc mam, lemon juice, and chilli.
    Serves 6 as a main course

The menu for an imperial-style banquet given today, whether in a fine restaurant or private home, might list up to a dozen dishes such as:

–**súp ga** (black pepper-laden chicken soup with lotus seeds)
–**nem rán** (spring rolls)
–**banh Hue** (rice flour pudding stuffed with minced shrimp)
–**thịt nướng** (grilled pork in rice paper, served with a peanut sauce)
–**càng cua nhồi thịt** (crab claws stuffed with pork)
–**chạo tôm** (minced shrimp wrapped around sugar cane)

Main dishes might include:

–**cá nướng lá chuối** (fish grilled in banana leaf)
–**bò lá lốt** (beef in wild betel leaves)
–**com Hué** (rice with vegetables)
–**tôm xào hành nấm** (sautéed shrimp with mushrooms)

These dishes can be found in other parts of Vietnam. What distinguishes them as being from Hué are the sophisticated cooking techniques and the artful presentation, and their generally smaller portions.

Chạo tôm (shrimp on sugar cane) seems a simple affair, but the complexity of its preparation is typical of Hué cookery. Small shrimp are shelled and marinated in nước mắm. Then they are pounded in a mortar with the pestle until they form a thick paste. Egg white, onion, garlic, sugar and pepper are added. The mixture is pounded again with a touch of pork fat, and finally wrapped around small sticks of split fresh sugar cane and grilled over charcoal. When eating these, the old saying, 'the closer to the bone, the sweeter the meat' seems apt.

Appearance is very important, not only in the use of colour and the arrangement of food on the plate, but also in the manner of serving. Rice might be served with a draping cloak of omelette, or cooked inside a lotus leaf and further enriched with lotus seeds. Chefs also employ unusual ingredients such as green bananas and unripe figs, banana flowers and green corn.

Virtually all the talented practitioners of imperial cuisine today are women, each able to trace descent to imperial households. Kitchen craft is reverently passed down in extended families, with young cooks-to-be taking an apprenticeship with an experienced cook. Only after much observation and training are the novices allowed to try with their own hands.

But not all of Hué's food was prepared for the kings and lords. There are many dishes for the common people prepared by the housewives of Hué whose handy hands and subtle imagination know how to fit the food to each season of the year. Unlike the south, the centre has seasons. The crops change with the weather, as do the appetites for this or that, and the body's needs according to tradition. Hué cooks are still keenly aware of the virtue of food diversity, and cooking techniques.

XI MA

On the old streets of Hoi An, past the shopfronts of flaxen-coloured walls and red-tiled roofs, I spot a sinewy old man with a pith helmet covering his grizzled hair. He bears a yoke. With every step, the large cooking pots at each end bow the bamboo perched on his shoulder.

He carries a three-generation tradition: **xi ma**, a viscous black pudding, served slightly warm, made according to a family recipe that's coveted throughout the central region. Mr Thieu carries medicine, and the taste is soothing and sweet. The medicine is particularly helpful for women suffering from menstrual pains. The dish is also good for children. All mothers in Hoi An know Mr Thieu.

The recipe is simple. The four ingredients are black sesame seeds, raw sugar, **rau má** and **bùi ngót**, two Chinese medicinal herbs. The trick is in the preparation and those details remain in the family.

Selling the valued fare is hard work. Mr Thieu and his wife rise at 3am daily. Preparing the first batch takes four hours. By 7.30, the old man is walking the streets of Hoi An bearing a full yoke weighing 50kg. He returns home at 2pm and prepares another load with the help of Mrs Thieu. At 3pm, he's walking the old quarter once again. He finishes selling his second batch by 6 or 7pm. That's been Mr Thieu's daily schedule for 60 years. He took over from his father at 15. When he dies his daughter will carry on.

Mr Chung, who runs a dress-making shop in Hoi An, continues, "when my mother was very young, she saw Mr Thieu on the Cam Nam Bridge one day. Seven men jumped him, trying to rob the hard-working man of his money. This was back when the bridge was made of only bamboo and wood. He kicked and punched all seven until each crashed through the railing and fell to the water below". The ones looking for easy money weren't aware that Mr Thieu is an expert in Kung Fu. He also eats the xi ma.

– *Garrett Culhane*

Food which must accord with the specific period of the year is a principle of Hué cuisine, as each of the four seasons has its specific good products and ingredients. During the cool days of spring, when the fruit trees are budding, Hué has a plentiful supply of vegetables such as aubergine (eggplant), pumpkins, calabash, as well as birds, crabs, prawn, cuttlefish and various species of fish.

In summer, when people believe it difficult to digest dried or fatty foods, vegetables and pickles, oysters, clams, prawns, crabs and fish are favoured. May is thought to be the best month for duck. All manner of fruits are taken with gusto in summer including mangoes, pineapples, longan, jackfruit, strawberries, papaya, mangosteen and custard apples.

With cooler autumn come beans, aubergine (eggplant), loofah, fish and prawns, and fruits such as persimmon, tangerine and grapefruit.

In the winters, people enjoy preserved vegetables with rice. While sea fish become less abundant, river fish and game birds come into season, and vegetables include beets, cabbage, green peas, bitter melon and pumpkin.

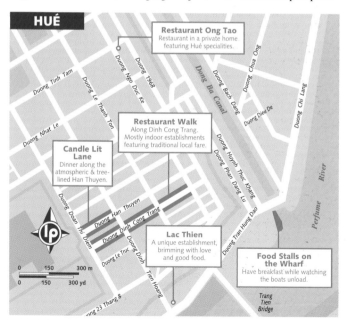

HUÉ

Restaurant Ong Tao
Restaurant in a private home featuring Hué specialities.

Restaurant Walk
Along Dinh Cong Trang. Mostly indoor establishments featuring traditional local fare.

Candle Lit Lane
Dinner along the atmospheric & tree-lined Han Thuyen.

Lac Thien
A unique establishment, brimming with love and good food.

Food Stalls on the Wharf
Have breakfast while watching the boats unload.

Duong Tinh Tam
Duong Le Thanh Ton
Duong Ngo Duc Ke
Duong 1968
Dong Ba Canal
Duong Bach Dang
Duong Chua Ong
Duong Dieu De
Duong Chi Lang
Duong Nhat Le
Duong Huynh Thuc Khang
Duong Phan Dang Lu
Perfume River
Duong Doan Thi Diem
Duong Han Thuyen
Duong Dinh Cong Trang
Duong Dinh
Duong Le Truc
Duong Tien Hoang
Duong Tran Hung Dao
Duong 23 Thang 8

0   150   300 m
0   150   300 yd

Trang Tien Bridge

LAC THIEN – Faces of Gastronomy

Le Van Trung sees us from across the street. As always, his face bursts into happiness and his mouth opens to let out a silent cry of welcome. Anticipating our thirst he picks up his signature bottle opener and waves it at us, still shouting joyously, soundlessly. Mr Le is both deaf and dumb. Of his eight siblings, only one can hear and speak. But he can communicate very well, thank you, in the language of food, hospitality and love.

His daughter, Thu, one of his nine children, has just returned home from school. She's been studying her English. "Why have you been gone so long?" she asks, "are you hungry? Do you want **bánh khoai**? Sit down", she insists. "I think you are too hot. Yes, yes. Sit down".

We first came to Lac Thien in 1991. Having been dumped by a third-world chicken bus in an unlit part of Hué in the dead of night, we shouldered our gear and trudged toward a distant glow. Near the left bank of the Perfume River we found the source of light – the Lac Thien restaurant at 6 Dinh Tien Hoang Street. While most of Hué closes by about 10pm, the Lac Thien stays open as long as anyone wants to eat or drink. We arrived late, dirty, smelly and looking thoroughly disreputable, yet to them a wondrous apparition. Within minutes we were seated, awaiting the local specialty of bánh khoai, or 'happy crepes' (see recipe). And we were the object of the fond attentions of Mr Le's children, one of whom was Thu, who sat in our lap and taught us to sing 'Frère Jacques'.

Happy crepes are in many ways the quintessence of Central Vietnam cookery. They employ the five flavours, yield a complex bouquet of aromas, have the textures of crunch, chewiness and crispness, are as pleasing to look at as a still-life painting, and the sounds they make when cooking or breaking under a fork or chopsticks are almost musical. In fact they are sometimes known as 'singing crepes'. They are made by pouring a rice flour crepe batter into a very hot pan. The hot side forms a crust while the cooler upper side cooks to a tender chewiness. They are filled with a stirfry mixture of ham, shrimp, onions and bean sprouts, and served with a rich and spicy sauce.

In the days before **doi moi**, even the most common and everyday items of manufacture could be scarce. Bottle openers were not on the commissars' list of important items of national use. Mr Le couldn't get even one, at least one that he could keep for long. And yet his customers wanted beer! So he drove a nut and bolt through a stick of wood and, voilà! The industrial planners be damned. Mr Le's opener used lots of leverage and produced a very satisfying 'pop'! So charmed were his customers by his ingenuity and the opener's festive report that they would take the opener home with them. And so now, if you wish, he will make one just for you, and sign it and date it.

We have since made Lac Thien our headquarters while in Hué because it is a place that brims with love. The adults constantly hug their children and pat their customers on the shoulder. The kids have no fear of any adult and are as eager to give hugs as to get them. In the kitchen, Thu will point out to you the three nubs on the traditional charcoal braziers that represent the kitchen gods.

Ask her, and she will tell you the story. The three nubs stand for what used to be three bricks laid end to end in a triangle, with the fire in the middle, a traditional hearth. According to the legend of the hearth, in a piece of misfortune, a woman was separated from her woodcutter husband. In the course of time she married a hunter. One day the woodcutter reappeared while the hunter was in the forest. The astonished wife had no time to react before the hunter came home with his catch, a deer.

"Quick!" she said to the woodcutter. "Hide under the haycock!" As the woodcutter hid, the hunter set the haycock alight to cook the deer. Seeing her first love go up in flames the wife leaped into the inferno to join him in death. The hunter, thinking he had somehow driven his wife to suicide, leapt in after her.

The Jade Emperor, that is, the Creator, took pity on them because they had all died for love. He appointed them as kitchen gods so they could be together. Their togetherness was represented by the three bricks that formed the triangle. They seem to put their heads close to one another against the fire. Every year at Tết the kitchen gods report to the Jade Emperor whether the kitchen is a place of love or strife, and the family is rewarded or punished accordingly.

At Lac Thien, the Jade Emperor always smiles. It was started by Thu's grandparents – grandmother Ho Thi Tra still makes the bánh khoai – and has been open continuously since 1965. They started serving only bánh khoai, but have gradually increased the menu to 89 selections, many of which are the result of recommendation from regular customers.

Next door is a similar-looking establishment, with a similar sounding name (we won't say). It was a furniture store until 1990. If you stand across the street and look at the two establishments, you can see Lac Thien (to the left) full of Vietnamese eating Lac Thien's food, and in the other you can see foreign tourists drinking beer. Your choice.

Banh Khoai (Happy Crepes)

These are good for breakfast, lunch, dinner or a snack. They require a lot of work, but are such a hit with guests that the effort is very well spent. If you have a large kitchen, invite your friends over and cook these as a group. The meal you enjoy together afterward will be all the more pleasant and memorable, and the Jade Emperor will be moved to smile.

Ingredients

1	cup (120g) rice flour
1/2	cup (60g) cornflour (cornstarch)
1/4	cup (30g) wheat flour
2 1/2	4 cups (560ml/18 fl oz) water
3	spring onions, green and white parts sliced separately
250g	minced pork
2	tablespoons nước mắm
2	cloves garlic, minced
250g	prawns, shelled, cleaned and split
250g	bean sprouts
1	onion, sliced
10	white mushrooms, sliced
3	eggs, beaten
	vegetable oil
	nước chấm

Combine all the flours and spring onion greens to make a batter. Combine the pork with half the nuoc mam, garlic, spring onion whites and pepper. Combine the shrimp with the remaining nuoc mam, garlic, spring onion whites and pepper. Arrange the above, and all the other ingredients, handily near the stove.

Heat a small skillet or an omelette pan to high. Add 1 tablespoon of oil, then 1½ tablespoons of pork and 2–3 pieces of prawn and cook for 2 minutes. Reduce the heat to medium and add 3 tablespoons of batter, 1 tablespoon of bean sprouts and a few slices of onion and mushroom. Cover and cook for 2 minutes. Uncover and pour 3 tablespoons of egg over the crepe then cover again for 2 minutes. Uncover and fold in half, adding more oil if needed. Continue cooking with the lid on, turning the crepe from time to time, until it is very crisp. Serve with nuoc cham.

Serves 6

A balance of simplicity and sophistication are the hallmarks of Hué cuisine both high and low. A good example of this is 'clam rice', originally from Con Island, a small island in the Perfume River, south of the Trang Tien bridge. The clams are collected from the river, and boiled until the meat falls from the shells. The shells are discarded, the meat and broth filtered through a cloth, and then served in two separate dishes of clam meat and clam soup. The two dishes are taken with cold rice and various aromatic vegetables, minced banana flowers, and a dipping sauce of thick soy sauce, chilli, nước mắm, pounded sesame, garlic and salt. The art of the saucier is alive in Hué. Each dish must go together with a specific sauce – to use the wrong sauce is a faux pas.

Another simple meal common among workmen in Hué is one of 'rice and three common dishes', which may include fish braised with nước mắm and herbs, fried water spinach with a sauce made of shrimp paste and lime, or a sour soup of small prawns and tamarind. Dessert might include a sweet soup of lotus seeds and longan, or locally available fruit.

Sweet soups are served in restaurants and parks, and in the shady groves along the Perfume River. Sweet soups are common in Hué, and include:

Chè đậu ván (sweet soup of broad beans)
Chè đậu ngự (sweet soup of royal beans)
Chè hột sen bọc nhãn (sweet soup of lotus seeds wrapped in longan)
Chè bt lọc bọc thịt quay (sweet soup of roast pork)

Hué's glory days were from 1802 to 1945, when it was the political capital of Vietnam. It's a rather a sleepy place these days. Alas, it has never quite recovered from the American/Vietnamese war. Bullet holes still mar stone walls. Monuments are in sad neglect. Ancient hostilities smoulder just beneath the surface of outward calm. The city that created the most sophisticated Vietnamese cuisine, and elevated vegetarian cooking to heights greater than those reached by Indian chefs, merits more of the government's attentions.

But there is renewed interest in the cuisine of Hué, and forward-looking Vietnamese chefs are looking upon it and making it their mission to restore the art of imperial cuisine to its rightful place of high esteem. Till then, to find the best of Hué you must look for the little pockets of culinary delight. Seek, find, and treasure.

You can always find a good feed and a good time at Lac Thien (see the boxed text Lac Thien earlier in this chapter). And if you would like to take a walk, wait till after dark. Start at the foot of Dinh Thien Hoang Street, where it meets Ong Ich Khiem. Head northeast on Dinh Thien Hoang past Lac Thien. Go through the gate into the old city and proceed for about 10 minutes. On your left you will begin to see what might be fireflies. But as you approach they reveal themselves as dozens and dozens of candles and little alcohol lamps. They sit on low tables along the sides of Han Thuyen Street between Dinh Thien Hoang and Doan Thi Diem, in the shadow of the citadel. Leafy trees overhang the tables, and a low hum and buzz of conversation is occasionally punctuated by a gentle laugh.

These portable tables and kitchens are not here in daylight. They only come out at sundown, and will be gone by 10pm. They all serve the same thing: noodles. The garnishes may vary, but to eat at one table is essentially to eat at all, as far as food goes. But you don't select your table here for the food – it's all good anyway – you select your table for the people who operate it, for the way the tree above hangs protectively over it, for the way its little light flickers. You select for your mood. If you come here to relax and dine in the moon and candlelight, no matter what your mood was when you arrived, it will be better by the time you leave.

BISTRO NO–NAME

Midway through our journey we stopped in a small town south of Hué. On the beach we were befriended by a young boy who, wanting to impress us with his English, recited the scores of all 53 World Cup soccer matches together with the key plays. By the time he finished we were not only amazed, but starved. We took up his suggestion to try an outdoor restaurant not far away. The roadside patio was empty. We casually ordered a few dishes, expecting nothing more than something to kill our hunger.

Just as Nina said, "I've never been hotter in my entire life", two young girls began to fan us. It was a quiet gesture we would never have been bold enough even to suggest. In the still heat of the afternoon these puffs of breeze silently skimmed the sweat away. I was somewhere between deep meditation and heat stroke when our food arrived. The fresh seafood was slightly piquant and among the best we tasted anywhere in Asia. We ate slowly. Two large pigs rooted around our feet waiting for scraps that would never fall. The tab came to US$3, fanning included. Paris had nothing on this bistro with no name.

– Robert Strauss, San Francisco

Hoi An

Hué is not the sum and total of the central region of Vietnam. The little port of Hoi An is only three hours' driving time to the south. It was formerly known as Faifo, and the principal trading port until the French period when they moved shipping operations to Danang. This was lucky for Hoi An because the world's attention, and the coming wars, passed it by. Unlike Hué, there is no ruin here, no simmering resentments. There is tranquillity, continuity, and a feeling of being far away. And all is graced with a patina of age.

Transporting wood, Hoa Lu

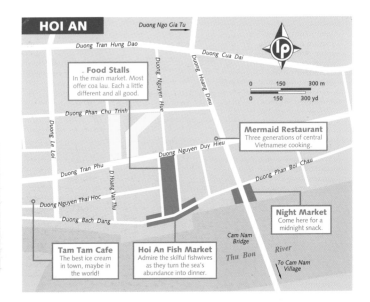

HOI AN

Duong Ngo Gia Tu

Duong Tran Hung Dao

Duong Nguyen Hue

Duong Cua Dai

Duong Hoang Dieu

Food Stalls
In the main market. Most offer coa lau. Each a little different and all good.

Duong Phan Chu Trinh

Duong Le Loi

Mermaid Restaurant
Three generations of central Vietnamese cooking.

Duong Nguyen Duy Hieu

Duong Tran Phu

D Hoang Van Thu

Duong Phan Boi Chau

Duong Nguyen Thai Hoc

Duong Bach Dang

Night Market
Come here for a midnight snack.

Cam Nam Bridge

Tam Tam Cafe
The best ice cream in town, maybe in the world!

Hoi An Fish Market
Admire the skilful fishwives as they turn the sea's abundance into dinner.

Thu Bon

River

To Cam Nam Village

0 150 300 m
0 150 300 yd

Coa Lau

In centuries past several foreign trading communities dwelt here: Chinese, Japanese, Portuguese, Dutch and so on. Many have left their marks architecturally, historically, and even gastronomically. The most famous dish, and what Hoi An is best known for, comes from the Japanese. It is based on the soba noodle soups of Japan, and known in Hoi An as **coa lau**. Word has it among foreign tourists that the true coa lau can only be made from water drawn from the Ba Le well, and that you can even taste the difference if someone tries to sneak a bastardised version to you. But this is just a tale. True, the Ba Le well is known for the clarity of its water, but it doesn't hold the key to coa lau. The one constant of coa lau is that the noodles for all the coa lau in Hoi An have been made by the same family for over 100 years. They've got the process down pat.

The noodles are made of rice that has been thoroughly rinsed in well water. Every house in Hoi An has had access to freshwater wells because Hoi An has always been a seaport and the river water is salty. Wells are the only source of fresh water. Hoi An was a freshwater stop for ships plying the north or south trade with China. Many of the old wells in the area have survived, although many others have caved in. Some are lined with wood or stone at the bottom or with bricks all the way down and stone pillars at the lip. They are a part of the town's architectural heritage. The famous Ba Le well is located in the alley of 35 Phan Chu Trinh.

After the rinse, the rice grains are squeezed to remove the water, then husked and polished. The flour is dried in a pan. While it is drying, the cook pours a little ash water into the flour, causing it to turn the distinctive pale yellow colour that identifies Hoi An noodles. To make the noodle dough, the flour is placed in the top level of a special double-boiler called a **xửng**, which has banana leaves on the bottom. The dough is then rolled out and cut by hand into noodles of varying size. They are cooked once more before serving.

Thin slices of lean pork are stir-fried with fish sauce or grilled until they become a toasty brown; the cooking juices are reserved. Fresh herbs are placed in a bowl along with bean sprouts, perhaps some sliced onion. The noodles are added next, the meat, and then the reserved sauce, some soy sauce, and some lime juice are poured over the whole.

Some people like to crumble up a flat crisp **bánh đa** (rice cracker) on top of the cao lau, as a sort of crouton. Bánh đa are made from old rice grains that retain most of the bran even after being soaked in water to acquire the right kind of 'sourness'.

These grains are then ground wet into a paste. A bit of previously cooked rice is added to the paste as it is being ground. Two layers of this smooth paste are spread on a hot metal plate on a large steamer. The two layers become one wet cracker, which is then removed, sprinkled with sesame seeds or chopped peanuts, and dried. Before eating it's

toasted over a charcoal fire which the cook maintains at just the right heat with a hand fan. You don't have to wait for a bowl of coa lau to enjoy bánh đa. They make a tidy little snack any time.

The South

The southern region focuses on Ho Chi Minh City, which began as an Indianised Khmer town in the 14th century called Prey Nokor. The Vietnamese took it in the 18th century, the French in the 19th century, and the Vietnamese took it back in the 20th century. The Chinese merchants have been there all along, and the south bears their imprint. And since Ho Chi Minh City is the country's centre of commerce and trade, with more foreigners both resident and transient, there is a greater awareness of and openness to outside influences. If ever a Vietnamese *nouvelle cuisine* should develop, it will begin in the south.

The south grows a greater variety of tropical and temperate fruits and vegetables, and more varieties of spice. Hence, the south favours spicy dishes. Curries have been around since earliest times, although, unlike the Indian originals, they are not hot but aromatic. They may be taken with noodles or rice as a family meal, or with French bread as a snack.

Another Indian influence is **bánh xèo**, which is akin to an Indian dhosa, or a large crepe filled with goodies. The Vietnamese make it with rice flour and coconut milk, and fill it with meat and shellfish, as well as vegetables. Bánh xèo is often referred to in English as a Vietnamese 'pancake'. While this is an unsatisfactory translation, there seems to be nothing we can do about it.

Almost anything cooked in coconut milk is a typical southern dish, such as **thịt kho nước dừa** (pork simmered in coconut). Southerners also use more sugar in their recipes, even the savoury ones. Sugar cane is abundant here, and besides using it in cooking, the southerners chew it for a snack, drink its pressed juice, put it in soups (in judicious amounts, of course), caramelise it, and use it as the chief flavouring agent in claypot cooking.

Tangy fruits like pineapple may be eaten as a fruit, or used as a vegetable, or as the acidic component in a cooked dish, taking the place of vinegar. Cooking times tend to be shorter, and stews and deep-fried dishes are less common than in the north.

Sweets are more popular in the south. Coconut sweets are made by boiling coconut milk with sugar over a fire of coconut shells until it is reduced to a thin taffy. Then it is turned out onto a work surface and kneaded like dough until it begins to set. Workers press it into moulds to form the candy into long, thin candy whips, then cut them into bite-sized lengths and wrap them in rice paper. You can eat the sweets, wrapping and all. You can watch it being made at the Ben Tre Candy Company, Dia Chi 2/30 Phuong 7, Thi Xa Ben Tre.

Boy on boat, Ha Long Bay

HO CHI MINH CITY

PHU NHUAN DISTRICT

DISTRICT 3

Restaurant Banh Xeo 46A
Traditional southern crepes.

Restaurant Houng Roung
Serving exotic species.
Get your cobra here.

Thi Sach Street
Pavement cafe walk
with oodles of atmosphere.

Restaurant Camargue
Elegant French Eatery.

**Restaurant Walk
on Pasteur**
Gritty and grotty but good.

La Biblioteque
Madam Dai's famous law
library turned restaurant.

Duong Dinh Tien Hoang

Duong Dien Bien Phu

Dai Lo Hai Ba Trung

Duong Nguyen Thi Minh Khai

Duong Nam Ky Khoi Nghia

Duong Vo Thi Sau

Duong Phan Dinh Phung

Nguyen Du

Thi Sach

Saigon River

River

400 m
400 yd
0   200   400
0   200   400

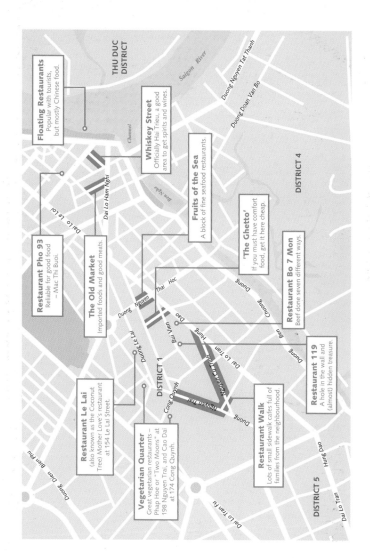

THU DUC DISTRICT

Saigon River

Duong Nguyen Tat Thanh

Duong Doan Van Bo

Floating Restaurants
Popular with tourists, but mostly Chinese food.

Whiskey Street
Officially Hai Trieu, a good area to get spirits and wines.

Channel

Dai Lo Ham Nghi

Ben Nghe

Fruits of the Sea
A block of fine seafood restaurants

DISTRICT 4

Restaurant Pho 93
Reliable for good food – Mac Thi Buoi.

Dai Lo Le Loi

The Old Market
Imported foods and good meats.

'**The Ghetto'**
If you must have comfort food, get it here cheap.

Restaurant Bo 7 Mon
Beef done seven different ways.

Duong Nguyen Thai Hoc

Duong Chuong

Duong Ben Chuong Duong

Duong Le Lai

Bui Vien

Dao

Hung

Tran

Dai Lo Tran

Restaurant 119
A hole in the wall and (almost) hidden treasure.

DISTRICT 1

Nguyen Cu Trinh

Nguyen Thai

Restaurant Le Lai
(also known as the Coconut Tree) Mother Love's restaurant at 154 Le Lai Street.

Cong Quynh

Restaurant Walk
Lots of small sidewalk cafes full of families from the neighbourhood.

Duong Dien Bien Phu

Vegetarian Quarter
Great vegetarian restaurants – Phap Hoe or "Two Moons" at 198 Nguyen Trai, and Cao Dai at 174 Cong Quynh.

Hung Dao

DISTRICT 5

Dai Lo Tran Phu

Dai Lo Tran

Bahn Xeo
(Southern Vietnamese 'Pancake' or Stuffed Crepes)

Ingredients

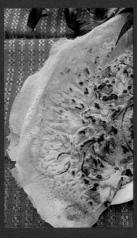

3	cups (750ml) water
1	pack (375g) bot ban xeo mix (rice flour with turmeric)
1	teaspoon sugar
2	cans/800ml coconut milk
4	spring onions (scallions), thinly sliced
500g	large prawns
250g	lean pork
2	yellow onions
	oil
4	handfuls fresh bean sprouts
1	head red leaf lettuce
1	bunch coriander, basil or mint
	nuoc mam

Prepare the crepe batter the night before serving. Place 1 cup (250 ml) of the water in a small pan on high heat. Thoroughly blend the flour with the remaining 2 cups (500ml) water until completely moistened. Dissolve the sugar in the boiling water and add to the batter. Add the coconut milk and spring onions and mix thoroughly. Refrigerate overnight.

The next day, peel and clean the prawns. Cut in half lengthwise. Cut the pork into 5cm slivers. Quarter the onion, then thinly slice.

Heat a few drops of oil on medium–high heat in a 25cm heavy-based frying pan. Add 3 slices of yellow onion and 2 slices pork, and cook for a few seconds until the onion is slightly translucent and the pork is white. Add 5 prawn halves and cook for 10 seconds. Pour in ½ a cup of batter and quickly tilt pan to form a large circle. Cover one half of the crepe with 1 handful of bean sprouts. Reduce the heat to medium. Cook until the batter looks solid. Cover partially (if you cover completely, water will condense on the crepe) and cook for 1 minute. Uncover and flip the crepe using a spatula. Cook for approx one minute, until slightly crisp. Serve immediately with fresh herbs and lettuce. To eat, tear off a piece of crepe, fill with coriander and wrap in lettuce leaf. Dip in sauce and eat.

Serves 4

Claypot cookery is very southern, and very satisfying. Claypots are usually small, often unglazed, with a lid, and look little different from a flowerpot with a lid. They were originally used by farmers and fishermen who had little to cook, few pots to cook in, and little fuel for the fire. When set on a small fire of leaves and twigs, the claypot distributes the heat evenly throughout its construction, making maximum use of the available heat. As cooking takes place from all directions, any herb or other seasoning will impart more of itself into the food than with other cooking methods.

Thit Kho To (Clay Pot Pork)

Ingredients

3	tablespoons dark brown sugar
¼	cup nuoc mam
2	tablespoons chopped shallot
½	teaspoon black pepper
250g	boneless pork, thinly sliced

Make a caramel by heating the sugar in a saucepan over low heat. Stir constantly until it darkens and thickens. Remove from heat and stir in the nuoc mam. Add the shallots and pepper and set aside to cool. Put the sauce and pork into a claypot, cover and set over a low heat for 30 minutes, stirring occasionally. The dish is done when the sauce has turned into a rich gravy.

Serves 2

One of the most important aspects of the varied southern diet is the existence of the mountain town and region of Dalat (see also the boxed text Street Congee in the Street Food chapter). With the intense light of the tropical sun, cool mountain air and rich soil, Dalat can grow just about anything from any part of the world. Long-stemmed artichokes, big fat carrots, what the Vietnamese call 'French bamboo' (asparagus), potatoes, tomatoes, cauliflower, and greens of all kinds. Watermelons, peaches, apples, avocados and white strawberries. Every morning, well before dawn, convoys of trucks make their runs into Ho Chi Minh City, Nha Trang, even as far as Hoi An, delivering the units of possibility for the great variety of southern cooking. Without Dalat, the south would be gastronomically impoverished.

Characteristically exuberant, dishes in the south are often served in a more festive way. A plate of fresh lettuce and herbs may come with unripe fruits such as mango, green banana or papaya, star fruit or pineapple. Take a little of the cooked food and place it in the lettuce leaf, add some herbs, wrap the lettuce around the food and dip it into whatever sauce is available. Dining in the south is very much a hands-on experience.

DON'T MISS

- A smoothie at Camargue
- Knocking for noodles
- A visit to a rice paper factory
- The fish market of Nha Trang
- Dragon fruit
- Breakfast at a floating market
- An after-dinner performance upstairs at La Bibliotheque

Nha Trang

Outside Ho Chi Minh City the best known tourist destination of the south is the beach resort of Nha Trang. You come here to stuff yourself with anything that once swam in the sea, then burn it off by bodysurfing or running on the beach. Or you could just be lazy and order another beer.

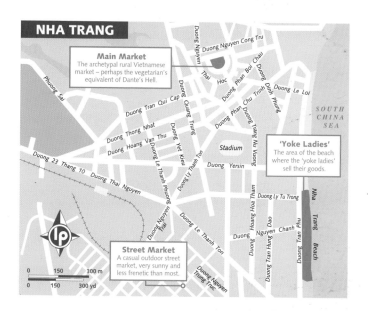

NHA TRANG

Main Market
The archetypal rural Vietnamese market – perhaps the vegetarian's equivalent of Dante's Hell.

Duong Nguyen Cong Tru
Duong Nguyen
Thai Hoc
Duong Phan Boi Chau
Duong Le Loi
Duong Tran Qui Cap
Duong Quang Trung
Duong Phan Chu Trinh
Duong Dinh Phung
SOUTH CHINA SEA
Phuong Sai
Duong Thong Nhat
Duong Hoang Van Thu
Duong Yet Kieu
Duong Tran Nu Vuong
Stadium
'Yoke Ladies'
The area of the beach where the 'yoke ladies' sell their goods.
Duong 23 Thang 10
Duong Thai Nguyen
Duong Le Thanh Phuong
Duong Ly Thanh Ton
Duong Yersin
Duong Ly Tu Trong
Nha Trang Beach
Duong Nguyen Trai
Duong Le Thanh Ton
Duong Hoang Hoa Tham
Duong Nguyen Chanh
Duong Tran Phu
Street Market
A casual outdoor street market, very sunny and less frenetic than most.
Duong Tran Hung Dao
Duong Nguyen Trung Truc

0   150   300 m
0   150   300 yd

But save at least one early morning to not be lazy. Get up before dawn and betake yourself across the Xom Bong Bridge to the north of town. You'll know you're at the right place when you see the darkened silhouettes of the Cham Towers of Po Nagar. Face the sea. At about 6am the colourful fishing flotilla rushes to shore, its holds bulging with the night's catch. Monstrous tuna requiring two men to haul ashore are landed before busy women with wickedly sharp knives quickly reduce them to manageable pieces. Smaller fish are scooped from small cockle-shell boats 'manned'

Cai Estuary, Nha Trang

PHAN THI NGUYEN – Faces of Gastronomy

Thi, as she is known, shoulders her **don ganh** (yoke) every working morning, hikes down to the morning market at the waterfront when the fishermen are landing their catch, and returns with a cargo of giant prawns. With the prawns in one of her two baskets and her little kitchen in the other, she is ready to feed you. You can find her, and ladies like her, any day on the beach at Nha Trang. Some carry prawns, others crab, a few might have oysters or molluscs or small fish. Still others, with baskets or wicker trays balanced on their heads, carry fritters and doughnuts or fresh fruit.

Find yourself a lazy place to relax a while in the sun or beneath a palm or beach umbrella, and the food ladies will find you. Call for Thi if you see her. She's not only adept at building a cook fire in a basket and making delicious dipping sauces from scratch – typical southern spice – but she speaks pretty good English. And she loves to laugh. She wants you to know that she was born in 1967, has two children, and she used to be a dressmaker in a shop. But she likes the beach, and being out on her own.

If she, or another, visits you at your spot in the sand, and you are hungry, take a few moments to chat to her. Get to know the person behind the don ganh. Let her get to know you. Soon she'll take a proprietary interest in you, and see that your gastronomic desires are satisfied. She doesn't have what you want in her baskets? She'll get it for you. She knows who has it. And she'll make sure you don't pay the 'tourist price'. Well, not all of it anyway. Just make sure to tell her we sent you.

exclusively by women. Their little craft are perfectly round and look like nothing more than large baskets daubed with pitch or tar. They each hold one fisherwoman and a catch of silvery fish.

The flotilla's abundance continues to flow ashore, the knife-wielding women pausing only to strop their blades on a stone or a brick or piece of old ceramic. Other workers chop away at great blocks of ice while others pack it into boxes, then layer them with fish, more ice, slam shut their covers and stack them onto waiting trucks for their runs to places across the south. And they're all done by sun-up, and the living, moving portrait of the fishery disappears like morning dew. Time for breakfast.

the
bold palate

If pho and banh aren't quite exotic or Vietnamese enough for you, it's very easy to take your taste buds off the gastronomic beaten track. The Vietnamese culinary palette features an array of alternatives you may wish to sample. However, if the likes of dog, snake and rat don't tickle your fancy, you should know what's out there – it's not for the squeamish. Then again, if you're craving for cobra...

No matter what part of the world you come from, if you travel much in Vietnam, you are going to encounter food that is unusual, strange, maybe even immoral, or just plain weird. Of course 'strange' depends upon your point of view.

The fiercely omnivorous Vietnamese find nothing strange in eating insects, algae, offal or fish bladders. They'll feast on the flesh of dogs, they'll eat a crocodile, or a dish of cock's testicles (see the boxed text 'A Cock's Tale' in the Where to Eat & Drink Chapter). They'll kill a venomous snake before your eyes, cut out its still-beating heart and feed it to you with a cup of the serpent's blood to wash it down, and say it increases your potency. They'll slay a monkey and then barbeque our distant cousin at your tableside. The menu at the Huong Rung restaurant (146 Hai Ba Trung St, Da Kao Ward, Ho Chi Minh City reads in part:

Barbequed turtle dove	$1.50
Grilled field mouse	$0.80
Roasted toad	$2.50
King Cobra done eight ways	$26.00/Kg
Three flavored bat	$5.00
Five flavored lizard	$2.50
Johnie (sic) Walker Red Label	$14.00/Bottle

To the Vietnamese there is nothing 'strange' about anything that will sustain the body. To them a food is either wholesome or it isn't; it's nutritious or it isn't; it tastes good or it doesn't. They'll try anything once – even Kentucky Fried Chicken. But they might find you strange, stranger.

The Bold Menu

First, restaurants that serve the macabre, the exotic and the dangerous are those specialising in such things. And since these 'indelicacies' are relatively expensive, so are the establishments that serve them; and expensive eateries always have English language menus, and the dishes are clearly spelled out. Therefore, you needn't worry about ordering an innocent omelette and getting pig brains scrambled in fertilised duck eggs.

The Huong Rung restaurant is widely known among expats, incorrectly, as 'the endangered species restaurant'. To our knowledge nothing on its menu is endangered, or even threatened. Items such as cobra are raised on snake farms and are plentiful. Field mice and toads are *too* plentiful and are captured regularly in rice paddies. Across the river, there is a restaurant dedicated to the gustatory enjoyment of the deadly crocodile. Like cattle and sheep ranchers, they breed and raise their own stock. We'd like to see the annual round up.

SNAKE WINE

Le Mat village in the Gia Lam district of Hanoi, and the famous Snake Farm of Mytho in the Mekong Delta, specialise in catching and raising snakes to be preserved in wine. Look for these jars of liquor and snakes known as 'snake wine' in almost any bar or restaurant. In the villages many restaurants specialise in snake dishes. The menus vary, with prices running between 30 000 and 100 000 dong. Traditional rice wine is free. (Hurrah!)

But perhaps the grandest venue for dining on the edge is the My Khanh Tourist Garden in Can Tho, in the Mekong Delta. Here, in a beautiful menagerie garden setting, you can wander among cages, ponds, aviaries and pens and, like the mighty hunter of ancient times, select your dinner. Ever look a live monkey in the face and then eat him? You can here. If you select fruit bat, eager boys will slip into the netted aviary with 5m-long bamboo cudgels and whack them from their roosts to render them senseless for the pot. Python is popular, but can only be sold whole, and at US$12 per pound they run about US$100-150 each. It's best to come with a group. A hungry group. Lizards great and small, colourful birds, dangerous looking creatures we have no names for, and the odd house pet are all available to those who would taste the thrill of darkside dining.

One small word of warning to the truly squeamish: while it is easy to avoid the exotic species restaurants, be aware that most Vietnamese do eat organ meats and other parts of an animal that we would normally discard or consign to pet food. You might find on the menu not only hearts and livers, but offal, blood, and what Gray's Anatomy describes as 'organs of generation'. If you see these things on the menu, just pass them by. If, at a com or other menuless eatery, you see something unrecognisable, just select something else that is comfortingly familiar and repeat to yourself, 'I am not a wimp. I am not a wimp'.

COBRA

The 2m-long King Cobra held up by the tail and writhing before me reminds me of a cowboy playing with a lariat (lasso). But this lariat is snapping his deadly jaws mere inches before my too vulnerable face. "Bravo!" (or something to that effect) the restaurant patrons shout, as the 'cowboy' displays his skill in controlling the 'Lariat of Death'. My interpreter, Miss Tran, leans forward and whispers in my ear, "don't worry. The handler is very good. He's only been bitten twice".

With tremendous effort I keep the smile I've been faking since they brought the beastie to my table. (I thought they would kill him first!) "I'm more concerned about myself being bitten once", I say in a raspy voice.

"Again", she assures, "don't worry. There is a complete aid station in the kitchen. And a hospital is nearby".

Before I had need of the aid station two of the handler's assistants appeared and the three of them grappled with the thrashing serpent, stretching him out lengthwise across the table. Another assistant slit his throat and drained the blood into a goblet. Now the beast lay still, and the handler cut out the still-beating heart and set it in a small ivory serving vessel. He mixed the blood with rice wine, and set the sanguine mess before me. "I guess I'm supposed to eat this, eh?" I asked Miss Tran.

"And drink the blood. It's an honour you know. And it will make you, how shall I say, strong". The term 'strong' was Miss Tran's delicate way of saying that it would supercharge my libido.

"There seem to be many dishes here that make men 'strong'".

Viperine

Viperine, or **rượu rắn**, is a white rice wine with a whole snake in the bottle, (remember the worm in a bottle of Mescal?) usually a pit viper and highly poisonous in its live state. Soused, as it is in the bottle, it is rendered benign. Like so many other things the Vietnamese eat and drink, it is said to revive the lagging libido. You'll see bottles of this stuff prominently displayed in many a bar, and at duty free shops. Drink a toast with it to establish your bona fides.

Dog

Along the Nhat Tan dyke, between the Red River and West Lake, there are about 20 dog meat shops in bamboo huts. At the end of each lunar month, diners come in such great numbers that motorcycles and cars clog the surface of the dyke. Vietnamese like to invite their foreign friends to taste this dish, perhaps because they like to watch them squirm.

"Yes. We have a high birth rate".

"Do ladies ever eat these things?" I asked, still regarding the thumb-nail-sized beating heart.

"No", she said. And for the first and only time I saw her blush.

Lifting the little ivory saucer to my lips I tilted my head back and the heart slid beating into my mouth. Almost of its own accord it snaked down my throat. I hardly had to swallow. Raising the goblet I toasted the skilful handler who has only been bitten twice and quaffed a goodly portion of the warm blood and sweet wine. Miss Tran looked on approvingly. I dabbed my lips with the starched white serviette, and it came away stained red, like a blotter a woman has used after her lipstick.

As I performed this ceremony a cook was adroitly deboning the snake. The bones, delicate as a small fish's, he broke into pieces, dredged in rice flour, and deep-fried to a savoury crisp. The meat he prepared as three separate dishes that I chose from a list of eight: curried, braised with wine, grilled then wrapped in tangy leaves. Miss Tran gamely tasted the flesh of the serpent, but deemed it unladylike to enjoy it. Perhaps believing that it would make her, shall we say, too strong. She contented herself with rice and vegetables and a small fish.

I, on the other hand, consumed all I could of Eve's betrayer. I continued to sip the vinous blood, and to dab my lips with the serviette until it was mottled with crimson. What did the serpent, the symbol of evil and deceit taste like? Was he bitter? No. Tough to chew? Hardly. I wish I could say that he tasted of sin. Or at least had an aftertaste of bad deeds. Or simply impure thoughts. But the fact is, he tasted like chicken.

At least seven different dishes of dog meat are served in restaurants specialising in what is sometimes called 'deer of the doorstep'. In the world of Yin & Yang, dog meat gives warmth, and consumers like to sit on mats close to the cool ground in well aired rooms. Getting together with friends to eat dog meat, quaff rice wine, and tell stories is what a Hanoi native of our acquaintance describes as "an inexpressible pleasure".

How is Fido prepared? Just like any other meat: roasted, fried, barbecued, boiled in a soup. Dog as a dish generally begins several days before the end of its days. It may be selected from a captive pack, or it may be captured on the street as is often the fate of common curs. (In addition to loving dogs as dinner, northerners also love them as pets. For this reason they are very protective of their house dogs, and never let them go a' roaming alone.) Their last days are days of ease, and of becoming tender and tasty by feeding richly on the finest table scraps and butchers' trimmings. The hound that's bound for the table top is a contented canine

CARE TO DINE AT DAI DUONG?

I was employed as a grill chef for the Dai Duong Restaurant in Ho Chi Minh City. My Vietnamese language skills and my pale skin were the only requirements for the job. Not the gutsy type, I went into this venture with a long-time French friend of mine, Christophe. Our uniform consisted of white chef's coat with red trim and black buttons and the unforgettable chef's hat. Thankfully, few expats dined here.

The Dai Duong featured Vietnamese specialities from bat to rat with a wide array of seafood in between. Bats, lizards, snakes, field mice, anteaters, doves, carp, and tiger prawns come to mind – all kept live in cages and aquaria for your dining pleasure.

The grill became my forte with minimum on-the-job training. I became an expert at shoving a large chopstick through the mouth of a **cá lóc** (live carp), skewering its innards and exiting through the trunk portion of the tail. This sounds harsh, but is nothing compared to the subsequent live grilling the truly fresh fish received next. Needless to say, it required some strength to keep the fish from flailing from the grill to the ground.

Prawns were another speciality. Though the large ones were fairly easy to handle one at a time – you grabbed the claws and held it to the grill until it stopped flopping – it was no small task to manage three in one go, although they were much easier to handle than the smaller shrimp, which were sold by the kilogram. Those bad boys would jump all over the place before simmering to a perfect, fire-red, ready-to-eat delicacy.

Generally, warm-blooded creatures were taken to the back where sadistic young lads took care of the killing and cleaning. The turtle dove usually required a thump to the head, while the field mice required a very skilled slam to the floor.

The mice were gutted and beheaded before presentation to the chef. The chef grilled them with a sauce cháo that made these little guys irresistible after the first, initial inhibitions.

The city sewer rat, on the other hand, is a nasty creature which should be avoided at all costs. They often reach cat-like proportions and are prone to myriad diseases which, if contracted, could land you in a scientific laboratory.

Bat was minced and served with a fresh salad – a must-try.

Though I specialised in the grill work, the upside of my job was being called from the grill to guests' tables, where I was plied with beer and fascinating stories of Vietnamese lore and legend. This aspect of the job helped to drive my colleague away. He didn't really have what it took to sit for long periods of time and drink much too much beer.

– Buddy Newell, Ho Chi Minh City

when he meets the knife. A deft and humane stroke to the jugular vein and the pooch is provender. The body is drawn, the ears and tail cut off, and the hair singed away. Looking very much like a roast piglet, it is then trundled to the December 19 market where it might be sold whole to a restaurant or chopped into quarters for private consumption.

What the dog tastes like depends on his pre-dinner diet. And the diner's attitude. If you have no qualms about feeding on Fido he tastes a bit like pork with some beefy undertones. And the flesh is firm, yet not tough. But if you have ever loved a dog as a pet and faithful companion, you may find him tasting of bitter betrayal. We have even known people to suffer hallucinations, seeing their dear doggies before them at the table, scowling their disapproval, minus their ears and tails. Beware.

Hot Vit Lon

We are sitting at the bar in Hien and Bob's pub on Hai Ba Trung Boulevard one fine Saigon afternoon. The BGI beer is the coldest in town, while the temperature outside hovers around 32°C with humidity to match. It's air-conditioned and dimly lit here, a respite from the heat and glaring light outdoors. The lovely Miss Yu, dressed in ao dai, sits primly behind the bar, about to have a snack.

We look curiously at what she holds in her hand. She places it in ours; an egg, still warm from cooking. By the appearance we guess, "duck?"

"Oh, so you know about **hột vịt lộn**," Miss Yu says.

She cracks the egg around the narrow end with a spoon and lifts off the top. Some of the contents run down the side of the shell. She holds forth spoon and egg, and invites us to partake. Inside the shell is what we can accurately describe as a duck abortion: a fertilised egg allowed to incubate till some days before maturity. It is dropped into hot water when it is no longer an embryo, but not yet a foetus.

Miss Yu's kind offering is a mass of blood vessels, with a suggestion of feathers, bones so nascent that they disintegrate at a touch. There's also a pudding-like substance, neither egg nor meat, that, left alone, would have congealed into the bird's musculature, brain and organs. And it smells rather ... tempting, like a duck confit. We decline the offer, knowing that she is simply being polite. She is hungry and we will not interfere.

She thrusts her spoon into the cavity, swirls it slightly to mix up the good bits. She draws it out full of tasty nourishment and brings it sensuously into her mouth. We are reminded of Brillat Savarin's assertion that 'a pretty gastronome' prepared to feed is one of the most charming sights in the world. She eats it like peanut butter, or Vegemite, or caviar, smiling with delight. A small gob of blood vessels clings to her lower lip. She licks it off, and smiles coyly. We agree with Brillat Savarin.

We have had this dish before, and esteem it a tasty treat. It has almost all the vitamins and nutrients a human needs. It's soft enough for a toothless babe, and is so digestible that if you have ulcers or other stomach complaints, this might be your perfect food. Try it. But take this advice, at least for the first time: close your eyes.

Durian Sense

The durian fruit does not smell. The odour comes from the rind. Try telling *that* to the airline steward who wants you to parachute out with your purchase.

– Harry Rolnik, New York

Durian

The most astonishing tropical fruit in Vietnam is the durian. A melon-like fruit with a yellow, pudding-textured flesh, its odour is best described as pig shit, turpentine and onions garnished with a dirty gym sock. It can be smelled from many yards off and can take your breath away. (See also Fruit in the Staples & Specialities chapter).

shopping

& markets

Western-style supermarkets and convenience stores are springing up all over the country. You can buy all manner of goods at these places but what you can't get, for any money, is the essential experience of Vietnam. It's only at the bustling markets, the focus of everyday life, where you can fill your senses with the aromas, flavours and sounds of Vietnam, its cuisine and its people.

The Vietnamese Market

Every city and town has one. Ho Chi Minh City and Hanoi have several; Can Tho has one that floats. In Vietnam you don't go to the Mom & Pop grocery on the corner. You don't need to seek out the butcher, the baker or the candlestick maker, you can get it all at the **chợ** (market). In Vietnam everything is under one roof. While it sounds a bit like a supermarket, it is not a commercial megalith operating on economies of scale. It's so much less and so much more. It is a village, a microcosm of this society. (For phrases on Shopping see the Eat Your Words chapter.)

FOR THE LOVE OF MEAT

All throughout South-East Asia, meat seems to be butchered with a bone in every bite. Maybe butchery is a lost art, or maybe they never had it to lose. So often they take whatever it is they are about to prepare, grab a big cleaver, and start whacking it into bite-size bits from head to toe. Vietnam is no exception. But one morning as my brother Paul and I walked through the Ben Thanh market in Saigon, I saw a wonderful sight, a glass display case full of long luscious white strips of what I took to be skinned and deboned chicken breast. My mouth watered. Finally, meat I could sink my teeth into, and through! I walked up to the food stall, pointed at the meat smiling from ear to ear. Not speaking any Vietnamese I just kept grinning and walked behind the counter.

The cook, not knowing what I was doing, had a perplexed look on his face, but caught on fast as I pretended to grab chilli, garlic and other assorted items from his makeshift kitchen, bring them to his chopping block and pretend to chop and then stir fry the lot. The cook and the crowd gathering were all laughing before I finally took a bow and then a seat at what looked like a little kid's table and chair set. Smells of garlic, chilli and fish sauce filled the air. I had him put the chicken breasts in whole! Within minutes my masterpiece was on a plate next to a large pile of rice. With my chopsticks I picked up a large piece of meat, showing it to Paul. "I'm in heaven, Bro," I told him. He just gave me a sheepish grin. I knew he was jealous. Slipping one end into my mouth I started to chew off a piece.

Aack!!! It's chewing back! My brother, noticing the look on my face started to laugh. "What in hell, this is tough as shoe leather," I cried. Paul was laughing so hard he couldn't even talk. He just pointed to the glass case that had held my prized "chicken breast."

"I'd take a closer look," he said. Now I knew why he was so hysterical. It was full of neatly stacked pigs ears!

– Bruce Harmon, Los Gatos, California

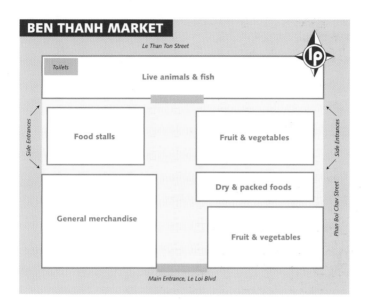

BEN THANH MARKET

Le Than Ton Street

Toilets

Live animals & fish

Side Entrances

Food stalls

Fruit & vegetables

Side Entrances

Dry & packed foods

Phan Boi Chav Street

General merchandise

Fruit & vegetables

Main Entrance, Le Loi Blvd

In the 'village' of the Cho Ben Thanh in Ho Chi Minh City you will find it, like any other, divided into little territories inhabited by merchants who pay a fee for their bit of commercial real estate. A market stall may be newly occupied by its merry merchant, or it may be held by the same family for three generations, serving three generations of customers. This explains why you will often see, side by side, several stalls selling the same merchandise. Vietnamese shoppers are not casual or impulse buyers. They generally know exactly what they want when they leave the house. If they want a cheesy romance novel, they won't buy it on a whim at the check-out counter. They'll go to the cheesy romance-novel seller, the one they've been buying from for years. Commercial transactions are personal here, especially for such intimate things as what the family will eat. Nothing is too good for the Vietnamese housewife's family table, and she will buy her aliments from people she knows and trusts. She does not merely 'go' to the market, she *visits* the market.

All the merchants of Ben Thành know each other. They constantly gossip and exchange stories. In slow times the ladies do each other's hair, or give each other pedicures. They call to each other from across the aisles.

"When is your daughter getting married?"
"How much did the tourist pay?"
"You're looking better today, Auntie".
"Have you seen Mr Tan's new grandson?"
"Is the price going up again?"
"My son-in-law is a rascal!"
"So is mine!"

You could start a tour of Ben Thanh at the perimeter, and explore in ever-decreasing concentric circles, as most tourists do. Or you can jump right into the middle of things.

In this land of spice you might do well to start at the spice merchant. Try following your nose till you reach him, or you could ask any merchant, or almost any shopper for that matter, to point you to Ong Tao Beo, 'Mr Big Chinese'. You will find his Buddha-like girth and wisdom surveying his wares and pondering new ways to use them. On his shelves you will see the palette used by Vietnamese cooks to colour the portrait of their cuisine. Here, you will see the genesis of that cuisine, in the Chinese and Indian spices that lifted a humble fare of rice, plain vegetables and meat seared by fire, to the heights of the present day.

Mr Big Chinese will sell you foot-long sticks of cinnamon and advise you to use it in a marinade for beef. He'll give you a good price on the star anise and peppercorns without which there would be no phở. He'll roast, grind and blend your spices to order, producing a curry, or a five-spice powder or an eight-spice powder, just for you. Or he'll sell you his own secret blends, wrapped in little paper packets for use in special dishes like **bánh xèo** batter, or special occasions like weddings. He might even make you a love potion.

From Mr Big Chinese it is a short walk to the coffee and tea merchant. Coffee and tea are just about the only kind of food items sold in shops outside the market as well as within. And it is sold from those outside shops mainly to tourists as a tasty souvenir to take home. The locals buy their coffee and tea in the market. There are many grades available, from fine flawless Arabica to the cheapest Robusta, with 50% broken beans from having been walked on by water buffalo while drying in the sun.

The culture of food is in this and every other market in Vietnam. It comes here in its raw form and is converted into the useful, nourishing and tasty icons of gastronomy. In the industrial world these processes occur in faraway factories, where we never see a tomato or a fish or a grain of wheat being turned by human hands into a thing of beauty and of use. We see the end result, the cans and boiler bags, and boxes with labels and warnings and lists of ingredients. We see the manufactured product.

Sleeping stallholder, Old Quarter, Hanoi

SHOPPING

But at Ben Thanh you will see the trucks arrive from Dalat and unloaded in hurried relays, the produce stacked and attractively arranged by your merchant. You'll watch as dexterous hands use razor blades to shred fresh lemongrass and spring onions (scallions) into yellow and green ribbons, chop vivid red chillies into sauce, crack crabs and mound the flaky meat into piles for sale by weight. They stack the young green coconuts and the older brown ones in separate pyramids. The green ones they open, and sell you the clean-tasting juice and scoop out the soft young meat for a snack. With the brown ones they'll grate and grind the flesh, then heat and squeeze out their rich white milk for use in curries and sweets. They julienne the perennial green papayas for tart salads tossed with crispy bean sprouts, onion, chilli and lime juice. For hours people will carve vegetables into attractive shapes and patterns for shoppers to take home and use to dress the table to their fancy.

From here walk to the fish and meat. It looks more like a zoo aquarium with its scores of live animals and sea creatures: crabs in baskets, fish swimming in tubs, tiger prawns scurrying about in glass tanks, and sea urchins kept for their roe. Select a carp or a catfish and the seller deftly kills it with one stroke of the knife to the base of the skull. She'll draw its entrails and set them aside, wrap your purchase in paper and bid you good morning.

Cages are full of chickens and ducks and geese. For those without cages, gaggles of geese and roosts of hens are tied together by their feet. And everywhere cleavers and knives are flashing and working at reducing them to dinner. Here the animals are killed to order. There is no such thing as a chicken trucked in frozen from Arkansas. Here you select the one you want and the merchant will casually cut its throat and drain the blood into a pan. If you want that, it will cost you a little extra. It's prized by sauce makers for its rich flavour and nutritional value. Be careful where you walk here so as not to step into a pan of blood or entrails. Everything is turned to kitchen use, for nothing is wasted.

The smells of blood, feathers and guts are ever-present in this part of the market. The sounds of protest from the birds and the thrashing of fish are constant. All the people are smiling and chatting as they do their bloody work, enjoying themselves in the midst of such bounty. This is no grim scene to the Vietnamese shopper, man or woman or child. This is life giving life, continuity, security and a full belly – the way of the natural world.

The Vietnamese are an artistic, aesthetic and highly civilised people. They are also mighty warriors. The earthy and visceral realities of life and death hold no dread for them. On the first and 15th days of the lunar month many of these market people will eat only vegetables in a sincere show of reverence for life. But they will still come to work, and wield their blades for those who choose a different way of life and diet.

Chicks & eggs for sale, Central Market, Cantho

Walk away from the slaughter now, past stalls selling bottles of nước mắm stacked to the ceiling. There can never be too much nước mắm in Vietnam. Pass the stalls with sheets of fresh vermicelli and rice noodles; then another selling rice papers, and on by others with dozens of different kinds of rice. In the north-west corner of the Ben Thanh market is your reward: lunch! About an acre of food stalls greet you. Stand at a distance and read the prominent signs and displays. Select your desire, then make a beeline for it. If you hesitate, you'll be accosted by food stall merchants who will block your path and urge you – no, insist – that you should patronise their concern.

"What do you want?!" they will demand. "Do you want noodle?"

"No", you say. "Uh ... I don't know yet ... I ..."

"You have noodle!"

"But, but ..."

"Noodle very good here! You eat! You have beer, too!"

"But ..."

"Okay, you have soda!"

Every market has its own personality, and its own way of living and working and dealing with shoppers. The Ben Thanh, granddaddy of them all and emperor of emporia, exudes confidence, bustle, city-slicker savvy and sophistication, as well as an almost New York aggressiveness. Well, we did say that they are mighty warriors.

SHOPPING

Floating Market

You must rise before dawn, for it begins when the sun rises and it doesn't last for long. This wil o' the wisp market reminds us of the mythical village of Brigadoon. It disappears with the mist. You should arrange for a boat the day before to pick you up at the riverbank in Can Tho to take you to market at Cai Ran a few miles upstream.

This market is entirely upon the water. Small boats laden with goods push off from the shore and from any number of places up and down the river to converge at this spot every morning at dawn. Like the on-shore market stalls, they tend to specialise. There are fruit boats, vegetable boats, fish boats, rice boats, potato boats and pig boats. They float gracefully about as in a colourful water ballet. Unlike the big-city markets, the merchants are quieter and less demanding of your attention. They

Duong Dong Market, Phu Quoc Island, Mekong Delta

paddle or motor slowly about, pausing at each other's gunnels to exchange goods or gossip, then part and couple anew with other vessels. A pomelo boat might drift by you, its occupant quietly watching you. If you show an interest in the fruits he may backwater and hover there to give you more time to ponder their taste. Then he'll float away.

You may collide gently with another and, before you can disengage, you're connected to another. Then another and another and another. Soon a little island of boats has formed, and you can get out of yours and walk across the conjoined decks from guavas to bananas to carrots and cabbages, all the way over to the breakfast boat. Here you can get a bowl of noodles or a baguette sandwich. Take it back to your boat and enjoy a leisurely repast. The cluster of boats will part when the current compels them. Then watch for a tea boat, and when you see it, hail the pilot. Tea is served. But do be careful about the beer boat, and the coffee boat, for there is no toilet boat.

Cai Rang floating market, Mekong Delta

Nha Trang Market

Laid out in concentric circles, this market reminds us just a little of Dante's Hell. This is a country market, and despite Nha Trang's status as a beach resort for foreigners, Nha Trang's people are country folk, and their market reflects that. If you're vegetarian, you might want to stay away. Almost all Vietnamese people are villagers, or villagers at heart, and they grow up using animals for labour and for food. They do not treat them cruelly, but neither do they try to make them happy. They try to make them tasty. You will find the market at Nha Trang a good reflection of rural life.

The outdoor portion, where all the food is, has a barnyard feel. That's where you want to go, to the first circle. As you approach the market at the main entry, you'll pass a few stalls under awnings selling snacks and soda. Keep going. Enter the first circle and make a right. Now all you have to do is go with the flow. On your right you'll see little cave-like eating establishments. The little stools and benches are only about 20cm high, and the tables are not much higher. The first cave offers vegetarian food. The others carry all the usual suspects. If you're hungry, go ahead and dine in the dim. The food is good country cooking. Scattered elsewhere through the market are tables and cooks who call out to you as you pass, and you can lunch in the sun.

Being on the coast, there is a plethora of seafood here. Fish of every description are sold fresh and dried, or cooked to order to take home to the family. At midday it can get crowded as people come in for lunch. The walkway is a jostle with humanity and yet the work must go on. Deliveries, made by motorbike and cyclo, must continue. They push their way through the crowd with shouts of 'Yo! Yo! Yo!' You can get run over here so when you hear that sound, get out of the way or take refuge behind the mendicant monks who come here with their begging bowls. People earn merit in Heaven by giving to them. They always seem to be well fed. We suppose the people of Nha Trang are very meritorious.

On the far side of the market are the animals. There is the usual collection of birds – geese, chickens, ducks – besides game birds such as quail. And here there is a live pig market. Portly pink piggies, just a few months old, are brought in on the backs of motorbikes (no helmets for them) singly or in litters and sold to those who want to fatten them up. Suckling pig is a rare thing in the Vietnamese diet. It costs very little to fatten up a pig, and when you do there is so much more of him. Families sometimes join together to buy a pig and raise it for Tết. They all bring their table scraps to feed it, and take turns keeping it. By New Year they all have a good supply of feast meat.

Music of the Market

One of the most delightful aspects of shopping in Vietnamese markets is the rich traditions surrounding the marketplace. There is the musical call of the **mì gõ**, the noodle knocker, but among the more traditional vendors there is a whole range of musical calls to buy. As you patrol the marketplace of Vietnam, listen for these songs.

Che Vendors

Chè is a sweet concoction (see the Staples & Specialities chapter) made of **đậu xanh** (green mung beans), lotus seeds, **bột khoai** (translucent noodles) and **bún** (vermicelli) and Chinese cherries cooked in a mixture of water and extract of coconut. A dish of sweet and warm chè thung is a popular night-cap here. You might not be hungry, but if the voice of the seller is lilting enough, you might change your mind. The chè business admits no male vendor. All dealers are women. So the nightingales sing:

Che ... ai an ... bot khoai ... bun ... tau ... dau xanh ... nuoc ... duà
   duong ... cat ong?
   (Who will eat potato flour, vermicelli, green beans, water,
   coconut sugar?)

Banh Bo Vendors

Bánh bò is made of rice flour, yeast and sugar. The dough is set in a mould and steamed. To call you to his place of business the vendor sings:

Banh ... bo ... gia ... cha ... quay ... ong?
   (Cake ... Creeping ... Doughnuts?)

Xoi Vendors

Xôi or glutinous rice should always be cooked in steam except when you want to make glue. It can be served either on a piece of green banana leaf with grated coconut and a mixture of sugar, salt and grilled sesame seeds, or on a plate with a piece of chicken on the side.

Xoi ... dau xanh ... nuoc ... dua ... duong ... cat ... ong
   (Glutinous rice ... green beans ... water ... coconut sugar ... powder?)

Nem Nuong Vendors

Tasty, often spicy, meatballs (usually pork) are grilled over charcoal on skewers. The fat drips down on the fire and the resulting smoke is song in itself. But just in case you don't smell it, you may hear:

Ai an nem nuong ong?
   (Who will eat meatballs grilled?)

Things to Buy

One of the most enduring memories you can bring home from Vietnam is a few Vietnamese coffee-makers (see Coffee in the Drinks chapter). They make only one cup at a time, very slowly, but if you are able to spend more than a week or 10 days in Vietnam you can easily get into the habit of letting an afternoon coffee hypnotically drip into your little glass as your mind empties of its cares. Repeating this ritual at home is a good way to stir up the memories. They're cheap and you can get them in any market.

While you're buying coffee-makers, buy some coffee. It will cost anywhere from a few pennies to a few dollars per kilo. It is roasted plain most of the time, but speciality coffee dealers, such as the one in the Ben Thanh market, often roast it with vanilla, or chocolate, or cinnamon, or whatever the dealer fancies. Most dealers can grind it to only one state: very fine. If that won't suit you at home, buy your beans whole.

HIDDEN TREASURES

It was still early morning but already the humid air of Ho Chi Minh City rose pulsating from the street, enveloping me in a miasma of ancient delta haze and modern diesel fuel. I retreated to the dubious shelter of the Nguyen Tri Phuong market, grateful for any protection against the pervasive heat. The proprietress of a small concern within smiled and gestured me over toward her fare that consisted of pâté-like meats, white sliced bread and, I looked again, baguettes! Surely the humidity would put them in a sorry state of sogginess, but out of curiosity I placed an order. Deftly she selected one, and as she split it, it crackled crisply. She began constructing a layered concoction of pate and various greens, the cucumber being the only one I could recognise. I got another smile when I motioned for her to add lots of Vietnamese fish sauce. She wrapped it quickly in a napkin and handed it to me. I paid the equivalent of 25 cents and sat down on a small stool near her concern. The crust of my baguette was firm and crunchy and had the tender, moist insides of those I loved to eat in Paris.

I never found out the name of the meat, but it tasted smooth and sweet and worked well with the pungent greens, salty fish sauce and the cleansing, cool bite of the cucumber. Delicious! Even the heat seemed less formidable, now. Each morning after that I returned to Tron's stand, that was her name, for my Banh Mi Thit with its exotic Indochine filling.

— *Gina Comaich - Oakland, California*

Crowds at Cholon Market, Ho Chi Minh City

Most coffee sellers also sell tea. It is available in a wide range of types and qualities. The chief designations are green and black. Briefly, green tea is gently roasted after drying. Black tea is the same stuff, but the leaves are broken after harvest and allowed to ferment, then dried and roasted. This gives it greater shelf-life and allows it to travel better, an important consideration in the days of sail when it could take literally months to make the passage from China or India to Europe and the Americas. Hence, the western penchant for black tea, and the Asian preference for the original brew. So buy both. Vietnamese tea is dirt cheap and earthily good. It is always sold in bulk (though the smart set now likes to buy Lipton tea bags). Ask the merchant to let you smell the various blends, and don't be shy about asking for a cup if he or she has the means to produce one. (And do the same with coffee.)

BINH TAY MARKET, HO CHI MINH CITY

Thap Muoi Street

Entrance

Roofless & crumbling buildings

Cao Van Lau

General manufactured goods; textiles, toiletries, utensils

General Goods

Meats

Central Courtyard

Food stalls

Food stalls

General food: canned & boxed goods

Staples: Rice, vegetables & fruit

Chu Van An

Colonial buildings

B Phan Van Khoe Street

I follow the long and wide street south to Cholon. I'm on the back seat of a Honda Om, a new and shiny moped. It is a long ride. My hands are firmly fixed on the metal rails of the rear seat rack. My driver is negotiating the traffic – trucks, cars, taxis, mopeds – all speeding toward us from every direction. Cyclos and bicycles follow in our wake.

Vietnamese cookware, especially the claypot, is delightful to look at and to use. Large claypots are commonly used for making hot and sour fish soup, and for lotus rice. They are useful as slow cookers, for the long, slow simmering of meats or stews. Smaller claypots are used for braising fish and pork, especially in caramel sauce. We find they work well for non-Vietnamese dishes such as mushrooms in red wine, and vegetables with herbs and butter. Although they are somewhat delicate, they are good for camp cookery as they were originally developed for use in the field by farmers and labourers who cooked over very small fires. Another good item is a **bánh khọt** mould, used to make a savoury pudding of coconut milk, rice flour and spices. The mould can be for one large bánh khọt or for several individual ones. It is made of aluminium and the lid is usually stamped with 'BK'.

Cholon. Reprobates and wanton hustlers of all sordid sorts collided here from the earliest of times. French and American adventurers gathered later to gamble, carouse, and wallow in vice. Cholon has a complicated past.

"This was the land of rebellious barons", noted Graham Greene, where "it was like Europe in the Middle Ages". Greene went on to wonder, "but what were the Americans doing here?"

Hmmm ... I would have to think about that. I walk the Binh Tay perimeter to grasp this market's difference and its noted past. I skirt the southern fringe, spotting rows of roofless and crumbling buildings. Testimony to the Tet offensive, I wonder? Fierce street battles raged around here in February 1968 as the Viet Cong were squeezed into this crowded district.

I walk on, cutting my way through to the centre courtyard. Local shoppers sit and rest. Visitors take pictures. Things certainly have changed. Cholon has been rinsed clean of its iniquities. Only the architecture belies a different time, particularly on the northern edge, where beautiful colonial buildings hopefully await restoration.

I spy a young noodle knocker (see the Street Food chapter) and follow him on his beat. It's time for lunch. He leads me to the market corner where food is served to the hungry. Ah yes! Spring rolls of all sorts. Noodles with slices of beef and coriander (cilantro). And my favourite: ground pork perfectly spiced, marinated, skewered, and grilled. I feast. I come to understand why, at least, I'm here. It's the food. Definitely the food!

– Garrett Culhane

Get some nice chopsticks made of polished wood. Hand-embroidered linen tablecloths are a real bargain, as are all kinds of crockery and table service. Vietnamese porcelain and china designs were hard to find a few years ago when the state decreed what would and would not be manufactured. Now, beautiful traditional designs for plates, bowls and such are being produced and sold in every market. Something uniquely Vietnamese for your table is a set of decoratively carved containers made from the wood of the cinnamon tree. Coffee, tea, sugar or toothpicks stored in these will acquire a faint suggestion of cinnamon. The aroma in the wood will last for years. Whenever you need to jog your sensual memories of Vietnam, have a cup of tea or coffee, or just pick your teeth!

where to
eat & drink

Ah, so many choices. And we poor mortals with only one mouth and one set of teeth. Envy the Hydra. Well, where to eat in Vietnam? Sometimes, on the boulevards and side streets of the cities, the best way to answer the question of 'where' is to simply start walking – or, if that seems like too much effort, you can just rest in the shade and wait for the noodle knocker to find you.

Where to Eat

In almost any district you will pass restaurants of every kind. Vietnamese culture and society require a plethora of restaurants, foremost because they are a gregarious people and draw sustenance from each other's company as much as from their food. Virtually all restaurants in Vietnam are 'family' ones; kids are always welcome.

Men and women work hard, and are often too tired to cook on a wood or charcoal stove with no modern conveniences. And most people have small kitchens, sometimes just a corner in a common room, which can be oppressively hot. In the north where the nights are cooler and the people more frugal, restaurants are more often for special occasions.

HOW TO ORDER

When ordering from a restaurant, menu don't worry – don't even think – about the proper succession of courses. There isn't any! Standard procedure is for all dishes to be placed in the centre of the table as soon as they are ready. Diners help themselves to whatever appeals to them regardless of who ordered what. This Vietnamese way allows you to try a little of everything without having to waste it if you don't like it. Just let the others eat it.

You should try to order as many tastes, textures and colours as possible. While you can eat your dishes in any order you like, try to start with the more delicate-tasting ones, and then proceed to the spicier and heavier items. Rice, in one form or another, may be brought out early or late in the repast. We recommend that you ask for it to be brought earlier so you can eat it with the other dishes. But don't try to control the order in which the other dishes appear – you will fail. It may seem like gastronomic Russian roulette, but just spin the cylinder, pull the trigger, and take your chance. The worst blast you can get will come from spices.

When dinner is over and it's time to pay, just catch the waiter's eye and make a writing motion across your palm.

Here are a few dos and don'ts for whether you're in a proper sit-down restaurant, a noodle stand, or a roadside stall:

Do …	**Don't …**
Just point to what you want on the menu or in the food display.	Ask for a change of ingredients.
	Change your order.
Remember what you ordered.	Ask for separate bills.
Accept whatever comes.	

Restaurants, or at least sellers of ready-to-eat foods have been common in Vietnam since time out of mind. What we think of as a proper sit-down restaurant with formalised service and tablecloths came with the French, but the public markets and the seaports and dockyards and the roadside rests have always been there. There have always been busy people in Vietnam with no time or no place to cook, and there have always been enterprising people to serve them.

The oldest continually operating restaurant of any kind in Vietnam, at least of our acquaintance, is Cha Ca La Vong of Hanoi, established circa 1899. At the time of its founding it was like so many other restaurants of its kind: a place where local merchants and tradesmen could get a good meal at a good price. A 'businessman's lunch'. You will still find this kind of restaurant throughout Vietnam: unprepossessing, a decor that might charitably be called 'early Spartan', often hard to find as it looks like the surrounding residences or commercial concerns, and yet retaining an ambiance and a quality of goods that keep it in business for generations. You will not often find these restaurants in guidebooks. They are too anonymous. But most Vietnamese can tell you where their favourites are. Just ask.

So what will you discover as you survey the restaurant landscape? To begin, you can find a lot of speciality restaurants. Many of Vietnam's favourite dishes are labour-intensive or require special kitchens, or ovens, which few homes have. You'll pass by any number of **phở** houses from grotty to grand (see Phở later in this chapter). Phở requires many hours and great bubbling cauldrons to produce the broth, and so is rarely made in the home.

Pancake houses are also popular but we're not talking flapjacks here. The word, **bánh xèo**, refers to a savoury dish more like a crepe or Indian dhosa. Their preparation requires counter space that most homes lack. They require so much space that in many establishments the actual cooking takes place outdoors, such as at Bánh Xèo (46A Dinh Cong Trang, Ho Chi Minh City).

Barbecue is a speciality and many such restaurants are easy to locate by the aroma wafting through the streets. Also popular is the dish known as Bo 7 Mon, which is beef prepared seven different ways – a good feed when you're feeling protein impaired. A good example is at Restaurant Bo 7 Mon (228 Tran Hung Dao Street, Ho Chi Minh).

A type of restaurant we see increasingly in Vietnam, as people become more entrepreneurial, is the family home being opened to anyone who has the price of a meal. Some can only accommodate a few diners, others can take in a crowd. Check out Ong Tao in Hué or the Phuong Anh restaurant in Hanoi.

Then there are those restaurants on the dark side of the street, as it were. Go see the dog meat restaurants along the Nhat Tan dyke in Hanoi. Houng Roung restaurant in Ho Chi Minh City will kill a cobra before your eyes and drain its blood into your glass of rice wine. Cheers. The My Khanh Tourist Garden in Can Tho raises all sorts of exotic animals from crocodiles to monkeys, and you can stroll among the cages and choose your victim. (See the Bold Palate chapter.)

For something a little less daring, just go to the north end of Thi Sac street in Ho Chi Minh City and find the best of family dining in the numerous sidewalk cafes. And don't neglect the remaining French and Chinese restaurants. They are not as common as they used to be, but they are an important part of Vietnam's culinary and cultural legacy.

The Noodle Knocker

One place you can eat well, at least in the south, is wherever you happen to be. It could be 10pm, and the streets of Ho Chi Minh City are quiet. Or it might be a bustling market day with a fierce tropical sun poised at the zenith and you don't want to leave the shade of the sycamore you've sheltered under. But you're hungry.

Noodle Knocker

And then you hear it. That musical knock-knock-knockety-knock of one bamboo stick beating rhythmically on another, as though a musician were trying to knock out a tune on one key of a xylophone. It's the sound of the **mì gõ** (the noodle knocker). It's usually a child, boy or girl, and the knocking announces that food is near and that he or she will bring it to you, wherever you are. As long as you are within earshot of the mì gõ, delivery is assured. It's usually noodle soup they go for, but it might be grilled meat or prawns with cold rice vermicelli (cold is a relative term). Or it could be spring rolls. One of these days it might be pizza. Oh well.

These days, some noodle knockers are knocking for noodles with a metal noodle knocker. We prefer not to patronise these peripatetic purveyors of pasta … we think they need a knock on the noodle! We are traditionalists, even if we are overly given to alliteration. Besides, when they use the bamboo, fine and useful souvenirs are to be had by offering the noodle knockers a generous tip in exchange for their knockers. Then, when you are home, and find yourself longing for the taste of Vietnam, just pick up your noodle knocker and knock-knock-knockety-knock …

The Com

Probably the single most common type of restaurant you will see is simply called a **cơm** – cơm being a word for rice. This is the same kind of linguistic usage as the English cafe. The word cafe means nothing more than coffee, but we get a lot more than java at a cafe. The standard meal at a cơm is a serving of rice, a meat, fish or fowl dish, and a vegetable, and cold weak tea. Cost is a set price, under US$1. You will see cơm everywhere and they are unmistakable. Their food is on colourful display out front on a tray or in a glass display case. The cơm might be nothing more than a nook the size of a broom closet, the operator possessing a single-burner cooker and a rice steamer which he or she works while squatting on the floor. There might be no place for you to sit but on the kerb. Or you may be offered a low stool a little larger than a golf tee. If you're in Hanoi, Com Hoan at 24 Duong Hoan at the edge of the old quarter is a good example.

More often the cơm will be a family operation about the size of a garage. It will have plain wooden or metal tables and folding chairs. Each table will be set with plastic

> ### Where's that Place?
> There is no better culinary thrill than embarking on your own adventure but if you want to sample the restaurants named in this chapter, check the maps in the Regional Variations chapter for locations.

pitchers of cold tea, a tray of condiments and little else. The floor could use sweeping. A glass refrigerator in the rear of the joint contains beer and soft drinks. There is no menu, no stuffy protocol, and no snooty head waiter. There is no waiter at all! You simply walk right up to the display and point to what you like. Father will dish it up for you, along with rice and soup, as mother continues to cook, and daughter or son or niece or nephew will follow you with it to your table. Other relatives will be washing dishes or peeling vegetables, usually in view. If you would like a little more variety in your meal, say for example you want two veg instead of one, simply point to the two you like. They will assume that you are asking for a half portion of each, and accommodate you. If you want two full portions you'll have to make that known and you'll be charged extra accordingly.

A cơm is usually named for the family that operates it, or for one of the children in the family. If the child was born under a lucky star it is hoped that some of that luck will rub off on the family business. Or it will be named for its address. After 1975, grandiose names such as Maxim's or the Jade Palace or Whiskey Mary's were condemned as bourgeois. And naming it after Marx, Lenin or – heaven forbid – Uncle Ho would have been impious. To be safe, restaurateurs were reduced to the expedient of calling their houses of good eats after their numerical locations on the city streets. Hence the very excellent com, restaurant 119 Bui Vien at, you guessed it, 119 Bui Vien Street, Ho Chi Minh City.

While the traditional com is a humble, though tasty, affair, in recent years many have become rather spiffy. They sport colourful furniture, serve imported beers, and occupy part of the wide, tree shaded sidewalks in downtown Ho Chi Minh City. They are excellent venues for relaxing and people watching. A com will open anywhere between 6am and noon, and will close by about 10pm. We have never been dissatisfied with the food at a com. It is always well varied, well prepared and presented. And penny for penny it is simply the best deal around.

CAFE TOILETTE

Be advised as you walk about; the cities of Ho Chi Minh City and Hanoi have grown a lot quicker than housing and services. Without explanation, many city walls are used as urinals, so much so that certain streets, especially those near the markets and other well-trafficked areas, cannot be walked in without gagging. Vietnamese Catholics, and others knowledgeable in the Bible, began to feel sympathy with King David, who swore the death of all the men of Nabal, all those who 'pisseth against the wall'. (It is not uncommon to see women availing themselves of open space either, but they do tend to seek a friendly tree or other screen.)

City authorities have been forced to act, if only out of aesthetic outrage. They have begun to install public toilets which cost about 500 dong to use. As there are no coins in the Vietnamese currency, and paper-money-reading machines are expensive, each pissoir must have an attendant to collect your tribute. Some of these are very enterprising. Need to wait your turn a while? Need a little rest after your relief? Sit down, then, on this little stool, or stand in the humble shade of the attendant's canopy, and have a cup of coffee. Only 10 cents. You want tea? You got it. Some of them will even serve you a soda or a beer, perhaps with the thought that you will soon be back for a return engagement.

The locals call these unconventional coffee concerns 'Cafe Toilettes'. Strictly speaking, they are illegal operations since they have no licence to sell food or drink. They tend to come and go where you come to go. We find them admirable, and we hope that cops on the beat, when called to serve justice upon these economic malefactors, will remember the last time that they had to 'pisseth against the wall'.

PHUONG ANH – A Typical Day in a Vietnamese Eatery

The Phuong Anh restaurant in Hanoi (see map in the Regional Variation chapter), isn't much to look at. From the street, it's hardly different from the hundreds or thousands of small eating places that line the roads all over Asia. But the food here is exceptional.

There are five or six different pork dishes, the same number of poultry and fish plates, and a dozen delicious vegetable selections. There is no menu – not that you need one. We didn't know the names of any dishes, and simply pointed to the ones that looked the tastiest. Ample servings, piled onto small plates, were brought to our table and lunch cost about US$1.

Nguyen Thi Bich, the 40-year-old owner, invited us to observe the goings-on of a typical day – it started at 6am. Most of Bich's supplies come from bicycle-peddling vendors who roll up to the restaurant with the likes of rice, salt, vegetables, roasted poultry and frozen fish. But for the key ingredients Bich goes to the market herself, cycling there and back within an hour.

At 7.30am, the restaurant is already buzzing. Bich's mother, father, aunt, and a variety of young relatives are all at work. The older women use razor blades to slice hundreds of spring onions into what seems to be thousands of thin green ribbons. They do this while squatting on the sidewalk, just inches from the street, where the earlier quiet of Hanoi has been drowned out by the flow of cars, trucks, bicycles, motorcycles and cyclos. In and around the restaurant, Bich's employees quickly and methodically go about the dozens of tasks needed in a country where prepared foods have yet to hit the shelves.

In an alley alongside the restaurant, several girls tend two woks and pots boiling with eggs and greens. An older woman squats further down the sidewalk, washing dishes. For the next 15 hours that's all she does.

Soon after Bich's return from the market, all activity centres on the middle of the floor. Twenty bowls and basins filled with meat, poultry, fish, mushrooms, spices, oils, fish sauce and molasses sit in the centre of a circle formed by Bich and her family. For the next three hours they hardly move from their squatting position. Basins of greens and boiled meats and fish come in from outside. The women quickly dice, slice, mix, knead, and roll these together with other ingredients and spices. Bich's mother measures out molasses in the palm of her hand. Bich's fingers are the scoop used to measure sugar, salt and pepper; everything is measured by hand. No one samples a thing. As quickly as the staff bring in new items, the now-seasoned dishes go back outside for steaming, boiling or deep-frying.

It's an assembly line with little talk. Everything happens with the precision of a Japanese manufacturing plant, except that it happens in a tiny space on the floor in the light of two dim bulbs.

Slowly, almost by sleight of hand, finished dishes gather on tables that have been pushed to the side of the room. Tray after tray of complicated dishes of fried fish, steamed vegetables, boiled pork and barbecued meats take shape as the crouching women work into their second and third hour of chopping, boiling, stirring, turning, flipping and steaming. For hours the women have crouched, barely inches from the floor.

Bich only stops work to quickly sharpen her knives and cleavers. She dashes them back and forth against the bottom of a plate with the same practised indifference as a barber sharpening a razor against a leather strap.

After four hours of tossing, mixing, shaking, kneading, chopping, hacking, slicing and cooking, it is time to move outside. Twenty different platters are ready for the lunchtime crowd. Spring rolls, shish-kebabs and eight other entrees are still waiting their chance in the wok or over the brazier. Thirty different dishes are stacked atop one another on the outside counter.

There are dishes of sea fish and river fish. Three different types of chicken. Six different types of pork. There is a shrimp dish and a squid plate. Several varieties of small, grilled birds. Salads of green beans, beansprouts, pickled eggplant and spinach. A fried tofu dish, something like a frittata. Spring rolls. For the refined diner, there is a platter of butterfly larva.

The sign above the entrance to the Phuong Anh restaurant, which is named for Bich's daughter, says **Cac Mon An** and **Com Binh Dan**, which roughly translate to 'all kinds of food' and 'everyday home cooking'. Evidently, Bich needn't say anything more because soon after she lays out the dishes, a crowd of lunchtime customers gather. For the next two hours, the small space is jammed. Bich stands at the doorway, now assuming the roles of maitre d', cashier, hostess and server. Meanwhile, in the alley, the staff continue cooking to replenish the most popular dishes.

By 1pm lunchtime business thins out and Bich stops moving for the first time in seven hours. She leans against a wall and lights up a '555'. The restaurant closes from 2 to 5pm although several workers continue cooking. There's another rush from 6 to 8.30pm and, by 11pm, the tables are put away, and all the food is eaten.

Out running at 6am the next morning, we spot Bich's mother already slicing onions on the sidewalk. Bich haggles with the meat sellers. She doesn't have time to waste. Lunch is only six hours away.

Robert Strauss, San Francisco.

Don Xuan Market, Hanoi

The Pho

A restaurant specialising in the national dish phở is called, well, a phở. A phở is rather like a cơm, but sells only phở, or phở and a few other tidbits. Very often they are tiny, as measured in real estate, and will spill out onto the sidewalk. In which case you can't miss them. Indeed you may trip over their minuscule tables and stools if you're not careful. Or it might be a stall set up on a street corner; a little hole-in-the-wall; or a garage size establishment like our typical cơm. And like the cơm it will be named for the family or family member, or for its address. Like the cơm and the market stall the phở is usually patronised by working people, people on the go, and travellers. Prices and operating hours are about the same as the cơm.

Pho 93, Ho Chi Minh City

Pho 93, in Ho Chi Minh City, is typical. It's just a spot on the sidewalk with a table and chairs, a few cooking pots and a display of delicious food. It's little more than a yoke or a cart. Open all day and into the night, it's like a gastronomic security blanket because you always know it's there, and you always know the comfort it will give you. Wherever you are in Vietnam, find your own little Pho 93. Use it as your regular stop for breakfast or lunch. Let the proprietor get to know you. Soon you'll be getting the best they have to offer. You can even bring your own baguette or a few bánh and just sit down with them for a drink. They'll tutor you gently in proper Vietnamese comportment if you need it and if you ask.

Can't find a Pho 93 to suit you? You can use ours. It's right next to the Luna Cafe, and just a few doors down from our favourite wine merchant, Le Tonneau. They won't even charge you corkage at Pho 93.

The Markets

The public markets in cities and larger towns have always been good places to eat. Most commonly, you'll find all kinds of noodle dishes: noodle soup, noodles with roast duck, noodles with vegetables, fried noodles with prawns, just about anything and everything that can be reduced to bite size and combined with noodles. The marketeers themselves eat here, and they know who has the best stuff because they sold it to them. The market food stalls operate all day and are a favourite with office workers, shoppers and nearby merchants. Prices tend to be a little higher than that of a com, but you would be hard pressed to spend more than US$2 unless you drink beer with your meal. Business tends to taper off in the later afternoon and stalls begin closing one by one until about 5pm when the market itself begins to close.

CHEF HO – Faces of Gastronomy

Many people will tell you that it was the Chinese, in particular the Cantonese, who taught the Vietnamese how to cook. And you could make a good argument for it. Certainly the Vietnamese have looked to the Chinese for inspiration, after which they caught the ball and ran with it themselves.

Chef Ho Wing Sang is one of those who throws the ball. He is the master of classic Canton/Hong Kong cuisine in the kitchens of the Dynasty restaurant in the New World Hotel, 76 Le Lai Street, District 1 of Ho Chi Minh City.

"A Chinese meal and a Vietnamese meal are alike in their structure", he says. "They use the same basic approach to seasoning, although our Vietnamese friends produce different tastes. And aromas, stronger ones. Garnishing is another big difference. We, Chinese, like to decorate a dish lavishly and it's one of my favourite things to do. In fact, I do all the vegetable carving that you see on my plates".

What Chef Ho calls his 'garnishing' looks more like sculpture: intricately carved birds, flowers, frogs and other flora and fauna grace his presentations. "This is just for your eyes to feast on, you won't see this kind of garnishing on a Vietnamese plate. It will be very pretty, but everything is for eating".

"Still", he says, "I have a Vietnamese *sous* chef. We exchange a lot of ideas while we work. Sometimes we experiment with mixing our two styles of cooking. And I think it's that kind of sharing and exchanging, the interest in trying something a bit different, that helped to produce the Vietnamese cooking style in the first place".

Upmarket Restaurants

After 1975, until relatively recently, there really were no upscale restaurants in the Socialist Republic of Vietnam – upscale being a relative term. But happy days are here again. A common sort in this class is the sidewalk or patio restaurant. In Ho Chi Minh City, they are especially plentiful along Thi Sac and Ly Tu Trong Streets. They are less common in the north as winter weather makes them seasonal. But in fine weather the growing middle class of Vietnam flock to these festive eateries nightly. Whole extended families come for dinner, businessman entertain clients,

WET TOWEL

Vietnam is a festive culture, always seeking the trappings and shows of festivity as well as the substance. Indeed, the trappings are substance. The sights and smells and sounds of a convivial dinner: colourful dresses on ladies, colourful food before you, waiters bustling; smoke wafting from braisiers grilling meats and fish on a dozen tables, and the sharp smell of lime and the perfume of lemongrass and the urgent smell of nước mắm; shouts of recognition of people or favourite dishes; calls for more of this and yet more of that; the cracking of crab legs; the clatter of glassware; laughter of new arrivals and happy farewells of well fed people; and one of the great constants and unifiers and most predictable sounds you will ever hear in the Land of the Ascending Dragon: POW! POW! POW! Like contrapuntal Champagne corks in the culinary concerto it punctuates every happy occasion in the land.

It's a wet towel. Yes, we know, it sounds like a party poop, but bear with us. In the heat and humidity of a tropical country we sweat a lot. We often get hot, clammy and icky. We find that we want to take a shower every hour. And who wants to sit down to a fine dinner and feel icky? At every restaurant of repute (good or ill), upon sitting down you will be given a cold, not wet but very moist, towel about 20cm square with which to swab your fevered brow, wash your dirty face, even bathe your tired head. During the meal you keep it alongside and use it as a serviette (napkin).

Whence the POW!? In most places they come in sealed plastic envelopes emblazoned with the establishment's name and address, like a calling card. Foreigners untutored in the art usually grab them with both hands and rip them apart in a brutal display of ignorance. But not you. You'll know to grasp it tightly in one hand till the air inside is forced to one or both ends of the envelope, making it balloon. Then just bash it against the palm of your free hand, or against your forehead, or your neighbor's forehead. POW! Dinner is on.

and local celebrities come to be seen. It is at this rung in the restaurant ladder that you begin to see printed menus. And in Vietnam printed menus are invariably printed in Vietnamese and English. Never fear about knowing how to order from the menu. It is nothing more than the com's display reduced to writing. There is no succession of courses, no right or wrong thing to have with this or that. The menu might, or might not, be organised by food type. It might just be alphabetical. As at the com, simply point to what you like. They are open from about 5pm to about 11pm. Dinner for one will normally cost between US$5 and US$10.

MOTHER LOVE – Faces of Gastronomy

When I first met Madam Tran Thi Huong in her Restaurant Le Lai, also known as 'The Coconut Tree', she was taking care of 40 children, 18 of them living in her own home. The other 22 were residing with various benefactors, persons in her arsenal of goodwill.

She's a keen business lady, having paid for 27 street children to emigrate to the US in 1990 alone. All told, Madam Huong figures she's provided a chance for more than 100 children to pursue a new life in America. And she's sent nearly 20 to the universities in Ho Chi Minh City, including our waiter.

Now in her 70s, she radiates goodwill. Ask her the secret of her longevity and success and she'll tell you, "I believe in God. I am at home in the church or the pagoda; both Christianity and Buddhism, because both teach us to do good, to help those who need our help", she says.

The government is aware of what Madam Huong is doing. "They've caught me several times", she says, speaking of what is tantamount to her own relocation service. "I don't need a licence because I don't use their money". Madam Huong has successfully managed to argue that her case is a private matter and not indebted to government.

And they tend to listen to the country's best-selling author. There is hardly anyone who is not familiar with her autobiography, *Fortune Misfortune*. Even Henry Kissinger is a fan, and she will be glad to show you the letter of wonderful praise she received from the man himself. And yes, that's his picture on the wall.

But you're probably wondering about the food at The Coconut Tree. It's excellent, traditional Vietnamese fare, including several game dishes. Care to partake? Order up from the extensive menu. Aside from the good food, you'll have the added reward of helping a good cause. (See the Ho Chi Minh City map in the Regional Variations chapter.)

– Garrett Culhane

There are also a growing number of what we can call tourist restaurants. We call them so because generally only tourists can afford them. These include the restaurants in the major hotels (which rarely serve Vietnamese food anyway, so we don't pay them much mind). Then there are the floating restaurants. In Ho Chi Minh City, they are converted ferry boats that take you on a dinner cruise up and down the river. There are about six of them at any given time, most serving Chinese food. One or two will offer a few Vietnamese dishes and a few 'French' dishes. Cruises depart around 8pm and return between 10 and 11pm. Dinner for one might cost about US$10 but can go quite a bit higher if you order delicacies and imports. In Hoi An and Huè there are floating restaurants anchored on the river or lake. They tend to be over-priced and attractive to mosquitoes.

French restaurants, of course, were once common in Vietnam. Nowadays hamburger joints are more numerous. There are a few French eateries which is good because Vietnamese cookery is, in part, defined by its 100-year association with French cookery. It's a very rewarding exercise to dine in a fine Vietnamese restaurant one night, and the next in a French restaurant. Note the differences and similarities, and how Vietnam impresses itself upon the French. This is delightfully noticeable at a place like restaurant Camargue in Ho Chi Minh City. Everything in the kitchen is done according to French tradition and technique, yet it all carries the perfume of Asia. The difference in the herbs is especially telling, as is the lightness of the bread and the sweetness of the butter. The sauces don't cloy but caress the tongue. This is not 'fusion cuisine'. We don't care for such schizophrenic falderol in the kitchen. It is a case of two of the world's great culinary regions meeting and, well, flirting. The story is much the same for the remaining Chinese restaurants, such as Arc d' Ciel. And in both you're starting to rise in price. You can easily spend US$40 for dinner.

One of the most hopeful developments in the Vietnam restaurant scene is the growing number of artful Vietnamese places; establishments that try to present the best of Vietnamese cookery in a setting that imbibes the best of the western restaurant tradition. Tables are set with starched white linen; waiters are attentive and softspoken; wine is served at the right temperature for its type; the menu is thoughtfully organised and the waiter can make intelligent suggestions. It's air conditioned and prices are still quite reasonable (for travellers and local businessfolk). Dinner might cost US$10-15. Some open for lunch, others only for dinner. All are closed by 11pm. Most of these places are in downtown Ho Chi Minh City at present. Vietnam House is an excellent example. A few are turning up in Hanoi and Hoi An. In Hanoi some of them are developing into supper clubs with superb local musicians playing soft, or swinging, jazz.

Vegetable vendor, Cantho

A COCK'S TALE

I hooked up with two Aussies, Rob and Leon, and went to Thi Sac Street for dinner. There is a cluster of densely packed sidewalk restaurants here, each alive with feasting. We picked our way through the crowd, climbed the steep and narrow stairs, and emerged onto a terrace happily strewn with lobster and crab shells, awash in beer, and afloat a thick cloud of hubbub and bustle.

A short, slim, intense-looking waiter beckoned, nay commanded, us to sit at a table from which he was sweeping the remnants of the previous meal. We took the proffered seats and ordered beer. Before the monosyllable was out, the scoundrel had disappeared. He returned a few minutes later with a single menu, dropped it on the table and ran. "Beer!" we shouted to his receding back. He returned at a near run, handing off bottles of beer like relay batons as he sped by. Mollified, we relaxed while I perused the menu. Rob and Leon declared that since I was the Indiana Jones of Gastronomy, and since we had only the one stingy menu, I should order.

Our surly servant returned with pen and pad, and stood sphinx-like, poised to take our order. "Well", I began, "we'll have..." and the beggar ran off again. "Beer!" Rob hollered after him. Miraculously he returned with more beer. I reopened the menu and glared at him, as if threatening to trip him if he should try to escape again.

I pointed to chicken on the menu and said, "this one". He nodded and wrote in his pad. And wrote and wrote. "And we'll have this", I said. Again he wrote and wrote. And by now Rob and Leon were beginning to snigger. "And we'll have..." whereupon he swivelled, hurled a stream of Vietnamese curses and ran off to punish some other diner!

When he returned I held him by the shirtsleeve, and pointed to beef on the menu. "Gimmie that". He wrote and wrote, then moved to leave. I held him fast, and pointed to fish and said, "and that".

"No!", came his first and only word.

"What?! Waddaya mean, no?!"

"No!"

"But I want fish. Fish, you rascal!"

"No!" He pointed to all the other items I had ordered and nodded, as if to say, "you may have that and no more".

"Blast you! Fish!"

It occured to me that the restaurant might be out of fish. In a conciliatory tone I pointed to a dish of pork cooked in a clay pot.

"No!"

"What, you're out of pork too? Then this one".

"No!"

"You can't be out of everything! I want this", I demanded, pointing to yet another item.

"No!"

"I want it I say!"

"No!"

"Bastard!"

"No!"

With the guys doubled over in laughter and me on the verge of apoplexy, I pointed to the last item on the menu and swore, "bring me this or I'll black your eyes!"

"Yes!" And with that he snatched the menu from my sturdy grip and disappeared out of sight.

Rob and Leon were still chuckling when a Vietnamese fellow diner approached, grinning. "He's afraid you won't be able to eat all you order. If there are any substantial leftovers, he has to pay a penalty. But he doesn't know how to say that".

"We'll eat every bite," Leon promised.

For my part, I resolved to grant the waiter a thousand pardons and to not tell the guys that the last dish I had been able to order was cock's testicles braised with garlic cloves.

Young Dr. No arrived unbidden with more beer and the chicken. It was a whole bird, rather small but roasted and spiced to a state of gustatory poetry. I prodded it with a chopstick and found it meaty and fat for all its puny size. Then came the water greens with ginger, dusted with that black pepper that is unique to Vietnam. It's less biting, flowery and almost sweet to the taste. Then the beef in sauce swaggered fatly to the table, done to blood rare perfection. Fluffy white rice sat chastely beside. And lastly came a dish of glistening gonads.

They were piled on a silver serving dish mounted on a pedestal. A twist of lime and a sprig of coriander balanced the presentation. The garlic cloves were fat and snowy. I noticed that the several roosters' family jewels were very like the cloves in size, shape and colour. Indeed, I had to look closely to tell which was which. The testes were distinguishable only by a more rounded appearance, rather like that of kidney beans. I was surprised and impressed at the very size of Foghorn Leghorn's endowment.

Rob had noticed the strange dish and recognised the garlic cloves. "Ah. Giahlic", he said, "smells good".

"I love giahlic", Leon concurred.

Lifting my chopsticks I gingerly fished out a rooster's best and brought it beneath my nose. The scent of garlic roiled up, mingled with some undefinable masculine aroma. I slipped it into my mouth and rolled it around between tongue and palate. It was firm yet pliable, like a grape. I rolled it over to the right side of my mouth, positioned it between my wisdom teeth, and bit down. The outer surface stretched and strained, and the little DNA factory burst, and spilled itself across the surface of my tongue.

In texture, consistency and taste, the rooster's physical connection with eternity was not unlike that of a mild and smooth goose liver pâté, expressing a bit of juice. I found the bird's instrument of continuity to be a bit salty, though you might have guessed that, with echoes of sweet, sour and bitter in such proportion as to obtain the sort of balance aspired to by the Chinese cook's philosophy of Yin & Yang. It was rich and creamy, and went down as easy as oysters.

Leon and Rob were enthusiastically helping themselves to the other dishes, so I picked up a testicle and put it in Leon's rice bowl. "Thanks, mate", he said, and popped it into his mouth and began to chew. Then he looked somewhat confused so I told him what it was. There is a certain gravity in the term 'cock's testicle' that makes it impossible to be a joke. If some one tells you that you have one in your mouth you know instinctively that it's true.

Leon continued to chew, but almost imperceptibly slowly, as though weighing his options. Rob reached across the table and took a morsel from the dish, chewed experimentally, and pronounced, "it tastes just like giahlic".

"That's because you just ate a clove of garlic", I said, and served him the genuine article. He boldly chewed, swallowed, then reached for another.

Leon choked, swallowed involuntarily, then turned pale. I selected the most garlicky looking gonad in the dish and handed it to him saying, "here, try the garlic now".

"Cheers mate", he said with visual relief, quickly followed by "you bastard!" But by then his mouth was no longer virginal. He gamely swallowed and we feasted. In the end the table bore only clean plates. Young Dr. No would pay no penalty this night.

As I sat in the afterglow, the diner at the next table asked, "how did you enjoy your dinner?"

"It was magic", I said. "Although we could have ordered more with no danger to the waiter. That chicken was very small."

"Oh, but it's large for its type", he assured me. "It's a small breed but this restaurant serves only the male of the species so that you always have the biggest possible".

The male of the species. That it might have been either one sex or the other had not occurred to me. So it was a rooster then. Well, suffice to say, we ate cock and balls for dinner that night, and we'll lick any man who says ought against it!

Vegetarians & Vegans

Well, there's good news and bad news. Fortunately, there are now more vegetarian options than ever. That's the good news. The bad news is that you have not landed in Veg Heaven, for the Vietnamese are voracious omnivores. While they dearly love their greens, they also dearly love anything that crawls on the ground, swims in the sea or flies in the air.

In keeping with Buddhist precepts, you'll find that many restaurants go vegetarian on the 1st and 15th of each lunar month. Otherwise, you should be on your guard.

Any dish of vegetables is likely to have been cooked with fish sauce or shrimp paste. You've got to ask. No one will think of you as a food fetishist or any other bad thing. They will be very willing to help you, but you've got to speak up.

If you're vegan, you've got a bigger challenge. Eggs are easy to spot, and if it's a crepe or a pancake, it includes eggs. However, the Vietnamese rarely cook with dairy products, though they do enjoy yoghurt and ice cream, and they use milk in their coffee.

If you're a fully-fledged vegetarian or have had just enough meat for the time-being, look for **chay** (vegetarian) in the name of the restaurant which indicates that the entire menu is without meat. Likewise, if you see it next to a specific dish on the menu, you're safe. (See Useful Phrases in the Eat Your Words chapter.)

Cao Dai

Dinh y restaurant, in Ho Chi Minh City, is owned and run by the Cao Dai religion. Service to humanity and reverence for life are among its chief tenets and this restaurant exists to satisfy both – Madam Thanh Hoa, chef de cuisine, is an award-winning cook. This is also a lot more than just a place to eat; there's a meditation space on the first floor and a charity out-patient clinic in the next building. "This is how we serve the people", the manager says.

The chef's specialities represent the best of vegetarian food, including pâtés of mushrooms and tofu, spicy noodle dishes with an array of vegetables, and aromatic rice plates.

The chef's excellence in the kitchen is a part of her religious service – the Cao Dai are a missionary faith, seeking to propagate their message, to extend reverence for life, and to popularise the vegetarian diet. It seems to be working.

(Dinh y restaurant is at 171B Cong Quynh, see map of Ho Chi Minh City in Regional Variations Chapter.)

Two Moons

Madam Nguyen Thi Ngoi Nga bursts from her law office into the dining room of her adjoining restaurant. "Hello, dear friends, everybody, welcome!" She radiates good humour, energy and a fierce interest in humanity. You suspect a bear hug somewhere in the offing. She is tall for a Vietnamese woman (or does her large personality simply make her seem so?). Her glasses are ever askew and she is ever on the move.

She grabs a shy woman by the arm and proclaims, "this is my sister. She is the chef de cuisine here in my restaurant. She is Miss Ho Minh Nguyen. Do you know what that means?" she asks excitedly. "Moon", she informs us. "And do you know what my name means'" she continues without interruption. "It's another word for Moon". Wrapping an arm around the blushing smaller woman, she laughs and says, "we are the 'Two Moons'". We decide to call them Big Moon and Little Moon.

Madam Nguyen and her sister operate one of the best loved vegetarian restaurants in Ho Chi Minh City. "The chief monk of Ho Chi Minh City asked me to open this restaurant", Big Moon says. "In 1994 the economy was improving and many people were able to eat well. But poor people could not. He knew that if you have a good cook, you can eat well on vegetarian food for very little money. And he knew that my sister was a very good cook. She can cook anything! I was busy with my law practice, but together we were able to open the restaurant, and now it is famous for her cooking!"

Miss Ho (Little Moon) specialises in making tofu look and taste like anything but tofu. She is the most tasty counterfeiter in the city.

"You see?" Big Moon says as a tray of Little Moon's special dishes arrives. "It all looks and tastes 'normal'". And delicious.

"All my dishes are Vietnamese", Little Moon announces, speaking for the first time, "and I use only local ingredients. I learned many of the recipes from my mother, but also from our customers. They are always giving me suggestions for their favourite dishes or for new ideas. I try to do them all".

We wonder how any kitchen can be truly Vietnamese without nước mắm. Little Moon produces a bottle of a dark, evil-looking potion, made from soy, she tells us. We smell...whew! Strong stuff. It doesn't really smell like fish sauce, but...

'The pungent aroma is an important characteristic of Vietnamese cooking", Little Moon explains. "It helps to set us apart from Chinese. We can't use fish but this satisfies the Vietnamese desire for a good smell. It's okay, yes?"

Oh yeah. It's very okay. Take our word for it.

Rice paddy, Mekong Delta

CHA CA LA VONG

Cha Ca is a small street in Hanoi's old town, 180m from end to end. In the 19th century, it was called Hang Son, or 'Paint Street', because paint sellers had their shops here. A restaurant was opened at no 14. a century ago. The owner was Mr Doan, and his speciality was chà cá (fried fish). In front of the shop, Mr Doan set up a small statue of an old fisherman, known locally as La Vong.

Because of the quality of his goods, Mr Doan was immediately successful. As time went by and more and more people came to dine, his place became known as La Vong. More time passed and the name of the street was changed to Cha Ca.

The restaurant, now known as Cha Ca La Vong, is still there today. The place looks as seedy, er... has as much character, as ever although tables are covered with cloth and sometimes graced with flowers these days. It's dimly lit, and the low ceiling makes the place feel a bit ... cosy. The wooden floor creaks, one assumes, a bit more than in decades past. Still, at the door, the old fisherman dangles his line in the empty air, as he has done for a century. He hooks a lot of customers. The best tables are by the windows looking down into the narrow street.

Several years ago a competitor opened up across the street. People said the service was better, and that regular customers could always get their favourite tables. Then another opened nearby, providing larger portions. Neither of these exist anymore and no one speaks of them.

Cha Ca La Vong lives on, using the same kind of fish – an almost boneless type of pike with firm flesh. Suppliers come from Haiphong on the last train of the day to ensure maximum freshness. The fish is boned, cut into bite-sized pieces, marinated in turmeric and other spices but the recipe is a tightly held family secret.

Unlike most restaurants in Vietnam, you must make a reservation. Before your arrival, the table is already set with a serving of rice vermicelli for each diner, and a plate of fresh spring onions (scallions), basil leaves, sweet dill and a choice of dipping sauces. A waitress brings in a clay brazier filled with red-hot coals and sets it right in front of you. She hurries off and returns with a frying pan heaped with hunks of fish, coloured yellow gold by the spices. So now you stir the herbs into the fish. Let it all bubble and sizzle a while before your hungry eyes.

Make a little bed of rice noodles in your bowl and spoon in a few pieces of crisply fried fish and herbs. Give it a dose of sauce. Now another. Now taste. Chew slowly, thoughtfully. See if you can recognise the herbs, the curry-like spices. See if you can deconstruct the recipe, because they won't tell you what's in it. What they will tell you, and we agree, is that it's one of the best dishes in town.

Tipping

There was a time when a graceful 'thank you' sufficed when leaving the table. It's still that way at the small and family restaurants but those catering primarily to tourists are developing a lust for lucre. It's a good idea to watch the locals if you can, or ask. Vietnamese are not shy about money talk. Do not tip if there is already a service charge printed on your bill. If there is no service charge, 10% of the bill is the general rule, depending on the quality of service. And you should always give a little something to your noodle knocker. Whatever it comes to, it will not be much by western standards.

The author playing Jenga, Ho Chi Minh City

Where to Drink

After a good dinner, how about a place to bend the elbow, do some 12 ounce curls, shout for a few rounds. Well, first off, you're not in Bangkok, Las Vegas, Club Med, or even King's Cross. You're still in a socialist country (yes, still) and for most people the lights go out by midnight. And even without what the constitution describes as "Marxism-Leninism and Ho Chi Minh Thought" you're not in a pub crawling culture (see the Drinks chapter). That said, you won't go thirsty, and you won't want for an evening's entertainment. But unless you are with some overseas Vietnamese, you will likely do your drinking with other travellers.

The 747 cafes are the most likely place to find locals drinking (see the Street Food chapter), though they will be drinking iced coffee and tea for the most part. All the major hotels have air-conditioned cocktail lounges, and there are many downtown pubs in the major cities that cater to thirsty foreigners. Most have attractive ladies tending bar, or waiting tables, or just … waiting. Some of the most pleasant places to wet your whistle in Ho Chi Minh City are the rooftop bars of the Rex and Caravel hotels. The grande dame of the city's hotels, the Continental, has a rooftop that was known by wartime journalists as the 'continental shelf', but it wasn't in use at the time of writing.

As with most of Vietnam, bars generally close by midnight. However, it is now possible to pull an all-nighter in Ho Chi Minh City. You've just got to know where to go. Earlier in the evening, hit the bars along Hai Ba Trung, Dong Koi and Thi Sac Streets. When they close, head for the nearby Apocalypse Now. Pace yourself, because when you come out of here between 2 and 3am you may have to run a gauntlet of pickpockets and you'll want to be in good form. Get a taxi if you're alone (which you shouldn't be), or a convoy of cyclos and keep them in close formation as you transit to the Rolling Stone bar on Pham Ngu Lao, just around the corner from 'The Ghetto'. The Rolling Stone is open daily from 5pm to 5am and specialises in music from, well, you know, The Rolling Stones. You will get satisfaction.

street food

Because so much of life is lived outside the home, street food is an important part of everyday life. Like much of South-East Asia, the Vietnamese are keen snackers. They can be found at impromptu stalls at any time of day or night, delving into a range of snacky things. Whether you want your tidbit wrapped, unwrapped, spicy, sweet, cakey or crunchy, chances are it is out there, somewhere in the streets of Vietnam.

It's all happening in the street. Every kind of human intercourse except the sexual (invitations thereto notwithstanding) goes on in the streets. You can get your hair cut in the street. You can have your eyes examined and glasses prescribed, then stroll down the block and take tea with friends, all on the street. Heel of your shoe falling off? Stop at the corner and let the boy sitting on the kerb with a box of tools fix it for you.

YOU'RE A MILLIONAIRE!

Food sellers and restaurants are so numerous in Ho Chi Minh City that the city fairly screams that she is a monarch of cuisine. Wonderful aromas are so thick on the streets that you think you might eat the air. The Vietnamese currency is called the dong, and US$1 buys 14 000. So upon arriving, exchange US$100 for over a million dong and, leaving the bank a millionaire, go looking for food.

Life here is lived in the street, so it is no wonder that it is also where life is sustained. You can eat, and eat gloriously, in the streets of Vietnam. As the cities awaken, just before dawn, the empty sidewalks begin to sprout little tables and chairs, and tiny plastic stools. The smells of sweet star anise and pungent ginger and insistent fish sauce are soon afloat upon the air. Office workers are among the first to occupy the tables as they sensuously slurp through a breakfast of phở while neat, well-scrubbed children troop off to school. Industrious artisans and mechanics begin work in dim, close shops. If they have no shops they set up operations on a street corner, or carry their tools in old American ammunition boxes and go from house to house. Finishing their breakfast, office workers pause to watch the lazy coffee drip, drip, drip into their cups. One last moment of calm before a busy day.

At midday the street cafes and stalls become an organised chaos of chopping, grilling and steaming; of hollering for orders of noodles, or rice cakes steamed in banana leaves, or spring rolls, and tumblers of freshly pressed sugar cane juice.

In Hanoi it might be raining as you sit on a bench beside the lake, but it is a rain so gossamer and fine and gentle that it embraces rather than falls, and you don't mind. Besides, the baguette seller working his way toward you has his wares covered with a plastic sheet and so will deliver your lunch to you unmarred by the weather.

In Hué there's a furious sizzle as rice-flour crepes turn crispy in a smoking hot pan being tended smack-dab on the sidewalk in the shade of the old city's walls. And in Ho Chi Minh City a hundred different dishes are being served on a thousand different side streets, intersections and alleyways. Everyone comes to dine on the street at some time.

In the evening, many people put their labours aside, and a graceful and refined cafe society emerges. Cafes in Vietnam are deep and narrow, no larger than a two-car garage. As though they were set in a Doonesbury cartoon, the word on the sign outside is often spelled 'Ca Phe'. They open completely onto the street and all the little tables and reclining beach chairs are arranged in neat rows facing outward, with an aisle running down the middle. They call to mind the fuselage of an airliner flying to the street. We have come to call them '747 Ca Phes'.

STREET CONGEE

Dalat. It was here that the French Governor General of Cochin China had his residence. Except for a few neo-Stalinist monstrosities put up in the 1980s, most of the buildings look like they were shipped in from a French village.

During the American/Vietnamese war Dalat served as a getaway for American, South Vietnamese and Vietcong officials. Each had their own villas, and the tacit truce that allowed them to share the place was never broken. "Disrupting the peace in Dalat during those days", we were told by an American veteran of those days, "would have been like shooting the piano player in a Western".

Though Dalat is not far from the sweltering heat of Ho Chi Minh City, its elevation makes it cool enough for jackets at night. And as the terrain and climate change, so do the people and their food. The Dalatois may lack the style and sophistication of the Saigonaise, but they also lack the frenetic pace of the city's lifestyle. Life in Dalat is quiet, the people warm and hearty.

In the chill air of evening the street vendors serve a unique style of 'congee'. Anywhere else, congee is little more than rice gruel or porridge, nourishing but bland. In Dalat the congee is rich with pork broth and chunks of meat, redolent of garlic and ginger, with a sheen of red chilli oil floating on top. Hefty portions are garnished with fresh bean sprouts and coriander (cilantro) and a good pinch of coarsely ground black pepper. Stand by the vendor's cart, or find a place to sit on the kerb, and take the steaming congee with gusto. There was never a better remedy for the sting of cold mountain air.

STREET SOUNDS

The sounds of Ho Chi Minh City affect everyone differently, but no one will argue that they assault or assuage the spirit in an endless cascade. Motorbikes sputter and whine along the crowded boulevards, their noise intensifying in the numerous and narrow backstreets. The sharp banging of bamboo sticks is heard all day, announcing the availability of the noodle knockers, people who will take your food orders and bring them back quickly, lifted high above their heads in covered trays. Street vendors hop along beside you, clamouring for your attention and vying with the incessant voices of cyclo drivers asking where you'd like to go. And always the undercurrent of voices in a city of 4 million where life in almost all its aspects is lived on the streets.

Experiencing the cacophony for the first time is like being infused with an invisible energy that buoys you up and carries you along in its wake. It can be overwhelming and there's nothing to do but to retreat to one of the numerous cafes strung along the thoroughfares. Even they

Patrons relax after another meal on the street. They sip tea, coffee and beer and watch their city go by. The river of life rushes by to the music from the cafes: lithe women in limpet hats and ao-dai dresses; porters in black 'VC' pyjamas bearing baskets balanced on bamboo poles; pedicabs, bicycles, motor scooters, pedestrians out for a walk. All busy-busy-busy, hurrying past the monuments, markets, tinker-toy apartment blocks. Insistent beggars, vendors and whores, people asking "hello, where you from?" The music of the cafes makes it all a pageant, something to lose yourself in.

The people and their lives have grace and poise. But the Vietnamese also have a boisterous, in-your-face aggressive side. Vendors need to be firmly shooed away. People will insist on practising their fractured English on you even when you want to be left alone. And never make eye contact with a souvenir seller – you won't be free of him till you buy!

By midnight most of the streets are dark, but safe – or at least safer than any streets you are used to. The few remaining vendors and other street denizens are about to retire. A woman squats on the sidewalk washing the last of the day's dishes. It's her last task before closing up. A pair of tourists on the way back to the hotel pass a corn-seller with a few ears unsold. They buy the last ones and move on. The seller unfolds a cot and sets it under the eaves or under the great tree growing out of the sidewalk. It's too hot to sleep indoors tonight. A cat curls up beneath the cot. The life of the street goes to rest. It all starts anew tomorrow.

are filled with pop music, played loudly to mask the street noises. It works. Soon I would hear nothing and find myself absorbed in watching the street scene as if it were some silent movie run at half-speed. Every motion slows down and the mere gesture of a hand settling a straw hat seems to take ages. The intricate weaving of motorbikes avoiding pedestrians and each other takes on the form of a sinuous dance.

Suddenly a boy of about seven comes tearing down the street. Behind him, almost grazing the heads of the crowd, bobs a white butterfly kite. The child, too, is supremely unaware of the noise and the rush and runs fluidly through my drifting crowd; he alone with momentum, intent only on keeping his kite afloat. Our eyes meet briefly and for a moment we are joined in a shared illusion.

I watch his progress down the street, a fleeting thing in my slow-motion world, until only the kite's fluttering tail marks his passage. Then it, too, is gone. Ho Chi Minh City's noise and bustle flow up and over me again. I pay my bill and ease myself into it.

—*Gina Comaich*

Often times in Vietnam you don't have to look for food. It looks for you. One of the world's oldest means of carrying a heavy load is the yoke. It's nothing more than a wooden or bamboo pole with a basket slung from either end and hefted up onto the shoulder. Simple, efficient and cheap. In Vietnam they are called **don ganh**, and they carry loads of bricks to construction sites, manure to the fields, vegetables to market, and even children too young or too tired to walk. On the street they can carry your dinner. Women – and it's always women – carry baguettes or spring rolls, fruits, bánh , whatever they think might sell, through the streets at all times of the day. If you see one, wave and you'll have a snack.

The most interesting don ganh carriers, in our view, are the ones who carry a portable kitchen in their yoke. In one basket they might have noodles and vegetables and meat, along with bowls, spoons, cups, and maybe a few bottles of soda or drinking water. In the other she might have a five-gallon pot of clear stock simmering over a small charcoal fire held in a ceramic basin. Wherever she sees a crowd of unfed people she can stop, unburden herself and set up shop.

Let her serve you a bowl of soup. It only costs 25 to 50 cents, less if you're a native. Stand or sit down on the kerb and have a meal on the run. You'll find she's very hygienic. She always manages to find water and scrupulously washes each bowl, spoon and pair of chopsticks after every use. After all, if she made people sick, they'd shoo her away.

The yoke lady's male counterpart is the cart pusher. He will bring you ready-to-eat foods such as baguettes and fruits like pineapple, mango, papaya, banana, etc. His fruits are peeled and cut into manageable pieces and kept cool on ice. As he tools down the street he rings his little bell to announce his approach. He is Vietnam's answer to the ice-cream man who drove through your neighbourhood in childhood days.

Other cart pushers will sell you soup, grilled meats, freshly pressed sugar cane juice, and coconuts with their tops lopped off so you can quaff their milk. If you're on a budget, yokes and carts are cheaper than the cheapest restaurant. It's a good idea, though, to observe the locals first as they purchase their dinners on the hoof. Get to know what the going rates are for a given city, for there are differences.

THE GHETTO – Faces of Gastronomy

In Ho Chi Minh City, on the stretch of De Tham Street between Pham Ngu Lao and Bui Vien Streets, you may see one of the most astonishing gastronomic sights in all of Vietnam – scores of foreign tourists feeding on hamburgers, pizza, chicken sandwiches, bangers and mash. And none of it tastes quite like the real thing. It's as though these strange folk have come to Vietnam for the taste of *faux* rather than *phở*. They crowd Kim Cafe and its half-dozen or so knock-offs from mid-morning to midnight, availing themselves of imported beer, vodka and whisky, listening to karaoke knock-offs of Western hit songs, thinking they're genuine.

This little foreign ghetto is surrounded on all sides by one of the better cuisines of the world, yet these queer fish school here. Cart-pushers and yoke-bearers pushing and bearing delectable Vietnamese goodies make daily forays into this Land of Bland, but generally they only feed the Vietnamese whose job it is to feed the foreigners with pale imitations of their homeland fare and sell them trinkets and gewgaws, T-shirts and chewing gum. It's a land apart, distinct and separate from Vietnam, clearly demarcated by the three streets.

But step across Bui Vien Street, through a culinary looking glass, and you're back to the land of taste and aroma. As though Heaven and Earth change places.

We don't know why these foreigners bother to come to Vietnam in the first place. Certainly it's not to dine. Nor, it seems, to hob-nob with the locals. Just for the warm weather? Why incur the cost of a transoceanic flight to Vietnam, why not just stay home and rent the video? Who are these strangers? We don't know. But we earnestly hope that a few of them will read this book, and find their way out of the wilderness. Amen.

Eat Cake

Bánh is a word for which there is no satisfactory English equivalent. Spring rolls can be called bánh, as can crepes. Sandwiches, and any baked goods are called bánh. Sweets and savouries wrapped in leaves to be steamed or grilled are called bánh. The only constant is that bánh are small culinary bundles or other constructions, often eaten with the hands. Vietnamese who speak English generally refer to them as 'cake'. You may be asked by some generous host if you would like a cake, and be given a cookie. 'Have a cake', the merchant says, and hands you what amounts to a sausage roll. But call it what they will, bánh are quintessential street food.

The oldest form of bánh, indeed, what is arguably the world's oldest form of cooking other than simply exposing meat to fire, are those wrapped in leaves. In every market, and on street corners of every city and town, you will see them. Tightly wrapped in green leaves and tied with complex knots that would make a sailor proud, they fill baskets with their abundance, sit neatly stacked on countertops, and hang in clusters from eaves, crossbeams, or stall corners – edible ornaments.

Thit Lon Nuong La Chuoi – Marinated pork cooked in banana leaves

What do they hide within? Don't ask. Just buy a few. Choose a fat cylinder whose weight tells you how much of your appetite it will satisfy. Select a few small ones, little culinary jewels, square, round, triangular. Take them to a shady corner and sit quietly with them for a moment. Run your fingers over the intricate lacings that bind them together. Bring them to your nose for a clue as to what might rest within. Strip the lacings off, and unfold them, layer by layer by yet deeper layer. Like a Russian doll or a dancer with seven veils, it slowly reveals itself. Is it a sweet rice cake? Perhaps a morsel of spiced ham? It could be minced pork, or a piece of sweet potato, a savoury rice cake, itself a wrapping for shrimp or mung beans. It could be any tasty thing in the world.

Each region in Vietnam has its own bánh, just as each region of France has its own wine. The various ethnic groups prepare different types of bánh with their local ingredients. People from the Tay ethnic minority wrap yams in banana leaves and call it **banh khoai so**. Hmong people use banana leaves to wrap **banh ngo non**, or young corn bánh. Sweet potatoes and cassava are other common ingredients in the highlands. Leaf-wrapped bánh are popular and enduring because they are so well suited to local materials and conditions. Leaves provide a container in which foods are cooked, and also help to preserve the food and keep it from getting dirty or mouldy. It is so compact and portable that if you have bánh, you've always got a movable feast, with no worries about disposing of a plastic wrapper.

The most common ingredient in bánh is rice, both sticky and fluffy. A popular type is 'square cake', known in the north as **banh chung**, a savoury sticky rice preparation filled with mung bean paste and minced pork, wrapped in banana leaves, or the leaves of rushes, and steamed. While these can be found any day of the year, they are also important as festival fare (see the Celebrating with Food chapter). In the central and southern parts of the country this cake is called **banh u**. The filling is the same, but the package is intricately folded into a little pyramid. You often see these placed on family altars, especially in farm villages, where they honour 'the soul of the rice'.

Banh tet, sometimes called **banh day**, is said to have been first prepared by votaries of the Hung temple, near Hanoi. This is sometimes called the birthplace of the Vietnamese people, and its bánh is meant to symbolise the continuity of the race, its determination to 'go forth and multiply'. Banh tet is always filled with rice, the gastronomic symbol of fertility, and in the form of a cylinder of a size that fits easily in your hand. Yes, you are eating a phallic symbol. But it always comes with round-shaped **banh day**, the female equivalent. Eat, and multiply.

Banh gio, a well-known treat in the north, is made from rice flour and pork wrapped in banana leaves. These round-shaped things are about the size of a hamburger. A similar recipe is used in Hué, but the bánh are rolled into long, thin cylinders and wrapped in leaves. These morsels are known as **banh la** or **banh nam**, depending on the thickness of the cylinders.

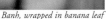

Banh, wrapped in banana leaf   *Banh, unwrapped*

In Hué you can also find **banh it**, little balls of sticky rice flour stuffed with shrimp and pork. They are served plain or wrapped in banana leaves. A variation is sometimes called black **banh it**. These are sweet rice balls filled with a paste of sweetened mung beans.

In northern Vietnam, people pound a type of leaf known as **lá gai** into sticky rice flour for **banh gai**. Now dark in colour from the gai, the bánh are filled with sweetened mung beans and wrapped in banana leaves.

Like banh gai, **banh com** are a speciality of the Red River Delta. Green ginger leaves are used to tint sticky rice, which is then filled with sweetened mung beans. After being cooked, the bánh cốm are wrapped in banana leaves. These particular bánh are a very popular wedding gift among traditionalists.

Also associated with marriage is **su se**. The original name of these bánh was **phu-the**, or 'husband–wife'. The sticky ingredients inside are said to bind like love. Made of tapioca flour, the su se banh dough is colourless so that the filling of shredded coconut and mung beans can be seen through the crust. The dough is sometimes coloured red or green with vegetable dye. In northern parts su se are not wrapped, but in the central region they are wrapped in boxes woven from palm leaves.

As you patrol the streets for treats, keep an eye out for **banh tro**. This sweet bánh incorporates the pits of Japanese lily fruit. These pits are first burned and the ashes mixed with water and lime. Rice is then soaked in this mixture and will then turn into a thick paste. After cooking, enjoy them with a sweet syrup such as molasses or caramel sauce. These are believed to be good for digestion. Be aware, though, that, like saffron, in higher doses, the ash of xoan stones is toxic. People of the Tay ethnic minority also prepare this kind of bánh, but form them into crescent shapes and call it 'cow horns'.

DRYING RICE

As you walk the streets of any Vietnamese city or town, here and there you may see woven grass or leaf mats lying on the walkways covered with rice that has been scraped from the bottoms of cooking pots. The still-moist rice is drying in the sun.

Some exotic treat being prepared, you wonder. An offering to the gods maybe? An obstacle course for pedestrians? No such thing. The people are making use of leftovers. The rice, hard dried on the street, will be pounded into meal and fed to chickens. In Vietnam, even chickens eat street food.

Tasty bánh wrapped in lovely green leaves are good for your tummy and good for the planet and good for your budget. But get your leafy bánh while you can, for 'progress' rears its ugly head in Vietnam. In the larger cities we see the beginnings of a disturbing trend among makers and sellers of bánh, who are replacing the ancient leaf wrappings with plastic or paper bags. Certain philistines in Hanoi have been spotted selling bánh cốm in blue boxes instead of fresh banana leaves. Be watchful of these 'innovations'. Accept no substitutes. Go for the green!

a vietnamese
banquet

So you've been to Vietnam and seen the light. Now is your chance to strut your stuff; it's time to give a great feast in true Vietnamese style. All the right dishes, seasoned just so. The right drinks and the right rice. All the right protocol and good manners, especially if you want to invite your Vietnamese neighbours. Here's your chance to shine.

The Vietnamese attach great importance to the protocol of a banquet, especially when it's associated with community events such as weddings or religious ceremonies etc. The seat of honour at the table, 'the table from above', is generally given to the eldest person in the party. 'The table from above' refers to the place nearest the ancestral altar. It is normally situated facing northwest. For a formal dinner for six the table setting would look like the following (in order of importance):

TABLE SETTING

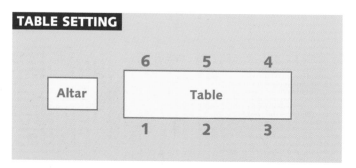

Traditionally, food will be served or passed 'down' the order of precedence, while alcohol makes the reverse journey. As the saying goes: 'eating goes from top to bottom while drinking goes from bottom to top'. If you are the host you will probably be forgiven if you don't follow this rule closely if the event is a birthday or simple social dinner. However, this kind of observation of the niceties will want to be closely adhered to in the case of a funerary feast. The place of the guest is determined by who he or she is closest to in the family. Friends of the father will sit near him, and so on.

With ethnic minorities, the custom is similar. In general, the father, as head of family, sits at the table end corresponding to the front of the house. After him come the sons, then daughters, and finally, the mother by the side of the kitchen.

But back to your feast. If it's to emulate a fairly standard family dinner, make it fun. Remember, the Vietnamese like to play with their food so give your guests something to play with. While it might not be practical to put a charcoal brazier on your dining-room table and serve **chả cá lã vọng** (Hanoi fried fish) and you won't be able to serve hotpot if you haven't got a portable burner, something like **bánh xèo** (Southern Vietnamese 'pancake' or stuffed crepe) is perfect (see recipe in the Regional Variety chapter). All you need is space.

Make the crepe batter in advance, and have two pans at the ready as it is fairly easy to do two at a time. Have the stuffing by the side of the stove, and the vegetable platter, garnishes and dipping sauces on the table by the time your guests arrive. Greet your guests and give them something to nibble like peanuts, a common Vietnamese snack. When they have all arrived, seat them and begin the crepes. You might want to enlist one guest to help you relay them to the table.

Bahn Xeo Crepes

When all are served, show the way. Using your chopsticks (or fork), break off a 5cm piece of bánh xèo. Place that in a lettuce leaf, and top it with herbs and vegetables. Roll it up as neatly as you can, then dip it into the sauce and enjoy. It's impossible to eat bánh xèo in a hurry. It's a perfect food for a convivial meal with lots of talk, lots of laughter as someone inevitably constructs the most ridiculous-looking roll of lettuce and mess. Let the beer flow and the conversation sparkle. Follow with Vietnamese tea and coffee and fresh fruit.

So to something more formal and fancy. Remember that the basic structure of a meal is rice and 'something else', although at a festive or formal meal rice will be less in evidence. You should show largesse. It's a time for indulgence. In the Vietnamese tradition a host should offer much more than the guests will consume in order to demonstrate generosity. And the guests will always leave something on the plate so as not to seem greedy.

MADAME DAI – Faces of Gastronomy

It's a mixed blessing, but people come to Madame Dai's restaurant, La Bibliotheque, less for the food and more to meet Madame Dai. They have heard about her, about how she was a high-powered lawyer and the speaker in the lower house of parliament in the old South Vietnamese regime. How she was suddenly out of a job in 1975 when the government ceased to exist. And how, unlike other South Vietnamese government officials, she never was sent for 're-education'. Rather, within weeks she had converted the library of her law office into a restaurant and was serving dinner to high and mighty potentates of the new regime. Since then, she has been serving presidents and ambassadors.

People think she must be some kind of Asian 'dragon lady', perhaps a beautiful seductress who turned the heads of the dour communist conquerors. In fact she is a very nice old lady who speaks perfect French and agreeable English. And she sets one of the more formal tables in town. Hers is the perfect place for entertaining, or for a private banquet. You must have a reservation. It's best to make one in person at 84A Nguyen Du, Dist 1, Ho Chi Minh City.

You can have a set piece Vietnamese dinner, or you can order French, á la carte. The formality is not the formality of the 'table from above'. It is a formality derived of Vietnam's association with France. And like all foreign influences in Vietnam it is no longer foreign, but a new Vietnamese. The set piece dinner is strictly Vietnamese food, but served in courses á la Francaise. The wine is French, but the after din-ner musical entertainment is classical Vietnamese. You'll find the most dignified aspects of both cultures, but neither are haughty or aloof.

Madame is very busy these days. She's back in the law trade as president of the Vietnam International Arbitration Center. But she does like to greet her guests whenever possible. She'll be happy, if she has time, to sit down with you and tell a story or drink a toast. She'll talk to you about fate and about politics and about the future of her country. And like Mother Love of the Coconut Tree, she'll tell you the secret of her success is her religious faith. She takes no credit for her tenacity, intelligence or courage. As she has done for a quarter of a century, she simply sets her table, commands her kitchen, and carries on. She wishes all 'bon appetit'.

Bicycle with bananas near the Cambodian border

Entertain in the style of the emperors at Hué. Begin with lots of little tidbits. If you've brought home any Vietnamese candies or salted fruits, offer them in little bowls. And be sure to keep everything 'little'. Your goal is to offer as much colour and variety as possible without stuffing your guests to bursting. Spring rolls can be offered either at the table or as an appetiser, but serve them now.

Graduate to sugar cane shrimp. You can buy foot-long lengths of sugar cane at Asian and Latin American markets. Use a hatchet to split the canes into quarters and cut them into 10cm pieces. Guests will ooh and ahh over this dish. Serve some champagne.

For an ordinary family meal you would want at least the four basic dishes: rice, vegetable, meat or fish, and soup. For your banquet you want meat *and* fish and maybe even fowl. Try this combination:

Elegant Menu

Canh chua ca (hot & sour fish soup)
Ca qua hap voi bia rau gia vi (steamed fish in beer)
Ga nuong xa ot (stirfried chicken with lemongrass)
Hit lon nuong ong tre (marinated pork in bamboo)
Rau xao (braised vegetables with nước mắm)
Com hoang bao (lotus rice)
Chuoi chien (fried sweet bananas)

If you want to serve wine with this meal, a semi-dry white with a bit of spice would go well with all the dishes. A gewürztraminer or a semillon would be good. If you have a beverage store with a large beer selection, you might be able to find Saigon or 333 beer. That would not only go well taste wise, but would lend an extra element of authenticity to your feast.

You should play some soft, almost contemplative, music. Many of the Vietnamese of our acquaintance enjoy the French impressionistic composers such as Satie and Debussy. And if you have the urge to burn incense, ignore it and it will go away.

fit & healthy

We all like to think that nothing untoward will come to us when we travel. Buses and trains will arrive and depart on time. Our immune systems will not be put to the test, and exotic bugs will remain foreign. But things happen, and you may discover a hitherto unknown allergy to coriander or rice. In this, and all cases, caution and common-sense are your best aides.

Above all, observe balance, moderation and variety. Food is important to your journey but, taken out of context, it is mere gorging. Balance your dining with visits to farms or wineries, museums and theatres etc. Moderate your intake.

If you're looking for a health guide to take on the road, look no further than Lonely Planet's pocket-size Healthy Travel Asia.

'HASH' FOR HEALTH

One of the best ways to exercise, eat, drink and meet new people at the same time is to hook up with the Hash House Harriers. Begun in 1938 at the Selangor Club of Kuala Lumpur in what was then British Imperial Malaya, this is arguably the oldest, and certainly the largest, international running club in the world. 'The Hash' has 1100 chapters worldwide in nearly every capital city and in such far-flung places as San Francisco, Turkmenistan and the South Pole. And it all began as an excuse to work up a thirst for beer and a hunger for the local food.

They meet once a week, customarily at 5 or 6pm on Mondays (it varies here and there), to run a 'paper chase'. One member is the 'hare' who runs ahead, leaving a trail of paper bits or chalk marks to show the route, but deviously interwoven with many false trails that can take the pursuers – the 'harriers' – through muddy ditches, cow pastures or city streets. It's non-competitive, recreational and wholly irreverent. The run is followed by wacky ceremonies, beer, food and revelry. The Hashers like to call themselves 'drinkers with a running problem'. As they say, 'If you have half a mind to try hashing, that's all you need'. Visitors and new members are always welcome.

In Ho Chi Minh City, the hash meets at the Caravel Hotel on Sundays at 2pm. It varies in Hanoi, but you can usually find out at the Press Club.

Don't plan on hitting the ground running, especially if you're on a long trip. It's worth allowing yourself time to adjust physically and mentally to your new environment and lifestyle. Factor in some time to take a breather, recover from jet lag and catch up on sleep. Don't overdo the booze or the chillies; work up to your usual party vigour slowly.

Hygiene

Many diseases associated with tropical countries are actually diseases of poor hygiene. Always wash your hands before you eat (there's usually a basin or jug for this in most restaurants) and after using the toilet. Short fingernails are easier to keep clean than long ones.

It's also worth observing local customs and perhaps adopting them yourself if they make sense to you, for example not letting your mouth touch a shared drinking vessel (pour the water into your mouth). The widespread custom of using the left hand for toilet duty and the right for eating and passing items is a sensible habit to adopt.

Having said this, Vietnam has achieved a very high standard of hygiene since 1975 and most foreign visitors to the country suffer no ill effect whatsoever from the food. Thoroughly cooked food is safest, but not if it has been left to cool or if it has been reheated. Uncooked or incompletely cooked shellfish such as mussels, oysters and clams should be avoided, as well as undercooked meat.

How food is prepared is more important than where – heating kills germs, so a plate of noodles cooked in a steaming hot wok at a street stall is probably safer than food left out on display in an upmarket hotel buffet.

Ice cream is usually okay if it is a reputable brand name, but beware of street vendors and of ice cream that has melted and been refrozen.

HANDY TIPS FOR KEEPING FIT

Use a calorie counter to help balance your intake and activity.

Avail yourself of local fresh fruit as much as possible.

Walk whenever you can, as often as you can.

If it's too far to walk, rent a bicycle.

Go swimming, in the hotel pool, in the nearby river if it's clean, in the ocean, at the ol' swimmin' hole.

Go dancing. If modern dance or shaking your booty in a disco is not your cup of tea, many ballrooms offer free or inexpensive lessons early in the evening. Shake a leg.

Take your running shoes. Ask the hotel desk for a good route.

Carry your skipping rope, flexgrips or other portable exercise equipment.

Make time for some kind of regular exercise, even if it's only 20 minutes in the morning before sallying forth to feast.

Pack a frisbee. It's good exercise and a good way to meet people in the park.

If you belong to any athletic or social/business club with athletic facilities, find out if clubs along your route have reciprocal privileges.

Don't rely on beer (sigh) to keep you hydrated. Alcohol is a diuretic and you'll just piss away the benefits.

Water

Vietnamese will drink tap water here, but you shouldn't. It's probably sanitary, but the mineral balance will be so different that it could make you sick. And besides, it tends to smell bad. Ask for **nước suối** (bottled drinking water), which will cost little.

Water used to make coffee or tea is of course boiled, rendering it safe to drink. Ice is produced from purified water under hygienic conditions and is therefore theoretically safe. During transit to the local restaurant,

---

THE BASICS

Everybody needs six basics for life: water, carbohydrates, protein, fat, vitamins and minerals (seven if you count beer). Foods aren't a pure source of just of one type of nutrient, they contain various elements in different quantities, so the best way to make sure you get enough of the right things is to eat a varied diet. You shouldn't find this difficult here, where the diet consists of a carbohydrate staple (rice, noodles) which you eat with a protein source (meat, fish, beans) and vegetables. Fresh fruit is widely available.

As a guide, you need to eat a variety of foods from each of five core groups:

* **bread** (baguettes), **other cereals** (rice, noodles) – eat lots of these, they provide carbohydrates, fibre, some calcium and iron, and B vitamins.

* **fruit & vegetables** – eat lots of these, they give you vitamin C, carotenes (vitamin A), folic acid, fibre and some carbohydrates.

* **milk & dairy products** – eat moderate amounts for calcium, zinc, protein, vitamin B12, vitamin B2, vitamin A and vitamin D.

* **meat, fish, nuts, beans** – these provide iron, protein, B vitamins (especially B12; meat only), zinc and magnesium; eat in moderation.

* **fat & sugary foods** (butter, oil, margarine, cakes, biscuits, sweets, etc) – eat sparingly from this group, which mainly provides fat, including essential fatty acids, some vitamins and salt.

Bear in mind that if you're already sick, your requirements change and you may need to increase the amounts of some food groups to increase your intake of protein, vitamins and minerals, for example.

however, conditions may not be so hygienic (you may see blocks of ice being dragged along the street), but it's very difficult to resist in the hot season. The rule of thumb is that if it's chipped ice, it probably came from an ice block (which may not have been handled well) but if it's ice cubes or 'tubes', it was delivered from the ice factory in sealed plastic.

When going out of town on day trips do not, we say again do not, go without a good supply of drinking water. In rural areas, you may not be able to conveniently find water when you need it. Along the highways there are usually roadside rests and small vendors' stands selling water and other basics but you could get very thirsty off the beaten path.

Eating the Right Stuff

Eating well should be fun, but it's also about making sure you get enough of the right nutrients to enable you to function at your best, mentally and physically. When you're on the road, your diet will be different from normal; in addition, a different lifestyle, stress and new activities may mean your nutritional requirements are increased.

With the help of this book you'll be able to identify available foods for a diverse and nutritious diet. But when you eat can be as important as what you eat. If you're on the move, be careful not to miss meals as this will make you more easily fatigued and vulnerable to illness.

Fading Away?

Losing weight when you're travelling is pretty common. There are lots of reasons for this, including getting sick, having a change in diet and perhaps being more active. You may have a bit of padding to spare, but keep an eye on how much weight you're losing and don't allow yourself to shed too much. Otherwise you'll be drained of your energy and you'll put yourself at risk of illness.

If you find you're losing weight, remember that with a vegetarian diet you generally have to eat larger quantities of plant foods to get the same amount of energy. Therefore, if you're eating mainly vegetarian, increase your quota of energy-giving foods, including fats.

If you've just turned vegetarian – or don't trust the meat here – be aware that your body takes a bit of time to adjust to getting some nutrients from plant sources, so it's worth taking a bit of care with your diet. Getting enough protein isn't generally a problem, especially if you eat dairy products or eggs. Note that proteins from plant sources often lack one or more amino acids (the building blocks of protein). Most traditionally vegetarian diets have dealt with this by basing meals around a combination of protein sources so that deficiencies are complemented. Examples of combinations include: pulses and rice, pulses and cereal, and nuts and cereal.

Because iron from plant sources is less well absorbed than iron from meat, iron-deficiency anaemia is a risk if you aren't careful, especially in menstruating women. Another vitamin you might not get enough of is vitamin B12 as it's only derived from animal sources. If you cut out all animal foods from your diet, you'll need to take a supplement to make up for this. Yeast extracts and fermented soybean substances like tempeh and miso contain a substance similar to B12 but it doesn't have the same effect in the body, so you'll still need B12 supplements. Good plant sources of nutrients include:

protein   soya protein, pulses, bread, grains, seeds, potatoes
calcium   tofu, seeds, green leafy vegetables, nuts, bread, dried fruit
iron   pulses, green vegetables, dried fruits, nuts; absorption of iron is increased by consuming a source of vitamin C at the same time (fruit, fruit juice or vegetables); tea, coffee, and phytate and oxalates from plants will reduce the absorption of iron

Diarrhoea

Don't let yourself get run down. Your immune system is suppressed when you're tired, so pace yourself and get sufficient rest. Practice the art of doing nothing now and then. If, despite taking precautions, you still get a bout of mild travellers diarrhoea, don't panic. A few rushed toilet trips with no other symptoms is not indicative of a serious problem. Diarrhoea caused by contaminated food or water is more serious.

Dehydration is the main danger with any diarrhoea, particularly for children where it can occur quickly. Drink plenty of fluids and check you're not getting dehydrated – weak black tea with a little sugar, carbonated drinks allowed to go flat and diluted 50% with water, are both good.

Note any other symptoms – diarrhoea can occur in many other illnesses, including malaria and hepatitis. Remember that diarrhoea is contagious so be scrupulous about washing your hands after using the toilet.

What to Eat

It's easy to get hung up about what, if anything, to eat when you have diarrhoea. But relax, use your common sense and try to tune in to what your body is telling you – if you feel like eating, go ahead, especially starchy foods which are known to promote salt and water absorption (such as rice, noodles and crackers). If you don't feel like eating, don't force yourself. Unless you're really roughing it, you're going to be basically well nourished and well able to withstand a couple of days with little or no food. It may make you feel a bit wobbly, so make sure you add a bit of sugar or honey to your drinks to keep your energy levels up.

Your overworked guts will appreciate small amounts of food at regular intervals rather than great big meals, and this may help make you feel less nauseated too. You may find that eating brings on cramps and you have to dash to the toilet. We all have a natural reflex whereby eating increases the activity of the gut, but this can get exaggerated in a diarrhoeal illness. It doesn't make you a great dinner companion, but you'll probably find that once you've answered the call of nature you can return to finish your meal! (But remember to wash your hands very thoroughly …)

> ## Food on the Runs
> **Eat** plain rice, plain bread, plain noodles, dry biscuits (salty or not too sweet) and bananas
> **Avoid** fruit & vegetables (except bananas), spicy foods, dairy products (including yoghurt) and greasy foods

Contrary to the spirit of this book, you should stick to a more limited diet while you have diarrhoea and as you recover. You should also go easy on fibre providers like fruit, vegetables and nuts. Bananas are good as they tend to stop you up, and they are a source of potassium and glucose. As the diarrhoea clears up and you start to get your appetite back, add in more foods gradually until you're back to normal and can resume your culinary adventures.

Indigestion

A change in diet, stress, anxiety and spicy foods can all make 'indigestion' (burning pains in your upper abdomen) and heartburn (burning in your gullet, often with an acid taste in your mouth) more likely when you're travelling. The discomfort is often worse when you're hungry or just after meals. Smoking and alcohol exacerbate it.

Simple measures you could try are to eat small, regular meals – don't eat a huge meal just before you go to bed. It can be difficult, but try to avoid spicy hot foods. Milk and yoghurt can be soothing, as can eating plain, starchy foods like noodles or bread. You could consider trying antacids (there are many products available without prescription), although stomach acid has a protective effect against infective agents, so taking antacids may make you more vulnerable to gut infections.

Children's Health

Like many places in South-East Asia, travelling with children in Vietnam can be a lot of fun, as long as you come with the right attitudes, equipment and the usual parental patience. All the usual health tips regarding food, heat and diarrhoea mentioned earlier should be followed with extra care, as kids tend to jump into everything with both feet.

For the most part, parents needn't worry too much about potential health concerns though it pays to lay down a few ground rules – such as regular hand-washing – to head off potential medical problems. Children are welcomed everywhere in Vietnam and more and more people are traveling with children here. If they get sick or sunburned, you'll be able to find ordinary medicines at a corner pharmacy. Children should be warned not to play with animals since rabies is relatively common in Vietnam.

Heat

Vietnam's full-on tropical climate can get to you, so take it slow until you've fully acclimatised. Drink plenty of liquids to replace all the water lost via perspiration. Use sunscreen, even when overcast.

Vietnamese bathe often and taking regular cool showers can be of great help. Use talcum powder to prevent 'prickly heat', an itchy rash caused by trapped perspiration.

Contrary to popular belief, salt tablets interfere with the absorption of water by the body. 'Dehydrating' or 'electrolyte' solutions can have a similar effect if consumed too often.

When the weather is hot, avoid the sun between noon and 4pm – stick to the shade, or find an air-conditioned building for temporary relief. Avoid overexerting yourself or eating a big meal at this time of the day – it's the perfect time for a siesta or for reading that airport novel.

Allergies

Anyone with an allergy to shrimp should be aware that a lot of Vietnamese dishes contain shrimp paste or dried shrimp.

Diabetes

If you are diabetic, bring plenty of supplies and everything you will need, then pack some more. If you're travelling with a companion it's a good idea to split your supplies between you in the event your luggage is lost. Also, leave some with a hotel or a friend. Carry your prescription or other documentation so the local police won't think you're dealing in drugs.

Last Word

Journey well, eat well, and return home well.

Recommended Reading

In *Down Highway One* by **Sue Downie** (St. Leonard's, 1993) take a trip down the length of Vietnam's national highway in the emerging society of the 1990s. A good look at Vietnam's "early" days of tourism after the American war. For a journalist's organised and thoughtful experience of modern Vietnam see **Henry Kamm's** *Dragon Ascending* (Arcade, 1996). This is a book that allows the reader to see Vietnam through the eyes of Vietnamese as the author meets and talks with people from all walks of life. **Karen Muller** travels the humble side of Vietnam in *Hitchhiking Vietnam* (Globe Pequot Press, 1998). She hitch-hikes, motorbikes and rides the rails of the country from south to north and back again. For a geographer's point of view nothing beats *Vietnam: A Country Study*, (1989) part of a series that covers most of the world published by the US government through the office of the Secretary of the Army. And for a culinary paean to the country you can't beat Vietnam on a Plate by **Annabel Doling** (Roundhouse Publications, 1996).

Resources

Barbara Cohen, *The Vietnam Guidebook*, Houghton Mifflin

Vietnam, Lonely Planet

Ngo and Zimmerman, *The Classic Cuisine of Vietnam*, Penguin

Robert Butler, *A Good Scent from a Strange Mountain*, Minerva

Bakaert and Hall, *Vietnam: A Portrait*, Elsworth Ltd

Internet Resources

For the most up-to-date information on Vietnam, try the following links:

Destination Vietnam
http://www.lonelyplanet.com

Destination Vietnam is a one-stop Vietnam electronic magazine:
http://www.destinationvietnam.com

Vietnam Adventures On-line has travel information, monthly adventures and special travel deals: **http://www.vietnamadventures.com**

Vietnam On-line offers travel lore, employment and business opportunities in Vietnam: **http://www.govietnam.com**

Vietnam at a Glance has a wide range of general information on travelling in Vietnam: **http://203.149.0.41/worldwide/world-info/asia/vietnam/glance.html**

For up-to-date news on Vietnam in English: **http://home.vnd.net/english/news/**
Jewels of the Mekong Delta, featuring the people, the countries and the river:
http://www.pata.org/mekong/index.html

The Ecotravel Centre, for information on travelling lightly:
http://www.ecotour.org/ecotour.htm

Photo Credits

Garrett Culhane p11, p12, p24, p37, p38, p39, p40, p41, p43, p48 centre, p49 centre, p49 bottom, p52, p53, p59, p68, p69, p73 top right, bottom, p74, p103, p108, p112, p117, p125, p127 bottom, p135 top left, bottom right, 151 left, p154, p160, p173, p175 bottom, p183, p191 bottom.

Richard I'Anson p5, p8, p9 top left, top right, bottom left, p17, p18, p23 top, p30, p48 top, p48 bottom, p67, p73 top left, p81, p95 bottom left, top right, p118, p135, p141, p142, p146, p151 bottom, p158, p170, p175.

Greg Elms Back cover, p23, p33, p36, p45, p46, p54, p57, p70, p83, p87, p95, p100, p106, p122, p123, p127, p129, p181, p185, p187, p191 top.

Jerry Alexander Front cover, p1, p20, p65, p92, p102, p151 top, p188.

Mason Florence p10, p23 right, p50, p77, p83 top left, p96, p143.

Bernard Napthine p25, p61, p66, p95 bottom right, p115.

S. J. Cleland p124, p139.

Juliet Coombe p28, p29.

Anders Blomqvist p13, p14.

Bethune Carmichael p9 bottom right.

Kraig Lieb p164.

Peter Ptschelinzew p55.

Neil Wilson p49.

eat your words
language guide

Pronunciation

As transliterations give only an approximate guide to pronunciation, we've included this guide for those who want to try their hand at pronouncing Vietnamese more like a native speaker.

Vowels

a	as the 'a' in 'father'
â	as the 'a' in 'father', but shorter
ă	as the 'u' in 'hut'
e	as the 'e' in 'keg'
ê	as the 'e' in 'pet'
i/y	as the 'i' in 'machine'
o	as the 'a' in 'saw'
ô	as the 'a' in 'about'
ơ	as the 'i' in 'bird'
u	as the 'oo' in 'too'
ư	between the 'i' in 'sister' and the 'u' in 'sugar'

Vowel Combinations

ai	as the 'y' in 'fly'
au	a + u
ay	as the 'ay' in 'day'
ie	i + e
oa	as in 'wa'

Consonants

c	as the 'c' in 'cat'
ch	as the 'ch' in 'cheese' at the beginning of a word; as the 'k' in 'king' at the end of a word
d	as the 'y' in 'yellow' in the southern dialect; as the 'z' in 'zoo' in the northern dialect
đ	as the 'd' in 'dog'
g/gh	as the 'g' in 'gone'
gi	as the 'y' in 'yes' in the southern dialect; as the 'z' in 'zoo' in the northern dialect
h	as the 'h' in 'hat'
ng/ngh	as the 'ng' in 'singer'
nh	as the 'ny' in 'canyon'
ph	as the 'ph' in 'photo'
q	as the 'w' in 'wet' in the southern dialect; as the 'qu' in 'quit' in the northern dialect
s	as the 's' in 'sugar'
t	as the 't' in 'stop', with no puff of breath following
th	as the 't' in 'top'
x	as the 's' in 'song'

Tones

Vietnamese has six tones, which can often determine a word's meaning.

ma	mid-level	ghost
má	high rising	mother
mà	low falling	which
mả	low rising	tomb
mã	high broken	horse
mạ	low broken	rice seedling

Transliteration Guide

The transliteration is intended to be as simple as possible, however to avoid confusion some aspects of Vietnamese transliteration need to be explained.

oh	as the 'oe' in 'toe'
ur-a	the final 'a' is very soft; as the 'a' in 'about'
ur-erk	the second syllable quickly follows the first
ur-u	the second syllable quickly follows the first
t	as the 't' in 'tiny'
t̲	heavy, voiced 't', almost like a 'd'

Accents

There are many accents spoken in Vietnam. However, the two main distinct and widely used accents are those in the south and north. Although they are spelled the same the pronunciation is quite different. These have been separated by a slash and placed in brackets throughout the transliteration (south/north).

Useful Phrases
Eating Out

restaurant
  nya hang   nhà hàng

cheap restaurant
  (wuan/kwuan) biny (yuhn/zuhn)   quán bình dân

Do you speak English?
  bahn biet noi tieng any kohng?   Bạn biết nói tiếng Anh không?

Table for (three), please.
  Mot kai bahn chaw (ba)   Một cái bàn cho (ba) nguoi.
  ngur-er-i

Do you accept credit cards?
  ohng/koh caw nyuhn trah bahng   Ông/Cô có nhận trà bằng thẻ
  te t̲in (yung/zung) kohng?   tín dụng không?

Do you have a highchair for the baby?
  bahn kaw geh ngoi chaw tre   Bạn có ghế ngồi cho trẻ em không?
  em kohng?

Just Try It!

What's that?
kai daw la (yi/zi)?

Cái đó là gì?

What's the specialty of this region?
**mon dahk sahn kwua vung nay
la (yi/zi) vay?**

Món đặc sản của vùng này
là gì vậy?

What's the specialty here?
er duhy kaw mon dahk biet (yi/zi)?

Ồ đây có món đặc biệt gì?

What do you recommend?
bahn (yer-i/zer-i) tieu mon (yi/zi)?

Bạn giới thiệu món gì?

What are they eating?
haw dahng ahn mon (yi/zi)?

Họ đang ăn món gì?

I'll try what she/he's having.
**ṭoh-i mu-on tur mon koh/any ṭa
dang (yung/zung).**

Tôi muốn thử món cô/anh ta
đang dùng.

The Menu

Can I see the menu please?
sin chaw sem turk dern

Xin cho xem thực đơn.

Do you have a menu in English?
**bahn kaw turk dern bahng tieng
any kohng?**

Bạn có thực đơn bằng tiếng
Anh không?

What are today's specials?
**mon dahk biet hohm nay
la (yi/zi)?**

Món đặc biệt hôm nay là gì?

I'd like the set lunch, please.
**chaw ṭoh-i goi fuhn
ahn trur-a**

Cho tôi gọi phần ăn trưa.

What does it include?
trong daw gohm nyurng (yi/zi)?

Trong đó gồm những gì?

Is service included in the bill?
**kaw tiny tien fuk vu trong
hoa dern kohng?**

Có tính tiền phục vụ trong
hóa đơn không?

Does it come with salad?
**fuhn nay kaw kem teo
sa-laik kohng?**

Phần này có kèm theo
sà lách không?

What's the soup of the day?
**hohm nay kaw mon
sup (yi/zi)?**

Hôm nay có món súp gì?

Throughout the Meal

What's in this dish?
  trong mon nay kaw (yi/zi)?   Trong món này có gì?

Do you have sauce?
  kaw nur-erk chuhm kohng?   Có nước chấm không?

Not too spicy please.
  sin durng chaw kay (wua/kwua)   Xin đừng cho cay quá.

Is that dish spicy?
  mon nay kaw kay kohng?   Món này có cay không?

It's not hot (temperature).
  kohng kay lahm   Không cay lắm.

I didn't order this.
  toh-i kohng goi mon nay   Tôi không gọi món nài.

I'd like ...
  toh-i mu-on ...   Tôi muốn ...

Can you please bring me ...?	**sin mahng chaw toh-i ...?**	Xin mang cho tôi ...?
an ashtray	**gaht tahn tu-ok**	gạt tàn thuốc
more bread	**tehm bany mi**	thêm bánh mì
a cup	**kai kohk**	cái cốc
a fork	**kai nea**	cái nĩa
a glass	**kai li**	cái ly
a knife	**kon (yao/zao)**	con dao
a napkin	**kahn (yuhy/zuhy)**	khăn giấy
some pepper	**it tieu**	ít tiêu
a plate	**kai (yea/zea)**	cái dĩa
some salt	**it mu-oi**	ít muối
a spoon	**kai mu-ong**	cái muỗng
a teaspoon	**kai mu-ong ka-feh**	cái muỗng cà phê
a toothpick	**kuhy tahm**	cây tăm
more water	**tehm nurk**	thêm nước
more wine	**tehm rur-u**	thêm rượu

This food is ...	**doh ahn nay ...**	Đồ ăn này ...
brilliant	**ngon twuet**	ngon tuyệt
burnt	**chay**	cháy
cold	**lany**	lạnh
spoiled	**hur**	hư
stale	**tieu**	thiêu
undercooked	**chur-a chin**	chưa chín

I'd like something to drink.
  sin chaw fuhn (yai/zai) kaht   Xin cho phần giải khát.

Can I have a (beer) please?
chaw toh-i sin (chai bea)?   Cho tôi xin (chai bia)?

Thank you, that was delicious.
kahm ern, mon ahn tuht twuet   Cám ơn, món ăn thật tuyệt.

Please pass on our compliments to the chef.
sin chwuen (yum/zum) ler-i ken   Xin chuyển dùm lời khen đến
dehn ngur-er-i dau behp   người đầu bếp.

The bill, please.
sin ṭiny ṭien   Xin tính tiền.

You May Hear
Anything else?
kuhn (yi/zi) nur-a kohng?   Cần gì nữa không?

Family Meals
You're a great cook!
any/chi la nya dau behp   Anh/chị là nhà đầu bếp
tuht (yoi/zoi)!   thật giỏi!

This is brilliant!
mon nay ngon twu-et!   Món này ngon tuyệt!

Do you have the recipe for this?
any/chi kaw bi kwu-et lam   Anh/chị có bí quyết làm
mon nay kohng?   món này không?

Is this a family recipe?
duhy kaw fai la bi kwu-et   Đây có phải là bí quyết gia
(ya/za) tru-en kohng?   truyền không?

Are the ingredients local?
kaw fai nyurng ngu-en lieu nay la   Có phải những nguyên liệu
er dia fur-erng kohng?   này là ở địa phương không?

I've never had a meal like this before.
ṭoh-i chur-a bao (yer/zer) ahn moht   Tôi chưa bao giờ ăn một bữa
bur-a ahn ngon nyur teh nay ka   ăn ngon như thế này cả.

If you ever come to (Australia) I'll cook you a local dish.
ki nao bahn dehn (Uk), ṭoh-i se nau   Khi nào bạn đến (Úc), tôi sẽ nấu bạn
bahn ahn moht mon kua dia fur-erng   ăn một món của địa phương

Could you pass the (salt) please?
nyer any/chi dur-a ṭoh-i chai mu-oi?   Nhờ anh/chị đưa tôi chai muối?

I really appreciate it.
ṭoh-i tuht sur kahm ern dieu daw   Tôi thật sự cám ơn điều đó.

Thanks very much for the meal.
kahm ern any/chi ruht nyieu   Cám ơn anh/chị rất nhiều
chaw bur-a ahn   cho bữa ăn.

Vegetarian & Special Meals

I'm a vegetarian.
t̲oh-i ahn chay   Tôi ăn chay.

I'm a vegan, I don't eat meat or dairy products.
t̲oh-i ahn cay, t̲oh-i kohng   Tôi ăn chay, tôi không
(yung/zung) tit va ber sur-a   dùng thịt và bơ sữa.

Do you have any vegetarian dishes?
bahn kaw nyung mon ahn   Bạn có những món ăn
chay kohng?   chay không?

Can you recommend a vegetarian dish, please?
bahn kaw teh (yer-i/zer-i) tieu   Bạn có thể giới thiệu
moht mon chay kohng?   một món chay không?

Does this dish have meat?
mon nay kaw tit kohng?   Món này có thịt không?

I don't eat ...	t̲oh-i kohng ahn ...	Tôi không ăn ...
chicken	**ga**	gà
cured/processed meats	**tit cheh bien**	thịt chế biến
fish	**ka**	cá
meat	**tit**	thịt
peanuts	**dau fung**	đậu phụng
pork	**tit heo**	thịt heo
poultry	**(ya/za) kuhm**	gia cầm
seafood	**hai sahn**	hải sản

Is it ...?	duhy la kohng ...?	Đây là không ...?
gluten-free	**chuht glu-ten**	chất glu-ten
lactose-free	**kaw chuht lak-tot**	có chất lác tốt
wheat-free	**kaw lua maik**	có lúa mạch
salt-free	**mu-oi**	muối
sugar-free	**dur-erng**	đường
yeast-free	**men**	men

Does it contain eggs/dairy products?
doh nay kaw trurng hay ber sua   Ủồ này có trứng hay bơ sữa
kohng?   không?

Can I get this without the meat?
chaw toh-i mon nay kohng tit   Cho tôi món này không thịt
dur-erk kohng?   được không?

Does this dish have gelatin?
mon nay kaw chuht gelatin kohng?   Món này có chất gêlatin không?

I'm allergic to ...
toh-i bi (yi/zi) urng ver-i ...   Tôi bị dị ứng với ...

Is this organic?
kaw chuht hur-u ker kohng?   Có chất hữu cơ không?

At the Market

Where's the nearest (market)?
cher guhn nyuht er duh-u?   (Chợ) gần nhất ở đâu?

How much?
bao nyieu?   Bao nhiêu?

Can I have a ...	**chaw toh-i sin moht ...**	Cho tôi xin một ...
bottle	**chai**	chai
box	**hohp**	hộp
can	**lon**	lon
packet	**goi**	gói
sachet/bag	**bao**	bao

Can I taste it?
toh-i kaw theh nehm tur dur-erk   Tôi có thể nếm thử được
kohng?   không?

How much is a kilo of ...?
bao nyieu tien chaw moht ki   Bao nhiêu tiền cho một kí lô ...?
loh ...?

Do you have anything cheaper?
kaw kai nao re hern kohng?   Có cái nào rẻ hơn không?

Is this the best you have?
duhy la mon toht nyat fai kohng?   Đây là món tốt nhất phải không?

What is the local speciality?
mon dahk sahn er duhy la (yi/zi)?   Món đặc sản ở đây là gì?

Give me (half) a kilo, please.
sin chaw toh-i (nur-a) ki   Xin cho toi (nửa) ký.

Will this keep in the fridge?
kai nay kaw kuhn trur tu lany   Cái này có cần trữ tủ lạnh không?
kohng?

I'd like (six slices of ham).
cho toi (sau mieng tit mu-oi)   Cho tôi (sáu miếng thịt muối).

No!
kohng!   Không!

I don't want to buy.
toh-i kohng mu-on mua   Tôi không muốn mua

I'd like some ...	cho toi mot it ...		Cho tôi một ít ...
bread	bany mi		bánh mì
eggs	trurng		trứng
flour	boht		bột
fruit & vegetables	trai kuhy va rau	kai	trái cây và rau
ham	tit mu-oi		thịt muối
jam	murt		mứt
margarine/butter	ber		bơ
milk	sur-a		sữa
pepper	tieu		tiêu
salt	mu-oi		muối
sugar	dur-erng		đường
yoghurt	sua chua		sữa chua

At the Bar

Shall we go for a drink?
miny kaw teh kung di u-ong   Mình có thể cùng đi uống
kohng?   không?

I'll buy you a drink.
sin mer-i bahn li nur-erk   Xin mời bạn ly nước.

Thanks, but I don't feel like it.
kam ern, nyurng toh-i kohng   Cám ơn, nhưng tôi không
tuhy hurng tu   thấy hứng thú.

I don't drink.
toh-i kohng u-ong rur-u   Tôi không uống rượu.

I was here before this lady/gentleman.
toh-i da kaw er duhy trur-erk   Tôi đã có ở đây trước
ba/onhg nay   bà/ông này.

What would you like?
bahn tik mon (yi/zi)?   Bạn thích món gì?

It's on me.
toh-i sin mer-i   Tôi xin mời.

You can get the next one.
fuhn bahn luhn ter-i   Phần bạn lần tới.

OK.
dur-erk   Được.

I'm next.
ter-i fien toh-i   Tới phiên tôi.

Excuse me.
sin loh-i

Xin lỗi.

I'll have (a) ...   **chaw ṭoh-i li ...**   Cho tôi ly ...
   beer   **bia**   bia
   brandy/cognac   **koh-nyahk**   cô nhắc
   champagne   **suhm bany**   xâm banh
   liqueur   **rur-u**   rượu
   rum   **rur-u rom**   rượu rom
   whisky   **wit-ki**   uýt ky
   wine   **rur-u**   rượu

Can I have ice, please.
sin chaw it da

Xin cho ít đá.

No ice, please.
sin vui long durng chaw da

Xin vui lòng đụng cho đá.

Same again, please.
sin chaw nyur ku

Xin cho như cũ.

Is food available here?
er duhy ko turk ahn kohng?

Ở đây có thức ăn không?

Where's the toilet?
fong veh siny er duh-u?

Phòng vệ sinh ở đâu?

This is hitting the spot!
da (wua/kwua)!

Đã quá!

Cheers!
mer-i kung li!

Mời cụng ly!

So, do you come here often?
vuhy bahn kaw tur-erng dehn duhy kohng?

Vậy bạn có thường đến đây không?

I really, really love you.
ṭoh-i ruht, ruht ieu bahn/koh/any

Tôi rất, rất yêu bạn/cô/anh.

I'm a bit tired, I'd better get home.
ṭoh-i her-i meht, ṭoh-i mu-on veh nya

Tôi hơi mệt, tôi muốn về nhà.

I'm feeling drunk.
ṭoh-i say (wua/kwua)

Tôi say quá.

I think I've had one too many.
ṭoh-i ngi ṭoh-i da (wua/kwua) chen roh-i

Tôi nghĩ tôi đã quá chén rồi.

I feel ill.
ṭoh-i kahm tuhy bi biny

Tôi cảm thấy bị bịnh.

I want to throw up.
toh-i bu-on nohn   Tôi buồn nôn.

She/he's passed out.
any/koh ta bi buht tiny   Anh/cô ta bị bất tỉnh.

I'm hung over.
toh-i tuhy chwu-ang vang   Tôi thấy choáng váng.

What did I do last night?
dehm (wua/kwua) toh-i   Đêm qua tôi đã làm gì?
da lam (yi/zi)?

Wine

May I see the wine list, please?
sin chaw toh-i sem turk dern rur-u?   Xin cho tôi xem thực đơn rượu?

May I taste it?
sin chaw tur moht ti?   Xin cho thử một tí?

Which wine would you recommend with this dish?
rur-u nao ti tik herp ver-i   Rượu nào thì thích hợp với
mon ahn nay?   món ăn này?

I'd like a glass/	**toh-i mu-on moht**	Tôi muốn một
bottle of ... wine.	**li/chai ... rur-u**	ly/chai ... rượu.
red	**daw**	đỏ
white	**trahng**	trắng
rose	**hohng**	hồng

This wine is corked.
rur-u nay da dong nut   Rượu này đã đóng nút.

A

abalone	*bao ngu*	bào ngư
adzuki bean	*dau daw nyaṯ ban*	đậu đỏ Nhật Bản
allspice	*(ya/za) vi erṯ koh*	gia vị ớt khô
almond	*hany nyan*	hạnh nhân
anchovy	*ka ṯrohng*	cá trồng
aperitif	*rur-u kai vi*	rượu khai vị
appetiser	*mon kai vi*	món khai vị
apples	*ṯrai ṯao*	trái táo
apricot	*(wua/kwua) mer*	quả mơ
apron	*iem*	yếm
artichoke	*ar ṯee show*	ar-ti-chô
asparagus	*mang ṯay*	măng tây
aubergine	*ka ṯim*	cà tím
avocado	*ṯrai ber*	trái bơ

B

baby corn	*bahp non*	bắp non
back bacon	*tiṯ lurng mu-oi*	thịt lưng muối
bacon	*tiṯ lern mu-oi*	thịt lợn muối
to bake	*nur-erng (bany)*	nướng (bánh)
baking soda	*mu-oi (yiem/ziem)*	muối diêm
bamboo shoot	*mang*	măng
banana	*chu-oi*	chuối
barbecue	*nur-erng (tiṯ)*	nướng (thịt)
barbecue grill	*vee nur-erng*	vĩ nướng
barbecue pork	*sa siu*	xá xíu
barley	*lwua maik*	lúa mạch
basil	*rau kwue*	rau quế
basmati rice	*gao hohṯ (yai/zai)*	gạo hột (yai/zai)
	dohng nam a	đông nam á
bass	*ka pecca*	cá pecca
batter	*bohṯ mi ṯrurng*	bột mì trung
bay	*la nguu-eṯ kwue*	lá nguệt quế
bean sprout	*(ya/za)*	giá
beef	*tiṯ baw*	thịt bò
beef jerky	*koh baw*	khô bò
beer	*bea*	bia
beetroot	*ku kai daw*	củ cải đỏ
berries	*(yau/zau)*	dâu
betel	*kay ṯrau kohng*	cây trầu không
bill (account)	*hwo-a dern*	hóa đơn

English	Pronunciation	Vietnamese
bird's eye chilli	*ert hiem*	ớt hiểm
biscuits	*bany kuk-ki*	bánh cúc-ki
bitter melon	*mur-erp dang*	mướp đắng
black bean	*dau den*	đậu đen
black-eyed bean	*dau nyan den*	đậu nhãn đen
blender	*may ngien*	máy nghiền
blood pudding	*(yoh-ilzoh-i) tiet*	dồi tiết
boil	*dun soi*	đun sôi
bok choy	*kai be trang*	cải bẹ trắng
boning	*ga rut sur-erng*	gà rút xương
bottle opener	*doh kui chai*	đồ khui chai
bourbon	*rur-u u-it-ki my*	rượu úyt-ki my
bowl	*chen*	chén
braise	*um*	um
bran	*kam*	cám
brandy	*rur-u ran-di*	rượu ran-đi
bread	*bany mi*	bánh mì
breakfast	*bu-oi ahn sang*	buổi ăn sáng
breast	*urk*	ức
brisket	*tit urk*	thịt ức
broad bean	*dau tahm*	đậu tầm
broccoli	*bong kai sany*	bông cải xanh
broth	*nur-erk xwit*	nước xúyt
to brown	*nau chin vang*	nấu chín vàng
brown rice	*gao lurk*	gạo lức
brown sauce	*nur-erk mau*	nước màu
buckwheat	*kieu maik*	kiều mạch
burnet	*chin vang*	chín vàng
bus boy	*ngu-er-i hau ban fu*	người hầu bàn phụ
butter	*ber*	bơ
butter bean	*dau trang*	đậu trắng
buttermilk	*sur-a nur-erk*	sữa nước
butterscotch	*keo ber kurng*	kẹo bơ cứng
button	*bup nuhm*	búp nấm

C

English	Pronunciation	Vietnamese
cabbage	*kai bahp*	cải bắp
cakes	*bany ngot*	bánh ngọt
can opener	*doh kui hop*	đồ khui hộp
candy	*keo*	kẹo
cane sugar	*(dur-erng) mea*	(đường) mía
cantaloupe	*yur-a daw*	dưa đỏ
capsicum	*ert daw*	ớt đỏ

caramel	*dur-erng tang mau*	đường thắng màu
caraway seed	*hoht carum*	hột carum
cardamom	*kay baik dau kau*	cây bạch đậu khấu
carrot	*ku ka rot*	củ cà rốt
carving	*tai/tark*	thái/tạc
cashew	*hoht dieu*	hột điều
cassava	*kwo-ai mi*	khoai mì
cauliflower	*sup ler*	súp lơ
caviar	*trurng ka tuhm*	trứng cá tầm
cayenne	*bot ert do*	bột ớt đỏ
celeriac	*re kan tay*	rễ cần tây
celery seed	*hoht kan*	hột cần
cereal	*ngu kok*	ngũ cốc
champagne	*sum bany*	xâm banh
chayote	*yur-a sany*	dưa xanh
cheap	*reh*	rẻ
check (account)	*hwo-a dern*	hóa đơn
cheese	*faw mat*	phó mát
chef	*dau bep*	đầu bếp
cherry	*kwa any dao*	quả anh đào
chervil	*rau mui*	rau mùi
chestnut	*hoht (yeh/zeh)*	hột dẻ
chick pea	*dau sany*	đậu xanh
chicken	*ga*	gà
chicory	*kay rau diep*	cây rau diếp
chilli	*ert ko*	ớt khô
chinese cabbage	*bahp kai tau*	bắp cải tàu
chips	*kwoai rahn lat mong*	khoai rán lát mỏng
chive	*la term mui hany*	lá thơm mùi hành
chocolate	*soh koh la*	sô cô la
chopping board	*tert*	thớt
chops	*tit sur-ern*	thịt sườn
chopsticks	*du-a*	đũa
chump	*tit lurng kur-u*	thịt lưng cừu
cilantro	*(rau) ngaw*	(rau) ngò
cinnamon	*kwue*	quế
citrus	*kam/kwuit*	cam/quít
clam	*kon trai*	con trai
clay pot	*kai toh*	cái tộ
clotted cream	*kem dak*	kem đặc
cocktails	*rur-u fa nur-erk hwoa kwua*	rượu pha nước hoa quả
cocoa	*soh koh la boht*	sô cô la bột
coconut	*yur-a*	dừa

cod	*ka moruy*	cá moruy
coffee	*ka fe*	cà phê
–decaffeinated	*ka fe da lwuai tru ka fe tiny*	cà phê đã loại trừ cà phê tính
–grinder	*may say ka fe*	máy xay cà phê
–maker	*may fa lok ka fe*	máy pha lọc cà phê
condiments	*doh (ya/za) vi*	đồ gia vị
congee	*chao*	cháo
cookies	*bany kuk-ki*	bánh cúc-ki
coriander	*(rau) ngaw*	(rau) ngò
corn	*bahp/ngoh*	bắp/ngô
corn meal	*boht bahp hoht*	bột bắp hột
courgette	*bi sany*	bí xanh
crab	*kwua*	cua
cracked wheat	*lwua maik say*	lúa mạch xay
crayfish	*tohm duht*	tôm đất
cream	*kem*	kem
credit card	*te tin (yung/zung)*	thẻ tín dụng
croissant	*bany surng bo*	bánh xừng bò
croquette	*ka va kwo-ai tay ngien ran*	cá và khoai tây nghiền rán
cucumber	*(yur-a/zur-a) chuot/leo*	dưa chuột/leo
cumin	*tia la*	thìa là
cup	*ly/kohk*	ly/cốc
to cure	*tit ur-erp say ko*	thịt ướp xấy khô
curry	*ka ri*	cà ri
curry powder	*boht ka ri*	bột cà ri
cutlery	*boh (yao/zao) nea*	bộ dao nĩa
cutlets	*lat tit; lap sur-erng*	lát thịt; lạp xưởng

D

dates	*trai cha la*	trái chà là
decaffeinated coffee	*ka fe da lwuai tru ka fe tiny*	cà phê đã loại trừ cà phê tính
deep-fry	*chian (yon/zon)*	chiên giòn
dessert	*mon trang mieng*	món tráng miệng
dessert spoon	*mu-ong ahn trang mieng*	muỗng ăn tráng miệng
dewberry	*(yau/zau) rurng do*	dâu rừng đỏ
dinner	*bu-oi ahn toh-i*	buổi ăn tối
distilled water	*nur-erk kut*	nước cất
dried fruit	*trai kay koh*	trái cây khô
drinking straws	*ohng hut*	ống hút

drinks	tuc u-ong	thực uống
duck	vit	vịt
dumplings	bany hahp	bánh hấp
durian	trai sau rieng	trái sầu riêng

E

eel	lur-ern	lươn
egg white	long trang trurng	lòng trắng trứng
egg yolk	long daw	lòng đỏ
eggplant	ka tim	cà tím
eggs	trurng	trứng
endive	rau (yiep/ziep) kwu-an	rau diếp quăn
entrée	mon dau bur-a	món đầu bữa

F

fennel	kay ti la	cây thì là
–seed	hoht ti la	hột thì là
fenugreek	(ya/za) vi nau sup hi lap	gia vị nấu sup hy lạp
fig	(wua/kwua) va	quả vả
fillet	tit ka lohk	thịt, cá lóc
first course	mon dau tien	món đầu tiên
fish	ka	cá
cha ka	chả cá
–paste
–sauce	nur-erk mahm	nước mắm
flank	tit sur-erng	thịt sườn
flavour	mui vi	mùi vị
flounder	ka bern	cá bơn
flour	boht	bột
food	doh ahn	đồ ăn
food processor	may che bien	máy chế biến
turk fuhm	thực phẩm
fork	nea	nĩa
fried chicken	ga chien	gà chiên
fried rice	kerm chien	cơm chiên
frog	eik	ếch
fruit	trai kay	trái cây
fruit cake	bany trai kay	bánh trái cây
fruit juice	nur-erk trai kay	nước trái cây
fruit punch	rur-u fa trai kay	rượu pha trái cây
to fry	chien	chiên
frying pan	chao chien	chảo chiên

G

galangal	*(yo/zo)*	giò
game	*tit sur-erng*	thịt săn
garden pea	*dau vur-ern tur-er-i*	đậu vườn tươi
garlic	*toi*	tỏi
garlic press	*doh bok vo toi*	đồ bóc vỏ tỏi
gelatin	*taik long*	thạch lỏng
ghee	*ber long*	bơ lỏng
gherkin	*(yur-a/zur-a) chuot sany long*	dưa chuột xanh
giblets		lòng
gin	*rur-u trahng*	rượu trắng
ginger	*gurng*	gừng
glutinous rice	*gao nep*	gạo nếp
goose	*ngohng*	ngỗng
gooseberry	*(wua/kwua) li gai*	quả lý gai
grapefruit	*bur-er-i*	bưởi
grapes	*nyo*	nho
to grate	*ngien*	nghiền
grater	*ban nao*	bàn nào
grease	*(yau/zau) mer*	đầu mỡ
green capsicum (sweet)	*ert sany*	ớt xanh
green pepper (sweet)	*ert sany*	ớt xanh
green split pea	*dau hwoa lan sany*	đậu hòa lan xanh
greens	*rau sany*	rau xanh
grill	*law nur-erng*	lò nướng
guava	*oh-i*	ổi
guyabano	*trai mang kau*	trái mãng cầu

H

haddock	*ka tu-et fin*	cá tuyết êfin
hake	*ka tu-et meluk*	cá tuyết meluc
halibut	*ka bern lur-er-i ngur-a*	cá bơn lưỡi ngựa
ham	*dui lern mu-oi*	đùi lợn muối
hard	*kurng*	cứng
hare	*to rurng*	thỏ rừng
haricot bean	*dau tay*	đậu tây
hazelnut	*(wua/kwua) fi*	quả phỉ
heart	*tim*	tim
herbal	*yur-erk tao*	dược thảo
herring	*ka trik*	cá trích
high chair	*nge kao chaw tre em*	ghế cao cho trẻ em
honey	*muht ohng*	mật ong
horseradish	*kay kai ngur-a*	cây cải ngựa

I

ice	*nur-erk da*	nước đá
ice cream	*ka rem*	cà rem
icing sugar	*kem dur-erng*	kem đường
ingredient	*tanh fun*	thành phần

J

jackfruit	*trai mit*	trái mít
jam	*murt*	mứt
jelly	*sur-erng sa; taik*	sương sa; thạch
juicer	*mong nur-erk*	mọng nước

K

kelp	*rong bien*	rong biển
kettle	*uhm nur-erk*	ấm nước
kidney	*tuhn*	thận
kitchen	*nya bep*	nhà bếp
kiwi	*(wua/kwua) kiwi*	quả kivi
knives	*(yao/zao) bahn*	dao bàn
knuckle	*kwiu chan/tay*	khuỷu chân/tay
kosher	*bur-a ahn kieng kwua (yo/zo) thai*	bữa ăn kiêng của Do Thái
kumquat	*kwua kwuat vang*	quả quất vàng

L

ladle	*tia kan yai*	thìa cán dài
lager	*bea nye*	bia nhẹ
lamb	*kur-u*	cừu
lard	*mer lern*	mỡ lợn
lavatory	*fong veh siny*	phòng vệ sinh
leeks	*ku kieu*	củ kiệu
leg	*chuhn*	chân
legumes	*kay ho dau*	cây họ đậu
lemon	*chany vang*	chanh vàng
lemon grass	*sa*	xả
lemonade	*nur-erk chany*	nước chanh
lentil	*dau lang*	đậu lăng
lime	*chany sany*	chanh xanh
liqueur	*rur-u many*	rượu mạnh
liquorice	*kam tao*	cam thảo
liver	*gan*	gan

lobster	*tom hum*	tôm hùm
loin	*tit tan*	thịt thăn
lollies	*keo*	kẹo
lotus root	*ku sen*	củ sen
lunch	*bur-a ahn trur-a*	bữa ăn trưa
lychee	*trai vai*	trái vải

M

macadamia	*hot dau ha wi yi*	hột đậu ha uy di
mace	*(wua/kwua) nyuk dau kau*	quả nhục đậu khấu
mackerel	*ka tu*	cá thu
madeira	*rur-u vang trang*	rượu vang trắng
main course	*mon ahn chiny*	món ăn chính
mango	*swo-ai*	xoài
manioc	*kwo-ai mi*	khoai mì
to marinate	*tum/ur-erp*	tẩm/ướp
marjoram	*kay kiny (yur-er-i/zur-er-i)*	cây kinh giới
market	*ler*	chợ
marmalade	*murt kwua ngien*	mứt quả nghiền
marrow	*twuy*	tủy
mayonnaise	*soht mayome*	sốt mayome
meal	*bur-a ahn*	bữa ăn
medium (cooked)	*vur-a, trung biny*	vừa, trung bình
melon	*(wua/kwua) (yur-a/zur-a)*	quả dưa
menu	*turk dern*	thực đơn
milk	*surh-a*	sữa
millet	*hoht ke*	hột kê
mince	*bahm/tai*	bằm/thái
mincer	*may say tit*	máy xay thịt
mineral water	*nur-erk su-oi*	nước suối
mint	*bark ha*	bạc hà
mixing bowl	*toh de trohn*	tô để trộn
mortar	*vur-a, hoh*	vữa, hồ
mung bean	*dau sany*	đậu xanh
mussel	*saw/hen*	sò/hến
mustard	*mu tak*	mù tạc
mutton	*tit kur-u (ya/za)*	thịt cừu già

N

neck	*fuhn co*	phần cổ
no smoking section	*ku kuhm hut thu-ohk*	khu cấm hút thuốc
noodles	*mi/bun*	mì/bún

nougat	*keo lark trung*	kẹo lạc trứng
nutcracker	*kep hat (yeh/zeh)*	kẹp hạt dẻ
nutmeg	*hoht nyuk dau kau*	hột nhục đậu khấu

O

oatmeal	*boht ngu kohk*	bột ngũ cốc
octopus	*baik tu-oht*	bạch tuột
offal	*boh long*	bộ lòng
oil	*(yau/zau)*	dầu
okra	*kay mur-erp tay*	cây mướp tây
olive oil	*(yau/zau) oh liu*	dầu ô liu
omelette	*trurng trahng*	trứng tráng
oregano	*bot za vi ee dai lur-er-i*	bột gia vị ý đại lợi
organic	*hur-u ker*	hữu cơ
oven	*law*	lò
oxtail	*du-oi baw*	đuôi bò
oyster	*saw*	sò

P

pancakes	*bany kep*	bánh kẹp
papaya	*du du*	đu đủ
paprika	*ert boht*	ớt bột
parasol	*oh/(yu/zu)*	ô/dù
to pare	*kat tia*	cắt tỉa
parsley	*kay mui tay*	cây mùi tây
passion fruit	*(wua/kwua) lark tien*	quả lạc tiên
pastry	*bany nur-erng*	bánh nướng
pea	*dau vur-ern tur-er-i*	đậu vườn tươi
peach	*(wua/kwua) dao*	quả đào
peanut	*dau fung*	đậu phụng
pears	*(wua/kwua) le*	quả lê
pecan	*kwua ho dao*	quả hồ đào
peeler	*kai bao*	cái bào
pepper (spice)	*tieu*	tiêu
pepper (vegetable)	*ert daw*	ớt đỏ
pepper mill	*doh say mu-oi tieu*	đồ xay muối tiêu
peppermint	*bark ha*	bạc hà
perch	*ka pecca*	cá pecca
persimmon	*trai hohng*	trái hồng
pestle	*(ya/za) vi koh*	gia vị khô
pickle	*rau kai nguhm (yuhm/zuhm)*	rau cải ngâm dấm
pickling onion	*ku hany hur-erng*	củ hành hương

English	Pronunciation	Vietnamese
picnic	*(yai/zai) tri va ahn ngu-ai trer-i*	giải trí và ăn ngoài trời
pigeon	*chim boh cau*	chim bồ câu
pineapple	*yur-a*	dứa
pinto bean	*dau dohm*	đậu đốm
pizza	*mon pee-za*	món pi-da
plain flour	*boht mi kohng men*	bột mì không men
plate	*yea*	đĩa
plum	*(wua/kwua) muhn*	quả mận
poach	*ko/rim*	kho/rim
pomegranate	*(wua/kwua) lur-u*	quả lựu
popcorn	*bahp rang*	bắp rang
poppy	*kay any tuk*	cây anh túc
pork	*tit heo*	thịt heo
pork (bbq)	*sa siu*	xá xíu
pork roll	*cha lwua*	chả lụa
pork sausages	*suk sik lern*	xúc xích lợn
port	*rur-u vang daw*	rượu vang đỏ
pot	*noh-i*	nồi
potato masher	*may ngien kwo-ai tay*	máy nghiền khoai tây
potatoes	*kwo-ai tay*	khoai tây
poultry	*(ya/za) kuhm*	gia cầm
prawn	*tohm to*	tôm to
prepared	*chuan bi san*	chuẩn bị sẵn
preservative	*(yung yik/zung zik) bao (wuan/kwuan)*	dung dịch bảo quản
pressure cooker	*noh-i ap swu-at*	nồi áp suất
prune	*mut muhn koh*	mứt mận khô
puffball	*nuhm trurng*	nấm trứng
pulses	*boht dau*	bột đậu
pumpkin	*(wua/kwua) bi daw*	quả bí đỏ

Q

| quail | *chim kut* | chim cút |
| quince | *kwua mohk hwoa* | quả mộc hoa |

R

rabbit	*to*	thỏ
radish	*kay ku kai daw*	cây củ cải đỏ
raisin	*nyoh ko*	nho khô
rare (cooked)	*long dao*	lòng đào

raspberry	(yau/zau) tim	dâu tím
ray	ka du-oi	cá đuối
receipt	(yay/zay) bien nyan	giấy biên nhận
red capsicum	ert daw	ớt đỏ
red kidney bean	dau daw	đậu đỏ
red onion	ku hany daw	củ hành đỏ
red pepper	ert daw	ớt đỏ
red wine	rur-u chat daw	rượu chát đỏ
reservation	dat choh trur-erk	đặt chỗ trước
restaurant	nya hang	nhà hàng
rhubarb	kay doi hu-ang	cây đôi hoàng
ribs	sur-erng	sườn
rice	gao	gạo
–paper	bany trang nem	bánh tráng nem
–(short-grain)	gao hoht tron nyo	gạo hột tròn nhỏ
–(wild)	gao rur-erng	gạo rừng
–vinegar	(yuhm/zuhm) gao	dấm gạo
–wrapper	bany trang nem	bánh tráng nem
ripe	chin mui	chín mùi
roast	(wuay/kwuay)	quay
rolling pin	chay lang boht	chày lăn bột
rosemary	la hur-erng tao	lá hương thảo
rump	fao kau	phao câu
runner bean	dau tuhn leo	đậu thân leo

S

saffron	mau vang ngeh	màu vàng nghệ
sage	kay soh term	cây xô thơm
sake	rur-u ngot sake	rượu ngọt sakê
salad	rau sa laik	rau xà lách
salad bowl	toh trohn sa laik	tô trộn xà lách
salt	mu-oi	muối
salt mill	doh say mu-oi tieu	đồ xay muối tiêu
salted pork	tit lern mu-oi	thịt lợn muối
sanddab (fish)	ka bern	cá bơn
sandwich	bany mi kep	bánh mì kẹp
sardine	ka trik	cá trích
sauce	nur-erk soht	nước xốt
saucepan	kai song	cái xoong
saucer	yea de kohk/taik	đĩa để cốc/tách
sauté	sao ap chao	xào áp chảo
savoury	hur-erng vi nohng	hương vị nồng
scales	chea murk doh	chia mực độ

scallions	*choi hany*	chồi hành
scallop	*kon so lo*	con sò lò
scissors	*kay keo*	cây kéo
seafood	*hai sahn*	hải sản
seaweed	*rong bien*	rong biển
semolina	*boht barng*	bột báng
serrated knife	*(yao/zao) rang kur-a*	dao răng cưa
service (at restaurant)	*fuk vu trong nya hang*	phục vụ trong nhà hàng
serviette	*kahn ahn (yay/zay)*	khăn ăn giấy
sesame oil	*(yau/zau) me*	dầu mè
sesame seed	*hoht me*	hột mè
shallot onion	*kay he tay*	cây hẹ tây
shallow-fry	*chien mong*	chiên mỏng
shandy	*bea fa chany*	bia pha chanh
shank	*sur-erng ong*	xương ống
sharpening stone	*da mai*	đá mài
shellfish	*hai sahn ko vo*	hải sản có vỏ
sherry	*rur-u vang tay bahn nya*	rượu vang tây ban nha
shiitake (mushroom)	*nuhm nyat bahn*	nấm Nhật Bản
short-grain rice	*gao hoht tron nyo*	gạo hột tròn nhỏ
shoulder	*ba vai*	bả vai
shrimp	*tohm*	tôm
shrimp paste	*mahm rwu-ohk*	mắm ruốc
sieve	*kai sang*	cái sàng
sifter	*kai ray*	cái rây
silverware	*boh (yao/zao) nea de ahn*	bộ dao nĩa để ăn
to simmer	*niny/nyo lur-a*	ninh/nhỏ lửa
sirloin	*tit than bo*	thịt thăn bò
skewer	*kai sien*	cái xiên
skimmed milk	*sur-a lwoai trur chat kem*	sữa loại trừ chất kem
skipper	*ka trik hung koi*	cá trích hung khói
smoked	*sohng koi*	xông khói
smoking section	*ku vurk hut thu-ohk*	khu vực hút thuốc
snacks	*mon ahn vat*	món ăn vặt
snap peas	*dau dwua ngan*	đậu đũa ngắn
snapper	*ka chi vang*	cá chỉ vàng
soda water	*nur-erk sohda*	nước sô đa
soft	*mem*	mềm
soft drink	*nur-erk ngot ko ga*	nước ngọt có ga
soup	*sup*	xúp

soup spoon	*mu-ong ahn sup*	muỗng ăn xúp
sour cream	*kem chwua*	kem chua
soy sauce	*si (yau/zau)*	xì dầu
soya bean	*dau nany*	đậu nành
–drink	*surh-a dau nany*	sữa đậu nành
–sauce	*nur-erk tur-erng*	nước tương
sparerib	*sur-erng sur-erng*	xương sườn
sparkling wine	*rur-u sui tum*	rượu xủi tăm
spinach	*rau (yen/zen)*	rau đền
spirits	*rur-u kohn*	rượu cồn
spoon	*tea*	thìa
spring onions	*choi hany*	chồi hành
squash	*kwua bi*	quả bí
squid	*kon murk*	con mực
star anise	*kay hoh-i*	cây hồi
star fruit	*trai ke*	trái khế
steak	*tit rahn*	thịt rán
steam	*huhp*	hấp
steamer	*noh-i huhp*	nồi hấp
steep	*nguhm*	ngâm
stew	*niny/hum*	ninh/hầm
stock	*(ya/za) suk nu-oi nyoht*	gia súc nuôi nhốt
stout	*bea den*	bia đen
straw mushroom	*num rerm*	nấm rơm
strawberry	*(wua/kwua) (yau/zau) tay*	quả dâu tây
string bean	*dau (wue/kwue)*	đậu que
sturgeon	*ka tum*	cá tầm
sugar	*dur-erng/mea*	đường/mía
sugar cane	*kuhy mea*	cây mía
sweet	*ngot*	ngọt
sweets	*keo*	kẹo
sweet basil	*hung kwue ngot*	húng quế ngọt
sweet potatoes	*kwo-ai lang*	khoai lang
syrup	*sea roh*	xia-rô

T

tablecloth	*kahn trai bahn*	khăn trải bàn
tamarind	*trai me*	trái me
tangerine	*(wua/kwua) (wit/kwit)*	quả quít
tap water	*nur-erk la*	nước lã
tapioca	*boht san*	bột sắn
taro	*kwoai mon*	khoai môn
tarragon	*kay ngai (yum/zum)*	cây ngải dấm

tartar	*kau rur-u*	cáu rượu
tea	*ṯra*	trà
tea spoon	*mu-ong ka fe*	muỗng cà phê
thyme	*kay hung ṯay*	cây húng tây
tip	*tiehn bohi bahn*	tiền bồi
toast	*bany mi nur-erng*	bánh mì nướng
to toast	*nuhng kok*	nâng cốc
toaster	*may nur-erng bany mi laṯ*	máy nướng bánh mì lát
tofu	*ṯau hu*	tàu hủ
toilet	*fong veh siny*	phòng vệ sinh
tomatoes	*ṯrai ka*	trái cà
tongs	*kai moh-i, (ya/za)*	cái môi , giá
tongue	*lur-er-i*	lượi
tonic water	*nur-erk kwoang quinin*	nước khoáng quinin
tray	*muhm*	mâm
tripe	*(ya yay/za zay)*	da dày
trout	*ka hoh-i*	cá hồi
tuna	*ka ngu*	cá ngừ
turkey	*ga ṯay*	gà tây
turmeric	*kay ngur*	cây nghệ
turnip	*kay ku kai*	cây củ cải

V

vanilla	*va-ni*	va-ni
veal	*tiṯ beh*	thịt bê
vegetable oil	*(yau/zau) tao mohk*	dầu thảo mộc
vegetables	*rau song*	rau sống
vegetarian	*ngur-er-i ahn chay*	người ăn chay
venison	*tiṯ nai ṯur-er-i*	thịt nai tươi
vermicelli	*bun/mien*	bún/miến
vinegar	*(yuhm/zuhm)*	dấm
vodka	*rur-u voṯ-ka*	rượu vốt ka

W

waffles	*bany (we/kwe)*	bánh quế
waiter	*ngur-er-i hau ban nam*	người hầu bàn nam
waitress	*ngur-er-i hau ban nur*	người hầu bàn nữ
walnut	*(wua/kwua) haik*	quả hạch
walnut	*ṯrai fi*	trái phi
water	*nur-erk*	nước
—distilled	*nur-erk kuṯ*	nước cất

–tap	*nur-erk la*	nước lã
–tonic	*nur-erk kwoang quinin*	nước khoáng quinin
water spinach	*rau mu-ong*	rau muống
watercress	*sa laik son*	sà lách son
watermelon	*yur-a hau*	dưa hấu
well done (cooked)	*nau tuht kee*	nấu thật kỹ
wet towel	*kahn tuhm ur-ert*	khăn tầm ướt
wheat	*lwua mi*	lúa mì
wheat germ	*lai hat lwua mi*	lai hạt lúa mì
where?	*duh-u?*	đâu
whipping cream	*kem dany*	kem đánh
whisk	*dany (trurng)*	đánh (trứng)
whisky	*rur-u uyt-ki*	rượu uýt ky
white poppy seed	*hoht any tuk*	hột anh túc
wholewheat	*hoht lwua mi*	hột lúa mì
wholewheat flour	*boht lwua mi*	bột lúa mì
wild boar	*heo rur-erng*	heo rừng
wild greens	*rau rur-erng*	rau rừng
wild rice	*gao rur-erng*	gạo rừng
wine	*rur-u*	rượu
wok	*chao sao*	chảo xào
wooden spatula	*bahn sen goh*	bàn xẻn gỗ

Y

yellow capsicum (sweet)	*ert vang*	ớt vàng
yellow pepper (sweet)	*ert vang*	ớt vàng
yoghurt	*sur-a chwua*	sữa chua

Z

zucchini	*bi sany*	bí xanh

Vietnamese Culinary Dictionary

The Vietnamese alphabet contains many letters not found in the English alphabet. These are listed in Vietnamese alphabetical order at the bottom of each page to help you find an entry. The tone marks are not included because they are not used in the alphabetical order. Sounds such as ch, ơ, qu, tr etc are seen as separate letters. This means that words beginning with kh for example appear between the alphabetical listings for k and l; for example, khô bò *koh baw* 'beef jerky' is listed after kiều mạch *kieu maik* 'buckwheat'.

Â

ấm nước *uhm nur-erk* kettle

B

bả vai *ba vai* shoulder

bạc hà *bark ha* mint/peppermint – the best is said to come from Lang village near Hanoi. Of the numerous Asian mint varieties, the round-leafed mint, a tropical variety of spearmint, is the one most commonly used by Vietnamese cooks. This fragrant herb is indispensable to Vietnamese cookery.

bạch tuột *baik tu-ot* octopus

bàn não *bahn nao* grater

bàn xẻn gỗ *bahn sen goh* wooden spatula

bánh *bany* cake; bun; pie pastry; (there are literally hundreds of varieties)

bánh bò *bany baw* foam/yeast cake

bánh cốm *bany kohm* frilled cake of fresh rice

bánh cúc-ki *bany kuk ki* cookies/ biscuits

bánh cuốn *bany ku-on* steamed rolls made of rice flour

bánh chay *bany chay* boiled dumplings

bánh chưng *bany churng* rice cake – boiled dumpling made of glutinous rice wrapped in bamboo leaves

bánh dày *bany (yay/zay)* a kind of rice cake

bánh đa *bany da* rice pancake/wafer

bánh giò *bany (yo/zo)* meat pie

bánh hấp *bany huhp* dumplings

bánh hỏi *bany hoi* rice vermicelli, extra-thin rice noodle variety used primarily as an accompaniment to grilled foods

banh Huế *bany hwu-eh* rice flour pudding stuffed with minced shrimp

bánh kẹp *bany kep* pancakes

bánh khoai *bany kwoai* sweet potato cake/crepe

bánh khọt *bany kọt* frilled pancake – small and round, made of rice flour and eaten with fish sauce

bánh mì *bany mi* bread

a ă â b c ch d đ e ê g gh gi h I k kh l m n

bánh mì kẹp *bany mi kep* sandwich

bánh mì nướng *bany mi nur-erng* toast

bánh mì thịt *bany mi tit* meat (pork, chicken) roll with vegetables

bánh nậm *bany nuhm* sweet cake

bánh ngô non *bany ngoh non* steamed bread made of corn flour

bánh ngọt *bany ngot* cakes

bánh nướng *bany nur-erng* pastry

bánh phở *bany fer* rice noodles

bánh phồng tôm *bany fohng tohm* shrimp chips – often called 'prawn crackers', these dried, reddish pink chips are made from ground shrimp, tapioca starch and egg whites. They're often eaten as a snack or as an accompaniment to salads.

bánh quế *bany (wue/kwue)* waffles

bánh trái cây *bany trai kuhy* fruit cake

bánh tráng *bany trahng* usually rendered in English as 'rice paper', this stuff is not very good for writing on. But it is very good for eating. We prefer to call it rice wrapper. It's a round, rather brittle sheet about eight inches across made from rice flour, salt and water. It's laid out on leaf mats to dry and adheres slightly to the mat, giving the rice wrapper a distinctive crosshatched design. Used as the outer wrapper for Vietnamese spring rolls.

bánh tráng nem *bany trahng nem* rice wrapper

bánh tro *bany tro* sweet cake made with the pits of Japanese lily fruit, water, lime and rice

bánh trứng đường *bany trurng dur-erng* meringue

bánh ú *bany u* a four-cornered rice dumpling

bánh ướt *bany ur-ert* rice noodle sheets usually cut up into thin strands for soups and stir-fries

bánh xèo *bany seo* turnover – country pancake eaten with vegetables and fish sauce

bánh xừng bò *bany surng bo* croissant

bào ngư *bau ngur* abalone

bát *baht* bowl

bằm *bahm* mince

bắp *bahp* corn

bắp cải tàu *bahp kai tau* chinese cabbage

bắp chuối *bahp chu-oi* banana blossom – looking like a big purple spearhead, sliced finely and soaked in cold water, it is used as garnish for noodle soup, and eaten raw in salads

bắp non *bahp non* baby corn

bắp rang *bahp rahng* popcorn

bí xanh *bi sany* courgette/zucchini

bia *bea* beer

bia đá *bea da* beer with ice

bia đen *bea den* stout

bia hơi *bea her-i* 'fresh beer', draught beer. This refreshing, light-bodied Pilsner was first introduced in

Vietnam by the Czechs. Decades later it's still brewed and delivered daily to drinking establishments throughout Saigon and Hanoi and points between. Brewed without preservatives, it is meant to be enjoyed immediately.

bia nhẹ *bea nye* lager

bia pha chanh *bea fa chany* shandy

bò lá lót *bo la lot* beef in wild betel leaves

bot gao *boht gao* rice flour – flour made from long-grain rice. Different from glutinous rice flour, which is made from sweet rice. Rice flour is the basis for many rice noodle dishes and sweets.

bộ dao nĩa *boh (yao/zau) nea* cutlery

bộ dao nĩa để ăn *boh (yao/zau) nea deh ahm* silverware

bộ lòng *boh long* offal

bội hương *boh-i hur-erng* star anise – dried pod of a tree of the Magnoliaceaes family, native to China. Mainly grown in north Vietnam, this bark-like spice has cloves that resemble an eight-pointed star. Not related to aniseed, it yields a strong licorice flavour and is used to enhance soups and stews. When chewed, it sweetens the breath and aids digestion.

bông cải xanh *bohng kai xany* broccoli

bột *boht* flour

bột báng *boht bahng* tapioca pearls – teardrop size balls made from the starch of the cassava root. Used as an ingredient in certain soups and sweet puddings to thicken and add texture.

bột bắp hột *boht bahp hoht* corn meal

bột cà ri *boht ka ri* curry powder

bột đậu *boht dau* pulses

bột gia vị ý đại lợi *boht (ya/za) vi ee dai ler-i* oregano

bột hạnh nhân *boht hany nyan* marzipan

bột khoai *boht kwoai* potato starch, used as a binder for meatballs and other dishes

bột lúa mì *boht lwua mi* wholewheat flour

bột mì không men *boht mi kohng men* plain flour

bột mì trứng *boht mi trurng* batter

bột năng *boht nahng* tapioca starch/flour from the cassava root. It gives a translucent sheen and chewiness to fresh rice wrappers.

bột nếp *boht nehp* glutinous or sweet rice flour, used to make sweet confections

bột nghệ *boht ngeh* turmeric – ground powder of a rhizome of the ginger family. Deep yellow in colour, this spice is often used as a dye.

bột ngũ cốc *boht ngu kohk* oatmeal

bột ớt đỏ *boht ert do* cayenne/ paprika

bột sắn *boht sahn* tapioca

bơ *ber* butter/margarine

ng nh o ô ơ p ph qu r s t th tr u ư v x y

bơ lỏng *ber long* ghee

bùi ngót *bui ngot* a type of leaf used for cooking soup

bún *bun* rice vermicelli, the thin variety is dried in 25cm lengths. Used in soups and noodle salads and often served cold at the table as an accompaniment to grilled or curried dishes.

bún ốc (khô) *bun ohk (koh)* rice noodles with cooked snail meat

buổi ăn sáng *bu-oi ahn sahng* breakfast

buổi ăn tối *bu-oi ahn toh-i* dinner

búp nấm *bup nuhm* button

bữa ăn *bur-a ahn* meal

bữa ăn trưa *bur-a ahn trur-a* lunch

bưởi *bur-er-i* pomelo, like a large grapefruit, pomelos (sometimes called pamplemousse) have thick skins and pith, and yield a sweeter, less acidic fruit than ordinary grapefruit. The coast of Central Vietnam produces the most prized varieties between August and November. They are often sold on the street and in train stations as a popular snack. They are often eaten with salt.

C

cá *ka* fish

cá bơn *ka bern* flounder/sanddab

cá bơn lưỡi ngựa *ka bern lur-er-i ngur-a* halibut

cá chỉ vàng *ka chi vahng* snapper

cá đuối *ka du-oi* ray

cá hồi *ka hoh-i* trout

cá lóc *ka lok* fresh water fish (carp)

cá moruy *ka moruy* cod

cá nướng lá chuối *ka nur-erng la chu-oi* fish grilled in banana leaf

cá ngừ *ka ngur* tuna

cá pecca *ka pecca* bass/perch

cà phê *ka feh* coffee

cà phê đã loại trừ cà phê tính *ka feh da lwai trur ka feh tiny* decaffeinated coffee

cà phê sữa đá *ka feh shur-a da* ice coffee

cá quả *ka (wua/kwua)* rock fish

cá quả hấp với bia rau gia vi *ka (wua/kwua) huhp ver-i bea rau (ya/za) vi* rock fish steamed in beer and seasoning

cà rem *ka rem* ice cream

cà ri *ka ri* curry paste – more pungent and spicier than curry powder, it's often combined with ordinary curry powder to strike a balance between the two

cá tầm *ka tuhm* sturgeon

cà tím *ka tim* aubergine/eggplant – also known as Chinese eggplant, this long, thin purple variety has a sweet flavour with little bitterness

cá tuyết êfin *ka twu-et eh-fin* haddock

cá tuyết meluc *ka twu-et meluk* hake

cá thu *ka tu* mackerel

cá trích *ka trik* herring/sardine

cá trồng *ka trohng* anchovy

cá trích hung khói *ka trik hung koi* skipper (fish)

cá và khoai tây nghiền rán *ka va kwoai tuhy ngien rahn* croquette

cái bào *kai bao* peeler

cải bắp *kai bahp* cabbage

cải bẹ trắng *kai be trahng* bok choy

cái rây *kai ruhy* sifter

cái sàng *kai sahng* sieve

cải tàu *kai tau* mustard greens – these have a sharp flavour, adding a nice clean taste when combined with other ingredients. They look a bit like head lettuce in size and shape but differ in that the leaves wrapping the heart are thick stalks. Parboiled, the stalks become tender and succulent and the assertive flavour mellows.

cái tộ *kai toh* clay pot

cải xanh *kai sany* cabbage – characterised by small yellow flowers when in bloom, firm, small stalks and crisp leaves, they are regarded as the best of Chinese cabbages and are much prized by Vietnamese cooks. The taste is mild and the texture tender but crisp.

cái xiên *kai siehn* skewer

cái xoong *kai song* saucepan

cám *kahm* bran

cam thảo *kahm tao* liquorice

canh chua cá *kany chua ka* hot and sour fish soup

cánh gà chiên *kany ga chien* fried chicken wing

cáu rượu *kau rur-u* tartar

cắt tỉa *kaht tea* to pare

cây anh túc *kuhy any tuk* poppy

cần *kan* a straw made from long and slender bamboo; also an alcoholic drink (*see* rượu cần)

cây bạch đậu khấu *kuhy baik duh-u kuh-u* cardamom

cây bạch hoa *kuhy baik hoa* capers

cây bách xù *kuhy baik su* juniper

cây cải ngựa *kuhy kai ngur-a* horseradish

cây củ cải *kuhy ku kai* turnip

cây củ cải đỏ *kuhy ku kai daw* radish

cây dâu tằm *kuhy (yuh-u/zuh-u) tahm* mulberry

cây họ đậu *kuhy haw duh-u* legumes

cây hẹ tây *kuhy he tuhy* shallot onion

cây hồi *kuhy hoh-i* star anise (*see* bội hương)

cây húng tây *kuhy hung tay* thyme

cây kéo *kuhy keo* scissors

cây kinh giới *kuhy kiny (yer-i/zer-i)* marjoram

cây mùi tây *kuhy mui tuhy* parsley

cây mướp tây *kuhy mur-erp tuhy* okra

cây ngải dấm *kuhy ngai (duhm/zuhm)* tarragon

cây nghệ *kuhy ngeh* turmeric

cây phòng phong *kuhy fong fong* parsnip

cây rau diếp *kuhy rau (yiep/ziep)* chicory

cây rau mùi *kuhy rau mui* coriander/cilantro

cây thì là *kuhy ti la* fennel

cây trầu không *kuhy truh-u kohng* betel

cây xô thơm *kuhy soh term* sage

CH ...

Words beginning with **ch** appear under a separate listing after all 'c' words (see next page).

con mực *kon murk* squid

con sò lò *kon saw law* scallop

con trai *kon trai* clam

cốc *kohk* cup

cơm *kerm* rice; also a restaurant

cơm chiên *kerm chien* fried rice

cơm hương giang *kerm hur-erng (yahng/zahng)* Hué Rice with vegetables

củ cà rốt *ku ka roht* carrot

củ cải đỏ *ku kai daw* beetroot

củ cải trắng *ku kai trahng* daikon – also known as Oriental white radish, a root that looks like a large white carrot. The flesh is crisp, juicy and mildly pungent and lends itself well to soups and stews. Also enjoyed raw in salads or pickled.

củ đậu *ku duh-u* jicama – brown-skinned root vegetable tasting like a turnip. It must be peeled and may be eaten raw in salads or cooked.

củ hành đỏ *ku hany daw* red onion

củ hành hương *ku hany hur-erng* pickling onion

củ kiệu *ku kieu* leeks

củ kiệu chua *ku kieu chua* pickled shallots – these are the very young, tender bulbs of spring onions (scallions), packed in vinegar, sugar and salt. They're used as a condiment to accompany grilled foods and noodle dishes or added as seasoning to sweet-and-sour dishes.

củ sen *ku sen* lotus root

cua *kua* crab

cừu *kur-u* lamb

CH

chả cá *cha ka* fish paste; also fried fish

chả cá lã vọng *cha ka la vong* fried fish dish where the fried fish is cooked with noodles and spring onions (scallions) in a charcoal brazier.

chả giò *cha (yaw/zaw)* spring rolls – often seen as the national dish of Vietnam. When we think of Vietnamese food they tend to be the first thing that comes to mind, and they do serve to set the Vietnamese apart from the Chinese, by their use of rice wrappings instead of wheat, and their different fillings. They're a tasty tidbit when wrapped in a lettuce leaf with a sprig of cilantro/coriander and dipped in **nước chấm**.

chả lụa *cha lua* pork roll

chanh vàng *chany vahng* lemon

chanh xanh *chany sany* lime

cháo *chao* congee

chảo chiên *chao chien* frying pan

chạo tôm *chao tohm* minced shrimp wrapped around sugar cane

chảo xào *chao sao* wok

chay *chay* vegetarian

chày lăn bột *chay lahn boht* rolling pin

chân *chuhn* leg

chè *che* dessert; a sweet snack, made of green mung beans. **Chè** shops are found everywhere on Hanoi streets and markets. Hanoians love to snack and so there is a kind of **chè** for every occasion and type of weather, each with different ingredients and appearance. The most popular type is a thick liquid with the consistency of custard or pudding and must be eaten with a spoon. Another type is dry and can be eaten by hand. The dry type is made simply of sticky rice or green mung beans and sugar while the pudding type is more complex. (See the **chè** section in the **Staples** chapter)

chè bal *che bal* type of pudding

chè bánh trôi *che bany troh-i* a sweet pudding with large and small round balls eaten with sweet sauce. The large balls are stuffed with sweet cooked green beans.

chè bánh trôi tàu *che bany troh-I tau* hot 'Chinese' **chè** taken on cold winter days

chè thái *che tai* Thai pudding

chè trôi nước *che troh-i nur-erk* sweet pudding (see **chè bánh trôi**)

chén *chen* bowl

chia mực độ *chea murk doh* weighing scales

chiên *chien* fry

chiên giòn *chien (yon/zon)* deep-fry

chiên mỏng *chien mong* shallow-fry

chim bồ câu *chim boh cu-hu* pigeon

chim cút *chim kut* quail

chín mùi *chin mui* ripe

chín vàng *chin vang* burnet

chồi hành *choh-i hany* spring onions; scallions

chôm chôm *chohm chohm* rambutan – fiery red and hairy skin give this fruit the look of tiny suns. Distantly related to lychees, they have a tender white flesh with a cool sweet flavour. Look for them during the rainy season (May-October).

chợ *ler* market

chuẩn bị sẵn *chu-uhn bi sahn* prepared

chuối *chu-oi* banana

D

dạ dày *(ya yay/za zay)* tripe

dao bàn *(yao/zao) bahn* knives

dao răng cưa *(yao/zao) rahng kur-a* serrated knife

dấm *(yuhm/zuhm)* vinegar

dấm gạo *(yuhm/zuhm) gao* rice vinegar

dấm lúa mõch *(yuhm/zuhm)* lua maik malt vinegar

dấm rượu *(yuhm/zuhm)* rur-u wine vinegar

dấm táo *(yuhm/zuhm)* ṯao cider vinegar

dầu *(yu-hu/zu-hu)* berries

dầu *(yu-hu/zu-hu)* oil

dầu hào *(yu-hu/zu-hu)* hao oyster sauce – thick sauce made from oysters, water, salt, cornstarch and caramel colouring, used primarily for stir-frying vegetables

dầu mè *(yuh-u/zuh-u)* me sesame oil – rich-flavoured, amber-coloured oil obtained from pressed roasted sesame seeds. A dash or two is added to marinades or at the last moment of cooking to flavour certain dishes.

dầu mỡ *(yu-hu/zu-hu)* mer grease

dầu rừng đỏ *(yu-hu/zu-hu)* rurng daw dewberry

dầu tím *(yu-hu/zu-hu)* ṯim raspberry

dầu thảo mộc *(yu-hu/zu-hu)* ṯao mohk vegetable oil

đĩa *(yea/ zea)* plate

đĩa để cốc *(yea/zea)* deh kohk saucer

đĩa để tách *(yea/zea)* deh ṯaik saucer

đôi tiết *(yoh-i/zoh-i)* ṯiet blood pudding

dung dịch bảo quản *(yung/zung)* *(yik/zik)* bao *(wu-ahn/kwu-ahn)* preservative

dứa *(yur-a/zur-a)* pineapple – grown chiefly in the Mekong delta region. Some are very good, others are rather dry but you can improve on them by using the little packet of salt and red pepper that is usually sold with cut pineapple. The juice is sometimes made into a perfumy liquor, or mixed with egg yolk to produce a high calorie beverage.

dừa *(yur-a/zur-a)* coconut

dưa chuột *(yur-a/zur-a)* chu-ọt cucumber

dưa chuột xanh *(yur-a/zur-a)* chu-ọt sany gherkin

dưa đỏ *(yur-a/zur-a)* daw cantaloupe

dưa hấu *(yur-a/zur-a)* huh-u watermelon

dưa leo *(yur-a/zur-a)* leo cucumber

dưa xanh *(yur-a/zur-a)* xany chayote – pear-shaped fruit usually used as a vegetable

dược thảo *(yur-erk/zur-erk)* ṯao herbal

Đ

đá mài *da mai* sharpening stone

đánh (trứng) *dany (ṯrurng)* whisk

đặt chỗ trước *daht choh ṯrur-erk* reservation

đậu ba tây *duh-u ba ṯuh-y* brazil nut

đầu bếp *duh-u behp* chef

đậu đen *duh-u den* black bean

đậu đỏ *duh-u daw* red kidney bean

đậu đỏ Nhật Bản *duh-u daw nyạt bahn* adzuki bean

đậu đốm *duh-u dohm* pinto bean

đậu đũa *duh-u dwua* long beans, 'chopstick beans' – immature pods of dry black-eyed peas. Just like the name says, long beans can measure over half a metre in length.

đậu đũa ngắn *duh-u dua ngahn* snap peas

đậu hòa lan xanh *duh-u hwua lahn sany* green split pea

đậu hu *duh-u hu* bean curd; tofu – sometimes called the poor man's meat. The pressed bean curd of the soy bean has all the essential amino acids, is low in calories and is devoid of cholesterol. It's bland but goes well with other ingredients, giving them no competition for you attention. It can be deep-fried, sautéed, steamed, baked, simmered, broiled or stuffed. It comes in three textures: the soft variety is added to soups or steamed dishes where cooking time is brief, the semisoft variety is used in stir-fries, and the firm variety is ideal for stuffing and deep-frying.

đậu lăng *duh-u lahng* lentil

đậu nành *duh-u nany* soya bean – used in the production of bean curd (tofu), they're the main ingredient in preparing soybean milk and a multitude of sauces and condiments

đậu nhãn đen *duh-u nyan den* black-eyed bean

đậu phọng *duh-u fong* peanuts – an important ingredient in Vietnamese cooking. Raw peanuts are preferred because they are usually roasted and ground just before serving to release their intense nutty flavour. Peeled raw peanuts are sold in Asian markets. They're used for texture and flavour in dipping sauces and as garnish for cooked food.

đậu phụ *duh-u fu* bean curd; tofu (see **đậu hu**)

đậu que *duh-u (we/kwe)* string bean

đậu tầm *duh-u tahm* broad bean

đậu tây *duh-u tuh-y* haricot bean

đậu thân leo *duh-u tahn leo* runner bean

đậu trắng *duh-u trang* butter bean

đậu ván *duh-u vahn* lentil

đậu vườn tươi *duh-u vur-ern tur-oi* fresh garden pea

đậu xanh *duh-u sany* mung beans. Dried green mung beans with the green skin removed are known as yellow beans. Usually soaked in water, they have a subtle flavour and a slight crunch. Yellow beans are used to make dipping sauces (yellow bean sauce) or other sauces to accompany vegetables and the starch from the beans is processed into cellophane noodles. Watered green mung beans develop into bean sprouts (see **giá**).

đinh hương *diny hur-erng* clove

đồ bóc vỏ tỏi *doh bohk vaw toi* garlic press

đồ gia vị *doh (ya/za)vi* condiments

đồ khui chai *doh kui chai* bottle opener

đồ khui hộp *doh kui hohp* can opener

đồ xay muối tiêu *doh say mu-oi tieu* salt and pepper mills

đu đủ *du du* papaya – high in vitamins A and C, the large, gourd-like fruit has a refreshing and sweet orange to red flesh, often taken with a squeeze of lime juice to bring out its subtleties. There are 45 species of papaya.

đũa *dwua* chopsticks

đùi lợn muối *dui lern mu-oi* ham

đun sôi *dun soh-i* boil

đuôi bò *du-oi baw* oxtail

đường *dur-erng* sugar

đường phèn *dur-erng fen* rock sugar – used to season Vietnamese sausages and meatballs. It's made from white sugar, brown sugar and honey, and is much sweeter than regular sugar.

đường thắng màu *dur-erng tahng mau* caramel

đường thẻ *dur-erng te* palm sugar – type of sugar made by boiling down the sap of various palm trees. It's used as a sweetener and also to help balance saltiness in savoury dishes.

Ê

ếch *eik* frog

G

gà *ga* chicken

gà chiên *ga chien* fried chicken

gà lôi *ga loh-i* pheasant

gà rút xương *ga rut sur-erng* boneless chicken cut in chunks

gà tây *ga tuh-y* turkey

gan *gan* liver

gạo *gao* rice

gạo hột dài đông nam á *gao hoht (dai/zai) dohng* basmati rice

gạo hột tròn nhỏ *gao hoht tron nyaw nam a* short-grain rice

gạo lực *gao lurk* brown rice

gạo nếp *gao nehp* glutinous rice – also called 'sweet rice', or 'sticky rice', there are two types of glutinous rice: the Chinese and Japanese short-grained type and the longer-grained Thai variety, which Vietnamese prefer. It has a soft, sticky texture and a slightly sweet flavour when cooked. Stuffed with mung bean paste or other savouries it is the basis of a variety of rice cakes.

gạo rừng *gao rurng* wild rice

gừng *gurng* ginger – not as common in Vietnamese dishes as Chinese, but still an important spice for both its medicinal properties and taste. It's commonly added to fish, seafood and offal. It not only adds to the flavour of food, it can also mask or remove objectionable odours.

GH

ghế cao cho trẻ em *geh kao chaw tre em* high chair for kids

GI

giá *(ya/za)* bean sprouts – mung bean sprouts, the most widely available variety, are found every-where in Vietnam. They are prized for the crunchy texture, their main characteristic. They can be eaten raw, added to soups or stir-fried.

gia cầm *(ya/za) kuhm* poultry

gia súc nuôi nhốt *suk nu-oi nyoht* stock

gia vị khô *vi koh* pestle

gia vị nấu súp Hy Lạp *vi nuh-u sup hy lạp* fenugreek

gia vị ớt khô *vi ert koh* allspice

giải trí và ăn ngoài trờ *(yai/zai) tri va ahn ngu-ai trer-i* picnic

giằm dấm *(yuhm yahum/zuhm zuhm)* pickled

giấm gạo *zuhm/yuhm gao* rice vinegar

giấy biên nhận *(yuh-y/zuh-y) bien nyuhn* receipt

giò *(yaw/zaw)* galangal

H

hải sản *hai sahn* seafood

hải sản có vỏ *hai sahn kaw vaw* shellfish

hạnh nhân *hany nyuhn* almond

hạt sen *haht sen* lotus seeds – resem-ble large, round peanuts. In Vietnam, where very fresh, young lotus seeds are available, they are eaten raw or used in stews, soups (especially in vegetarian cooking) and also sweet confections.

hầm *huhm* stew

hấp *huhp* steam

heo rừng *heo rurng* wild boar

hến *hehn* mussel

hóa đơn *hwua dern* bill/check

hoa huệ *hwua he* chives – thin, stiff flowering stems from Chinese chives, with a single, conical bulb at the tip of each stem. Sold fresh by the bunch, the stalks are tender and taste mildly of garlic.

hoisin *hoi sin* hoisin sauce is a sweet, piquant brown paste made from soybeans, red beans, sugar, garlic, vinegar, chilli, sesame oil and flour. Vietnamese cooks often mix it with broth, fresh chilli pepper and ground peanuts to make a dip. It's also used as a barbecue sauce for meat and poultry.

hồ *hoh* mortar

hồi hương *hoh-i hur-erng* star anise *(see* **bội hương***)*

hột anh túc *hoht any tuk* white poppy seed

hột cần *hoht kuhn* celery seed

hột carum *hoht ka-rum* caraway seed

hột dẻ *hoht (ye/ze)* chestnut

hột đậu hạ uy di *hoht duh-u ha wi (yi/zi)* macadamia

hột điều *hoht dieu* cashew

hột điều đỏ *hoht dieu daw* annatto seeds – seed of the 'lipstick plant' commonly used as food colouring. The seeds are fried in oil to extract the orange colour, then discarded.

hột kê *hoht keh* millet

hột lúa mì *hoht lwua mi* wholewheat

hột mè *hoht me* sesame seed

hột nhục đậu khấu *hoht nyuk duh-u kuh-u* nutmeg

hột thì là *hoht ti la* fennel seed

hột vịt lộn *hoht vit lohn* boiled embryonic duck egg

húng quế ngọt *hunh (we/kweh) ngot* sweet basil

hương-liệu *hur-erng lieu* five-spice powder – this fragrant reddish brown powder, a blend of ground star anise, fennel or anise seed, clove, cinnamon and Sichuan peppercorns, is used to flavour barbecued meats and stews

hương vị nồng *hur-erng vi nohng* savoury

hữu cơ *hur-u ker* organic

K

kem *kem* cream

kem chua *kem chua* sour cream

kem đánh *kem dany* whipping cream

kem đặc *kem dahk* clotted cream

kem đường *kem dur-erng* icing sugar

kẹo *keo* candy/sweets/lollies

kẹo bơ cứng *keo ber kurng* butterscotch

kẹo lạc trứng *keo lahk trurng* nougat

kẹp hạt dẻ *kep haht (ye/ze)* nutcracker

kiều mạch *kieu maik* buckwheat

kim châm *kim chuhm* lily – the buds of a special type of the Hemerocallis-fulva lily. Also called 'golden needles', the golden dried buds are often added to stir-fries, soups and vegetarian dishes.

KH

khay *kay* tray/salver

khăn ăn giấy *kahn ahn (yuh-y/zuh-y)* serviette/napkin

khăn tắm ướt *kahn tuhm ur-ert* wet towel

khăn trải bàn *kahn trai bahn* tablecloth

khế *ke* star fruit – has a smooth and shiny skin with a pod-like shape. It can be yellow, orange or green and cut into cross sections its star shape is revealed. It's intensely juicy and biting into one can cause droplets to fly.

kho *kaw* poach

khoai lang *kwoai lahng* sweet potatoes

khoai mì *kwoai mi* manioc/cassava – large tuber

khoai môn *kwõai mohn* taro root – oval-shaped tuber with brown, hairy skin and encircling rings. It tastes a bit like a potato and the flesh can be white to creamy, sometimes speckled purple. Vietnamese cooks use it the same way you would potato or sweet potato, often adding previously steamed chunks to a stew or sweet pudding.

khoai rán lát mỏng *kwoai rahn laht mong* chips

khoai tây *kwoai tuh-y* potatoes

khô bò *koh baw* beef jerky

khổ qua *koh (wua/kwua)* bitter melon – hard gourd, thought to have healthful benefits, it looks like a fat, knobby cucumber and is often pickled. Green and firm, it has a very crisp texture and a strong, bitter taste. Before cooking, the seeds and inner membrane are removed and the outer pod is sliced into small, crescent-shaped pieces and fried or added to soups. It's also hollowed out, stuffed with minced pork and braised.

khu cấm hút thuốc *ku kuhm huṭ tu-ohk* no smoking section

khu vực hút thuốc *ku vurk huṭ tu-ohk* smoking section

khuỷu chân giò *kwu-uy chuhn (yaw/zaw)* knuckle

L

lá chuối *la chu-oi* banana leaves, used to wrap foods either for steaming or carrying, but the leaf is not eaten. They preserve moisture, and impart a light green colour, but no flavour.

lá gai *la gai* pinnate leaf

lá hạt lúa mì *la hahṭ lwua mi* wheat germ

lá lốt *la lohṭ* betel leaves – peppery leaf of a vine related to piper nigrum, which yields black pepper. The large, round, crinkled leaf is used as a leafy green in soups, as an outer wrapping for spring rolls and as part of the standard garnish.

lá nguyệt quế *la ngu-eḥṭ (wu-eh/ku-weh)* bay (leaf)

lá thơm mùi hành *la term mui hany* chive

lát thịt *lahṭ tiṭ* cutlets

lạp xưởng *lahp sur-erng* cutlets

lẩu *luh-u* hot pot

lẩu dê *luh-u (yeh/zeh)* lamb/goat hot pot

lẩu lươn *luh-u lur-ern* eel hot pot

lẩu thập cẩm *luh-u tuhp kuhm* 10-items hot pot

lò *law* oven

lò nướng *law nur-erng* grill

lòng *long* giblets

lòng đào *long dao* rare (cooked)

lòng đỏ *long daw* egg yolk

lòng trắng trứng *long ṭrahng ṭrurng* egg white

lúa mạch *lwua maik* barley

lúa mạch xay *lwua maik say* cracked wheat

lúa mì *lwua mi* wheat

lươn *lur-ern* eel

lưỡi *lur-er-i* tongue

ly *li* cup

M

măng cầu *mahng kuh-u* custard apple – a smaller version of the durian (see **sầu riêng**), this is apple-sized with a bumpy green skin that blackens as it ripens. It's full of black pips that get in the way of its enjoyment, but persevere for its sweet peach custard taste and texture.

màu vàng nghệ *mau vang ngeh* saffron

máy chế biến thực phẩm *may cheh bien turk fuhm* food processor

máy nướng bánh mì lát *may nur-erng bany mi laht* toaster

máy nghiền *may gien* blender

máy pha lọc cà phê *may fa lok ka feh* coffee filter/maker

máy xay cà phê *may say ka feh* coffee grinder

máy xay thịt *may say tit* mincer

mắm nêm *muhm nehm* anchovy sauce – blend of fermented anchovies and salt

mắm ruốc *mahm rwu-ohk* shrimp sauce – very pungent product made from pounded, salted and fermented shrimp. It's commonly used to flavour soups, salads, dipping sauces, fried rice and dishes containing pork or beef.

măng *mahng* bamboo shoots – fresh, pickled or dried (the most delicious), bamboo shoots are popular in Vietnam. Fresh shoots, which have a savoury sweetness and crunch, are peeled and boiled for about 30 minutes before using. Dried shoots are soaked and boiled.

măng cụt *mahng kut* mangosteen – looking like a dull purple peach the mangosteen seems pretty ho-hum. But inside is a transparent white flesh with a delicious sour-sweet flavour. In the balance of yin and yang, it is the complement of durian (*see* **sầu riêng**).

măng tây *mahng tuh-y* asparagus

mâm *muhm* tray

mật ong *muht ohng* honey

me *me* tamarind – originally thought to be from India, these brown seedpods resembling vanilla beans contain a tart mushy flesh. Their high acidic content make them useful as a flavouring agent in savoury dishes and desserts.

mè *me* sesame seeds – used both hulled and unhulled. A common ingredient in Vietnam, they are toasted and crushed and used to flavour dipping sauces and marinades or to coat sweets and other foods.

men *men* yeast – normally sold in pharmacies, it's a dry yeast used in making rice wine. Small round, greyish balls are usually sold in pairs.

mềm *mehm* soft

mì *mi* noodles

mì gõ *mi gaw* mobile noodle stall; also noodle knocker

mía *mea* cane sugar – used raw, brown and refined, sugar is an essential element of Vietnamese cookery, especially in the south. It's cultivated widely as a food crop and as a source of sugar. The pressed juice from the cane is served as a soft drink in the summer, and people enjoy simply chewing the cane and spitting it out.

miến *mien* vermicelli

mít *mit* jackfruit – giant pear-shaped fruit containing chewy yellow segments. The wood of the tree is often used for sacramental carvings.

món ăn chính *mon ahn chiny* main course

món ăn vặt *mon ahn vaht* snacks

món đầu bữa *mon duh-u bur-a* entree

món đầu tiên *mon duh-u tien* first course

món khai vị *mon kai vi* appetiser

món tráng miệng *mon trahng miehng* dessert

mọng nước *mong nur-erk* juicer

mỡ lợn *mer lern* lard

mù tạc *mu tahk* mustard

mùi vị *mui vi* flavour

muối *mu-oi* salt

muối diêm *mu-oi (yiehm/ziehm)* baking soda

muỗng ăn tráng miệng *mu-ong ahn trahng miehng* dessert spoon

muỗng ăn xúp *mu-ong ahn sup* soup spoon

muỗng cà phê *mu-ong ka feh* tea spoon

mực khô *murk koh* dried squid

mướp *mur-erp* flavour

mướp đắng *mur-erp dahng* bitter melon

mứt *murt* flavour

mứt *murt* jam; also sugared dried fruits and vegetables

mứt mận khô *murt muhn koh* prune

mứt quả nghiền *murt (wua/kwua) ngien* marmalade

N

nấm *nahm* mushrooms

nấm hương *nahm hur-erng* Chinese black mushrooms – expensive but popular for their distinctive flavour, fragrance and texture, they have thick caps and are light brown with prominent white cracks on their surface.

nấm mèo *nahm meo* tree ear mushrooms – also called cloud ears or wood ears. Named for their convoluted shape, reminiscent of a human ear. Their texture is somewhat jelly-like and translucent, yet crisp. They are mainly used to add texture to stir-fries and stuffing.

nấm rơm *nahm rerm* straw mushrooms – pretty little umbrella-shaped caps with a yellowish brown colour

nấm nhật bản *nuhm nyuht bahn* shiitake

nấm trứng *nuhm trurng* puffball

nâng cốc *nuhng kohk* toast

nấu chín vàng *nahm chin vang* to brown

nấu thật kỹ *nuh-u tuht ki* well done (cooked)

nem *nem* pork sausage

nem nướng *nem nur-erng* grilled meatballs usually eaten with rice noodles and fish sauce

nem rán *nem rahn* spring rolls (north Vietnam); (see **chả giò**)

nem sài gòn *nem sai gon* spring rolls (see **chả giò**)

ng nh o ô ơ p ph qu r s t th tr u ư v x y

nĩa *nea* fork

ninh *niny* stew

ninh nhỏ lửa *niny nyaw lur-a* simmer

nồi *noh-i* pot

nồi áp suất *noh-i ahp swu-aht* pressure cooker

nồi hấp *noh-i huhp* steamer

nước *nur-erk* water

nước cất *nur-erk kuht* distilled water

nước chấm *nur-erk chuhm* dipping sauce for spring rolls – the main ingredients being chilli, garlic, carrot and fish sauce

nước chanh *nur-erk chany* lemonade

nước dừa *nur-erk (yur-a/zur-a)* coconut milk – the main ingredient in curries and sweets. The milky liquid squeezed from grated and heated coconut meat. The clear juice inside the shell is called coconut water, mainly used as a drink or as a meat tenderiser.

nước đá *nur-erk da* ice

nước hoa *nur-erk hwua* flower waters/essences – in Vietnam, flower waters and essences are popular for flavouring sweet drinks and desserts. They're produced by distilling the fresh petals of flowers, the most popular being jasmine, grapefruit and orange-blossom.

nước lã *nur-erk la* tap water

nước màu *nur-erk mau* brown sauce

nước mắm *nur-erk mahm* fish sauce – the one ingredient that is quintessentially Vietnamese, it's different from fish sauces made in other countries and lends a distinct character to Vietnamese cooking. The simplest way to describe it is as the liquid drained from salted, fermented fish. Its uses are many and it is used in virtually every dish in much the same way that soy sauce is used in Chinese food. Very often used as a dipping sauce, it takes the place of salt.

nước ngọt có ga *nur-erk ngot kaw ga* soft drink

nước sô đa *nur-erk soh da* soda water

nước suối *nur-erk su-oi* bottled water

nước tương *nur-erk tur-erng* soy sauce – traditional light brown sauce prepared from a naturally fermented soybean product in which the ground beans are mixed with water, roasted rice powder and salt

nước trái cây *nur-erk trai kuh-y* fruit juice

nước xốt *nur-erk soht* sauce

nước xúyt *nur-erk xwit* broth

nước chấm *nur-erk chuhm* sauce

nướng (bánh) *nur-erng (bany)* to bake

nướng (thịt) *nur-erng (tit)* barbecue

NG

ngâm *nguhm* steep

ngò *ngaw* coriander/cilantro – Vietnamese cookery, as we know it, would not exist without this herb, also known as Chinese parsley. This leafy green herb, resembling watercress, is highly scented, with a clean, refreshing taste.

ngọt *ngọt* sweet

ngô *ngoh* corn

ngỗng *ngohng* goose

ngũ cốc *ngu kohk* cereal

ngũ vị hương *ngu vi hur-erng* five-spice powder (*see* **hương-liệu**)

người ăn chay *ngur-er-i ahn chay* vegetarian

người hầu bàn nam *ngur-er-i huh-u bahn nam* waiter

người hầu bàn nụ *ngur-er-i huh-u bahn nur* waitress

người hầu bàn phụ *ngur-er-i huh-u bahn fu* bus boy

nghiền *ngiehn* grate

NH

nhà bếp *nya behp* kitchen

nhãn *nyan* longan – tasty tiny fruits that grow in the Mekong Delta and in the North. Smooth, light brown skin covering a translucent white pulp covering a large black seed. The thicker the pulp, the juicier and more fragrant the fruit.

nho *nyaw* grapes

nho khô *nyaw koh* raisin

nhồi nhét *nyoh-i nyẹt* stuffing

Ô

ô mai *oh mai* apricots (or other small fruits) perserved in salt, licorice and ginger

ốc *ohk* snail

ốc cuốn chả *ohk ku-ohn cha* rolled snails

ốc hấp bia *ohk huhp bea* snail cooked with beer

ốc xào cả võ *ohk sao ka vaw* stir-fried snails (still in their shells)

ổi *oh-i* guava –the fall-apart pink flesh of the guava is sheathed in a thick green avocado-shaped skin. Eat it raw or use it for juice.

ống hút *ohng hụt* drinking straws

ông Táo *ohng Tạo* the Kitchen God

Ơ

ớt *ert* chilli – Vietnamese cooks generally use two varieties of chilli. The first is a large, elongated red or green chilli, resembling the Italian pickling pepper, mildly hot, and used either sliced or whole. The other type is a tiny, fiery hot pepper called 'bird's eye pepper', used for seasoning.

ớt bột *ert bọht* paprika

ớt đỏ *ert daw* red capsicum/pepper

ớt hiểm *ert hiehm* bird's eye chilli

ớt khô *ert koh* chilli

ớt vàng *ert vang* yellow capsicum/pepper (sweet)

ớt xanh *ert sany* green capsicum/pepper (sweet)

ng nh o ô ơ p ph qu r s t th tr u ư v x y

PH

phao câu *fao kuh-u* rump

phần cổ *fuhn koh* neck

phó mát *faw maht* cheese

phở *fer* noodle soup usually served with beef or chicken

phở bò *fer baw* noodles served with beef

phục vụ trong nhà hàng *fuk vu ṭrong nya hahng* service at restaurant

QU

quả anh đào *(wua/kwua) any dao* cherry

quả bí *(wua/kwua) bi* squash

quả bí đỏ *(wua/kwua) bi daw* pumpkin

quả chà là *(wua/kwua)cha la* dates

quả dâu tây *(wua yur-u/kwua zur-u) ṭuh-y* strawberry

quả dưa *(wua yur-a/kwua zur-a)* melon

quả đào *(wua/kwua) dao* peach

quả hồ đào *(wua/kwua) hoh dao* pecan

quả hồ trăn *(wua/kwua) hoh trahn* pistachio

quả hạch *(wua/kwua)haik* walnut

quả kivi *(wua/kwua) ki vi* kiwi

quả lạc tiên *(wua/kwua) lahk tiehn* passionfruit

quả lê *(wua/kwua) leh* pears

quả lựu *(wua/kwua) lur-u* pomegranate

quả lý gai *(wua/kwua) lee gai* gooseberry

quả man việt quốc *(wua/kwua) mahn vieṭ (qu-ohk/kwu-ohk)* cranberry

quả mận *(wua/kwua) muhn* plum

quả mận cà *(wua/kwua) muhn ka* plum tomatoes

quả mộc hoa *(wua/kwua) mohk hoa* quince

quả mơ *(wua/kwua) mer* apricot

quả nhục đậu khấu *(wua/kwua) nyuk duh-u kuh-u* mace

quả phỉ *(wua/kwua) fi* hazelnut

quả quất vàng *(wua wu-uht/kwua kwu-uht) vahng* kumquat

quả quít *(wua wiṭ/kwua kwiṭ)* tangerine

quả vả *(wua/kwua) va* fig

quay *(way/kway)* roast

quế *(weh/kweh)* cinnamon

R

rau cải ngâm dấm *rau kai nguhm (yuhm/zuhm)* pickle

rau đền *rau (yehn/zehn)* spinach

rau diếp quăn *rau (diehp wu-ahn/ziep kwu-ahn)* endive

rau má *rau ma* pennywort

rau mùi *rau mui* chervil

rau muống *rau mu-ong* water spinach – unrelated to the true spinach but used in much the same way, it's considered Vietnam's national vegetable. Although an aquatic plant it grows equally well on wet or dry land and is characterised by hollow stems and light green, arrow shaped leaves. Vietnamese cooks value it for the contrast in texture between the crunchy stems and tender leaves and for its spinach-like taste. It's sold by the bunch at Chinese and Viet-namese greengrocers and is used in stir-fries and soups or added raw to salads.

rau ngò *rau ngaw* coriander/cilantro (see ngò)

rau quế *rau (weh/kweh)* basil – also known as Thai basil, a herb with exceptional flavour it is necessary for garnishing **phở** (beef and noodle soup). In the tropics it has purple stems and flowers.

rau rừng *rau rurng* wild greens

rau sống *rau sohng* vegetables

rau xà lách *rau sa laik* salad

rau xanh *rau sany* greens

rễ cần tây *reh kuhn tuh-y* celeriac

riềng *riehng* galangal – rhizome related to ginger, it resembles ginger but has zebra-like markings and pink shoots. It's not a substitute for ginger. Dried galangal is used only in soups and stews. In the spirit world, galangal represents silver; ginger represents gold.

rim *rim* poach

rong biển *rohng biehn* seaweed/kelp

rượu *rur-u* wine

rượu cần *rur-u kuhn* rice wine – it's as old as the hills, consumed at lunch by men, or used in religious ceremonies or to greet guests. City

folk look upon it as the drink of country bumpkins, but it's gaining acceptance.

rượu cồn *rur-u kohn* spirits

rượu chát đỏ *rur-u chaht daw* red wine

rượu khai vị *rur-u kai vi* aperitif

rượu mạnh *rur-u many* liqueur

rượu mạnh uýt ky *rur-u many wit ki* rye whisky

rượu pha nước hoa quả *rur-u fa nur-erk hwoa (wua/kwua)* cocktails

rượu pha trái cây *rur-u fa trai kuh-y* fruit punch

rượu ran-đi *rur-u ran-di* brandy

rượu rắn *rur-u rahn* snake that has been soaked in wine (used as a kind of medicine)

rượu trắng *rur-u trahng* gin

rượu uýt ky *rur-u uyt-ki* whisky

rượu vốt ka *rur-u vot-ka* vodka

rượu xủi tăm *rur-u sui tahm* sparkling wine

S

sà lách son *sa laik son* watercress

sầu riêng *suh-u riehng* durian – the most praised and the most damned of fruits, you either love it or you hate it. Its Vietnamese name means 'one's sorrows' and you may well regret breaking the chain mail skin of a durian as the powerful aroma will linger long in your memory. But if you hold your breath you can enjoy the creamy dense flesh and its complex flavour reminiscent, to speak kindly, of olive oil, peanut butter, ripe cheese, and honey. This gigantic and very expensive fruit is in season May-August.

sò *saw* oyster/mussel

sô cô la *soh koh la* chocolate

sô cô la bột *soh koh la boht* cocoa

sốt mayome *soht may yohm* mayonnaise

súp lơ *sup ler* cauliflower

súp ga *sup ga* pepper laden chicken soup with lotus seeds

sữa *sur-a* milk

sữa chua *sur-a chua* yoghurt

sữa đậu nành *sur-a duh-u nany* soya-bean drink

sữa loại trừ chất kem *sur-a lwai trur chuht kem* skimmed milk

sữa nước *sur-a nur-erk* buttermilk

sườn *sur-ern* ribs

sương sa *sur-erng sa* jelly

T

tan xai *tan xai* preserved vegetables – a mix of pickled Chinese cabbage and seasoning. Very pungent, and used only in small amounts to add flavour to soups and noodle dishes it's sold in small crocks in markets.

tàu hủ *tau hu* bean curd; tofu (see đậu hu)

tẩm *tuhm* to marinate

tiền bồi bàn *tiehn bohi bahn* gratuity/tip

tiêu *tieu* pepper (spice)

tim *tim* heart

tỏi *toi* garlic

tô để trộn *toh deh trohn* mixing bowl

tô trộn xà lách *toh trohn sa laik* salad bowl

tôm *tohm* shrimp

tôm đất *tohm duht* crayfish

tôm hùm *tohm hum* lobster

tôm khô *tohm koh* dried shrimp – shelled, dried and salted shrimp with a pungent flavour. They are usually used in small quantities to season certain dishes such as soups and stir-fries, but they can be found sprinkled on cupcakes as well.

tôm to *tohm taw* prawn

tôm xào hành nấm *tohm sao hany nuhm* shrimp with mushrooms

tổng phí tiền *tohng fi tiehn* the total amount

tủy *twi* marrow

tương *tur-erng* soy sauce (*see* **nước tương**)

tương cà-ri *tur-erng ka ri* curry paste (*see* **cà ri**)

tương hoisin *tur-erng hoi-sin* (*see* **hoisin**)

tương ớt *tur-erng ert* chilli sauce – this hot sauce is made from ground fresh chilli peppers, garlic, sugar, salt and vinegar. It's used as a table condiment and seasoning in soups and salads and any other thing you may wish to put it on.

a ă â b c ch d đ e ê g gh gi h I k kh l m n

tương ớt tươi *tur-erng ert tur-er-i* chilli paste – spicy hot mash of fresh red chillies, garlic, salt and soybean oil. Used as a table condiment and seasoning for sauces and stir-fries, it's a necessity of Vietnamese cookery.

TH

thạch cao *taik kao* gypsum – chemical agent used as a coagulant for bean curd; tofu, sold in pharmacies. Chemically known as calcined calcium sulfate, gypsum is also called plaster of Paris or plaster stone.

thạch đen *taik den* grass jelly. Made from seaweed and cornstarch, this black jelly tastes and smells, well, strange. It is sold in cans like soda, try it on ice.

thạch hoa *taik hwoa* agar-agar – gelatin derived from processed seaweed. It looks like crinkled strips of cellophane and is widely used in the tropics for jellied sweets, as it sets without refrigeration in very high temperatures.

thạch lỏng *taik long* gelatin

thái *tai* mince

thành phần *tany fuhn* ingredient

thận *tuhn* kidney

thìa *tea* spoon

thìa cán dài *tea kahn (yai/zai)* ladle

thìa là *tea la* cumin

thính *tiny* roasted rice powder

thịt bê *tit beh* veal

thịt bò *tit baw* beef

thịt bò bằm miếng dẹp *tit baw bahm miehng (yep/zep)* hamburger

thịt cá lóc *tit ka lok* fillet

thịt cừu già *tit kur-u (ya/za)* mutton

thịt chó *tit chaw* dog meat – along the Nhat Tan dyke, with the Red River on one side and West Lake on the other, there are about twenty dog meat shops in bamboo huts. At the end of each lunar month diners come in such great numbers that motor-cycles and cars clog the surface of the dike.

thịt heo *tit heo* pork

thịt kho *tit kaw* braised pork

thịt kho nước dừa *tit kaw nur-erk (yur-a/zur-a)* pork braised in coconut milk

thịt lợn muối *tit lern mu-oi* bacon; salted pork

thịt lưng cừu *tit lurng kur-u* chump

thịt lưng muối *tit lurng mu-oi* back bacon

thịt nướng *tit nur-erng* grilled meat

thịt rán *tit rahn* steak

thịt săn *tit sahn* game

thịt sườn *tit sur-ern* chops/flank

thịt thăn *tit tahn* loin

thịt thăn bò *tit tahn baw* sirloin

thịt ức *tit urk* brisket

thịt ướp xấy khô *tit ur-erp say koh* to cure

thỏ *to* rabbit

thỏ rừng *to rurng* hare

thớt *tert* chopping board

thực đơn *turk dern* menu

thực uống *turk u-ong* drinks

thượng hống *tur-erng hahng* topping

TR

trà *tra* tea

trái bơ *trai ber* avocado

trái cà *trai ka* tomatoes

trái cây khô *trai kuh-y koh* dried fruit

trái chà là *trai cha la* date

trái hồng *trai hohng* persimmon

trái khế *trai keh* star fruit

trái măng cầu *trai mang kuh-u* guyabano

trái me *trai me* tamarind

trái mít *trai mit* jack fruit

trái phi *trai fi* walnut

trái sầu riêng *trai suh-u riehng* durian (*see* **sầu riêng**)

trái táo *trai tao* apples

trái vải *trai vai* lychee – you'll see clusters of dark red, lumpy lychees throughout the country, especially in the north. Connoisseurs say the best of these fruit come from Hung Yen province, where they are the juiciest and sweetest.

trăm phần trăm *trahm fuhn trahm* 'one hundred percent' – cheers!

trung bình *trung biny* medium (cooked)

trứng *trurng* eggs

trứng cá tầm *trurng ka tuhm* caviar

trứng tráng *trurng trahng* omelette

U

um *um* braise

Ư

ướp *ur-erp* to marinate

V

vai *vai* lychee (*see* trái vải)

va-ni *va-ni* vanilla

vĩ nướng *vi nur-erng* barbecue grill

vịt *vit* duck

vừa *vur-a* medium (cooked)

vữa *vur-a* mortar

X

xả *sa* lemon grass – this is an aromatic tropical grass that informs both Vietnamese and Thai cuisine. It imparts a lemon like taste and smell without the acidity.

xá xíu *sa siu* barbecue pork

xào áp chảo *sao ahp chao* sauté

xâm banh *suhm bany* champagne

xì dầu *si (yuh-u/zuh-u)* soy sauce (*see* **nước tương**)

xia-ro *sea-roh* syrup

xíu mại *siu mai* marinated pork mince

xò nhỏ *saw nyaw* cockle

xoài *swo-ai* mango – the fibrous coral coloured flesh of the mango comes in several varieties, the sweetest are the large rounder ones with a bright yellow skin that can weigh up to half a kilo. The most prized come from the Mekong Delta, and are in season March-June.

xôi *soi* glutinous rice *(see* **gạo nếp***)*

xông khói *sohng koh-i* smoked

xúc xích lợn *suk sik lern* pork sausages

xúp *sup* soup

xương ống *sur-erng ohng* shank

xương sườn *sur-erng sur-ern* sparerib

xửng *surng* wooden mould used to cook cake; also a double boiler

Y

yếm *iem* apron

Boxed Text

Maps

Recipes

INDEX

More World Food Titles

Brimming with cultural insight, the World Food series takes the guesswork out of new cuisines and provide the ideal guides to your own culinary adventures. The books cover everything to do with food and drink in each country – the history and evolution of the cuisine, its staples & specialities, and the kitchen philosophy of the people. You'll find definitive two-way dictionaries, menu readers and useful phrases for shopping, drunken apologies and much more.

The essential guides for travelling and non-travelling food lovers around the world, look out for the full range of World Food titles including:

**Deep South (USA),
Italy,
Mexico,
Morocco,
Spain,
Thailand,
Turkey,
France,
Ireland &
Hong Kong.**

Out to Eat Series

Lonely Planet's Out to Eat series takes its food seriously but offers a fresh approach with independent, unstuffy opinion on hundreds of hand-picked restaurants, bars and cafes in each city. Along with reviews, Out to Eat identifies the best culinary cul-de-sacs, describes cultural contexts of ethnic cuisines, and explains menu terms and ingredients.

Updated annually, new Out to Eat titles include:
Melbourne, Paris, Sydney, London and San Francisco.

Planet Talk

Our FREE quarterly printed newsletter is full of tips from travellers and anecdotes from Lonely Planet guidebook authors. Every issue is packed with up-to-date travel news and advice, and includes:

a postcard from Lonely Planet co-founder Tony Wheeler
a swag of mail from travellers
a look at life on the road through the eyes of a Lonely Planet author
topical health advice
prizes for the best travel yarn
news about forthcoming Lonely Planet events
a complete list of Lonely Planet books and other titles

To join our mailing list, residents of the UK, Europe and Africa can email us at go@lonelyplanet.co.uk; residents of North and South America can do so at info@lonelyplanet.com; the rest of the world can email talk2us@lonelyplanet.com.au, or contact any Lonely Planet office.

The Lonely Planet Story

Lonely Planet published its first book in 1973 in response to the numerous 'How did you do it?' questions Maureen and Tony Wheeler were asked after driving, bussing, hitching, sailing and railing their way from England to Australia. Written at a kitchen table and hand collated, trimmed and stapled, *Across Asia on the Cheap* became an instant local bestseller.

Eighteen months in South-East Asia resulted in their second guide, *South-East Asia on a Shoestring*, which they put together in a backstreet Chinese hotel in Singapore in 1975. The 'yellow bible', as it quickly became known to backpackers around the world, soon became the guide to the region. It has sold well over ¾ million copies and is now in its 10th edition, still retaining its familiar yellow cover.

Today there are over 400 titles, including travel guides, walking guides, language kits & phrasebooks, travel atlases & maps, diving guides, restaurant guides, first time travel guides, condensed guides, illustrated pictorials and travel literature. The company is the largest independent travel publisher in the world.

The emphasis continues to be on travel for independent travellers. Tony and Maureen still travel for several months of each year and play an active part in the writing, updating and quality control of Lonely Planet's guides.

They have been joined by over 120 authors and over 400 staff at our offices in Melbourne (Australia), Oakland (USA), London (UK) and Paris (France). Travellers themselves also make a valuable contribution to the guides through the feedback we receive in thousands of letters each year and on our web site.

The people at Lonely Planet strongly believe that travellers can make a positive contribution to the countries they visit, both through their appreciation of the countries' culture, wildlife and natural features, and through the money they spend. In addition, the company makes a direct contribution to the countries and regions it covers. Since 1986 a percentage of the income from each book has been donated to ventures such as famine relief in Africa; aid projects in India; agricultural projects in Central America; Greenpeace's efforts to halt French nuclear testing in the Pacific.

Lonely Planet Offices

Australia
90 Maribyrnong St, Footscray, Victoria 3011
☎ 03-8379 8000
fax 03-8379 8111
email:talk2us@lonelyplanet.com.au

UK
72-82 Rosebery Ave, London EC1R 4RW
☎ 020-7841 9000
fax 020-7841 9001
email: go@lonelyplanet.co.uk

USA
150 Linden St, Oakland, CA 94607
☎ 510-893 8555 TOLL FREE: 800 275 8555
fax 510-893 8572
email: info@lonelyplanet.com